If These WALLS *Could* TALK:
DETROIT RED WINGS

If These WALLS Could TALK:
DETROIT RED WINGS

Stories from the Detroit Red Wings Ice, Locker Room, and Press Box

Ken Daniels with Bob Duff

TRIUMPH
B O O K S

Library of Congress Cataloging-in-Publication Data available upon request.

This book is available in quantity at special discounts for your group or organization. For further information, contact:

Triumph Books LLC
814 North Franklin Street
Chicago, Illinois 60610
(312) 337–0747
www.triumphbooks.com

Printed in U.S.A.

ISBN: 978-1-62937-461-1

Design by Amy Carter

Page production by Nord Compo

All photos are courtesy of the author unless otherwise noted.

To my beautiful son, Jamie: his life story never got to be written, but his 23 years could have filled 300 pages with joy, caring, laughter, and loyalty, as his years did for us.

—K.D.

CONTENTS

AUTHOR'S NOTE

It's not the years in the life, but the life in the years.

For my first 20 years here in Detroit, for some reason, every now and again, I'd hear, "Hey, Ken Holland."

Nope. Missed that by about 2 million bucks a year. I told Red Wings general manager Mr. Holland that story and he said, "It might be closer to 3 million." Now those dollars make more sense.

And then I'd hear, "Hey, Ken Kal." That's a notion I can't quite grasp. I suppose if his name were Bill, I would never be confused with our radio voice.

Kal has been with the Wings two years longer than I have, but his face isn't on television upwards of 80 nights a season (no face made for radio jokes here by me). Maybe it's just his shorter last name that rolls off the tongue. I wish he had kept his birth name of Kalczynski.

The case of mistaken identity has happened to Ken Kal, too. One night, KK was hosting a banquet and the guy introducing him reads his bio, and then says, "Ladies and gentlemen, Ken Daniels."

It seems crazy right? And to think we used to have goaltender Ken Wregget on our team, too. Now we only have one other Ken, besides the aforementioned, and that's our security guy.

If people didn't get my name correct by calling me using the surnames of one of the other too-many Kens, I would also be known as "There's that Red Wings guy. He's the one who does the games on TV."

Now it's become, "There's that guy whose son passed away."

That's how I feel I've become known. And you know something, I don't mind that at all. If that's what it takes to keep my son in people's thoughts, then I will gladly be known as "Jamie's dad."

My son, Jamie, died suddenly in December 2016, as I was working on this book. It was a shock, a personal tragedy that no parent should ever know, being left to bury a child.

To me, my son is the mirror image of Xavier Ouellet, the Red Wings' fine young d-man. When Jamie was in the Red Wings room a few years back standing near "X," Xavier's nickname, Tomas Tatar walked past and saw the two of them and joked, "Same mother?"

I was lucky enough to meet X's parents near my home in Birmingham, Michigan, shortly after my son had passed, and I showed Xavier's dad, Robert, how similar they looked. Even he couldn't help but notice the uncanny resemblance. And, to take this one step beyond crazy, Robert and I share the same March 18 birthday.

I've often felt that hockey people are just the greatest athletes with which to have a conversation. They are personable and for the most part genuine.

When Jamie was with me for a game against Chicago midway through the 2015–16 season, we sat in seats at the Joe so Jamie could watch his favorite player, Patrick Kane. Patrick was "sick," Jamie would say (i.e., "sick" being a tribute to his sick skills). I wasn't doing that midweek game against Chicago since it was on NBCSN.

As much as I'd love to call every Red Wings game, I have enjoyed those nights off to spend with my son; or my biggest fan, my daughter, Arlyn; or my wife, Rebecca, and her kids, Zoe and Ian, at a game. It's a nice change of pace.

And for those wondering, no, I do not do the play-by-play while I am watching from the seats. I do think of things I might have said while I'm watching, but only to myself, or if one of my kids or my wife had asked about a certain play.

Despite all my years with the Red Wings, Jamie had still not met Patrick Kane. He'd met a lot of his favorites over the years from Marty Brodeur to Alex Ovechkin, but not Kane.

We made our way down to the Blackhawks dressing room and stood there waiting for him to emerge from the change area. Patrick walked right over to me and said, "Ken, how are you? Patrick Kane." As if I didn't know. But truthfully, I was surprised he knew me. I was flattered even more so since Jamie was standing right beside me.

Now over the years I have been in those media scrums where we all gather around a player and stick microphones in his face. But I'm usually on the periphery listening, so Kane and I had never actually met.

Well, my son couldn't have had a bigger smile on his face except for the one that was on his dad's face.

Kane then said, after I introduced him to Jamie, that he had been watching for years. "I grew up watching you and Mick, when I used to live at Beeker's [Pat Verbeek's] place." Kane billeted with Pat Verbeek and his family while he was playing hockey for the HoneyBaked youth program in Metro Detroit.

And then he added, "I love listening to you and Mick." He then turned to Jamie and said, "Your dad is the best."

Well, that made my day, month, and year.

So I snapped a picture of Patrick with Jamie. They shook hands. Jamie grabbed my phone, looked at the photo, and immediately said, "Oh my God, you rocked this, Dad. You even got [Chicago captain Jonathan] Toews in the background." Kane and Toews in the same photo with my son. Now that was lucky!

Like Patrick, Todd Bertuzzi is also a first-ballot personality. I was with Jamie at the Joe back in 2010, in Todd's second go-around with the Red Wings.

Todd would give his shirt off his back to anyone who needed one. He was a great Red Wings teammate and a great friend to me. I believe Todd trusts me after all these years, in part because I have never mentioned the Steve Moore incident. I can't imagine what Todd has had to live through this past decade nor what Steve Moore has had to endure. It's none of my business nor anyone else's not directly involved. I just hope all can move on successfully in the years ahead.

Jamie came down to the room during a morning skate on the day of a game, and I introduced him to Todd. Big Bert said, "I got him," and took him around the inner sanctum of the room.

A little while later, Jamie returned and I asked my son how it went. And he replied, "Todd said, 'Listen to your dad. In this business, there aren't many you can trust, but he's one of the good guys. He does it right.'" That meant a lot to me then and even more so today.

Hearing what both Patrick and Todd said goes a long way in the eyes of a child, even if they aren't as impressionable as they were in younger years.

Sometimes as parents, we wonder how our children view us. We know they love us. But it's always nice to hear the unsolicited thoughts about us from the perspective of others.

During Jamie's time as a student at Michigan State, he was working with the Spartans hockey team. Now a Red Wings video coach, Adam Nightingale, previously a MSU alternate captain from

2003 to 2005, went on to become the team's director of hockey operations and hired Jamie as its student manager. Over the next three seasons, Jamie would video practices and games and break down tape.

The NHL was locked out to start the 2012–13 season, and it was early October. I went to Munn Ice Arena in East Lansing to go to lunch with Jamie, and from the last row of seats, we watched a pick-up game of Spartan players, since their season wasn't yet underway.

Jamie and I were both in awe watching this one player's rush up the ice as he slashed through three defenders before scoring a spectacular goal. I remember saying, "Who the hell is that?" Jamie noticed a No. 8 on his helmet, but said, "No way that was Chris Forfar," Michigan State's No. 8 at the time. Chris was a hard worker for Michigan State but couldn't school players like that, not even players from his own school.

After practice we ventured down to the room and out walked Red Wings forward Justin Abdelkader. Justin was a former Spartan who needed a place to play, since the NHL players were locked out of the Joe. I quickly realized why that No. 8 rushing up the ice looked so seasoned. Jamie and I both knew no college player was walking around his mates as easily as Justin did. For the most part, the gap is wide from pro to college and that was pretty evident on that one play. It just took us an hour to figure it out.

Most importantly during his time at MSU, Jamie developed some great friendships with Spartan players—guys like Brent Darnell, Matt Berry, and Mackenzie MacEachern, to name just a few. All were terrific players during their time at State and, best of all, wonderful people who were always great to my son.

You never forget the people who touch your life, and that's why I know no one who ever met Jamie will ever forget him, for he was a young man who touched the lives of everyone he met.

FOREWORD

As smooth as silk—that's how I'd describe Ken Daniels' work in the booth.

When you are first working with a new partner there's always a transition period. But when I first started working with Ken Daniels in 1997, I don't think it took very long and I don't think it was difficult. I don't really recall any issues we would have had. It's like the bad goal for a goalie. You don't remember all the saves but you do remember the bad goal.

It was a smooth transition. And it was probably more of a transition for him because he was coming from a national broadcaster with *Hockey Night in Canada* to working for an individual team. There's a lot of things you have to learn with how a team does their advertising and their promos, the stuff that we do in any given telecast.

In a strange way, I describe it as though Ken has to please me first, because his voice and his information comes through my ears before it gets to anybody watching on television. We joke about that. He got a kick out of that when I first told him, "You've gotta understand man, you're coming through my ears first, so be careful what you say. If what I'm hearing is good stuff, I expect it to be good stuff for everybody else, because I'm just a fan like everybody."

In any partnership on the air the key is giving and taking. You have to learn when to give and when to take. That's the biggest adjustment any two people will have in the booth and I think it is up to the color guy because he has to learn the cadence of the play-by-play voice. It's not a big thing, but it's the biggest thing that a color guy has to adjust to, making sure he's not stepping on the play-by-play guy's voice.

For us that was easy, because he was a professional broad-caster when he got here. He'd paid his dues. I think he understood what his role was. The biggest challenge for him was understanding that we were Detroit Red Wings broadcasters now. We're here to deliver the game and the information about the game and not to hunt for news like it would be if we were doing a national game.

I started in 1979 and then I went to *Hockey Night in Canada* from 1980 to 1985, although I was still doing Red Wings games through those five years. It's an entirely different role as a broad-caster when you work with one team. I think when you get close to a team like we do and you're traveling with them, it's a different hockey world. As broadcasters, we need to maintain our credibility with our fans but at the same time we don't want to embarrass the players on the team or the organization. Still, we have to be reasonable with what we are calling, because the majority of fans are educated about the game. We shouldn't be trying to hide things and cover them up. The challenge as a team broadcaster is to know how to deliver that information and the message.

I think one of those most important things to learn, whether it's play-by-play or color, is to know your place. We have to know when to be in and when not to be in. Where to go and where not to go. Where are the landmines? How to work around all that stuff and connect all the dots on how we go about our job and what is expected of us. For Ken coming in, that would have been a bigger challenge, because I was already here for many years. He's the new guy on the block. My job was to make his transition as easy as possible and try to give him as much information as I possibly can, so that he can make that change easily.

For me, it was to let him know, as I would anybody coming into that situation, that we are a team, just like a team on the ice. We've got 40 to 50 broadcast people all over the building, including working in our mobile TV truck. They're in our ears.

Nobody sees them; nobody ever hears their names. You just see the guys who deliver the message when the light comes on. Nobody is bigger than the game, and as long as we remember that and know when to get out of the road, we all fit in very well at what I think is the best job in the world.

Away from the rink, Ken and I have developed a strong bond as friends. He was there for me when I went through my battle with cancer in 2002 and my ongoing issues with celiac disease. I tried to be a shoulder for him as Ken dealt with the shocking death of his son, Jamie, in 2016.

It isn't a necessity for broadcast partners to be pals, but it really helps to have a life outside the press box, and from behind the microphone.

We don't have a lot of time to socialize because we're on the go so much. Still, it's great to be able to have that relationship beyond the professional one. We can sit across the kitchen table, have a pop, and talk about whatever, whether it's family, friends, or the game.

Hopefully that shows on the air. Whether it's the exchange of laughter or jokes, or on the serious side, explaining the game and calling the game, I think it shines through when both broadcast partners are on the same wavelength.

I've worked with some icons in this game such as Danny Gallivan, Bob Cole, Dick Irvin, Dave Hodge, Brian McFarlane, Jim Hughson, all those guys from *Hockey Night*. There was Dave

Strader for the first 11 years here in Detroit. I've been very fortunate to not only work with some of the best in the business, but some of the best people in the business. I was able to learn from them how to open the door to people and allow them an opportunity to grow.

I guess I can say that right from the beginning I felt that Ken was right there with them. He's got the voice. He's got the delivery. He's got the work ethic. And as far as I'm concerned he's one of the top play-by-play guys in the game. He's one of the best in the business.

I guess, as a former winger, I would liken it to—and I've often talked about this—having Hall of Famer Alex Delvecchio as my center, who was a winger's dream. To have a play-by-play guy like Ken Daniels is a color man's dream.

—Mickey Redmond
March 2017

INTRODUCTION

I've just completed my 20th season and have called more than 1,500 games with an iconic franchise in Detroit.

In many ways, I'm still the kid living the dream I had as a Toronto youngster at the age of 10 when my parents sent me to bed with the Toronto Maple Leafs game still not completed on television.

I would sneak my radio under my pillow, listening as Foster Hewitt, the Leafs' play-by-play voice, painted a vivid picture of the action from Maple Leaf Gardens.

I'd then fall asleep to Foster's words, wishing I could one day see the game as Foster did. Literally, dreams do come true.

I am doing today what I've wanted to do since that young age. It was then that I discovered my passion for this glorious game and turned that passion into my life's work.

I was never the greatest student nor a voracious reader, except for the hockey pages in the daily sports section of the newspapers, back when the paper would be delivered at four in the afternoon just as I'd be getting home from school.

Studying those scoring summaries and memorizing everything there was to know about the hockey world became my version of homework. Sure, it was a little easier then because in 1969 there were only 12 NHL teams. Who knew then how much the research and time I put in to learning about the game would pay off so handsomely for me?

The first book I ever read on my own was Bobby Hull's *Hockey Is My Game*. It was my game, too.

As for music, I grew up on rock and roll and The Beatles. But hockey has been my symphony. The game was a new orchestra every night. The conductor was the man behind the microphone, Hewitt. Foster coined the phrase "He shoots, he scores" in the 1920s. But it was always the sound of the game for me, and not the score.

My son, Jamie, and me, celebrating with the Stanley Cup at his FJA school in 2008 in West Bloomfield. He was so proud we could share with his classmates.

My favorite score, and for that matter my national anthem, was Dolores Claman's "Hockey Theme." She wrote it in 1968, and it was performed by a 20-member orchestra. That tune became the sound of *Hockey Night in Canada* until 2008, when TSN's Bell Media in Canada bought the rights.

Twenty years later I did my first ever hockey play-by-play on the same radio station that was previously owned by Foster Hewitt and from the same 56-foot distance above the ice and in the same building that Foster called Maple Leafs hockey for more than 40 years.

Foster opened a door for this wide-eyed youngster who dreamed big, a window into my imagination of the possibilities that might lay ahead, and my life has been spent on the other side of it, making certain it wouldn't close on me.

I guess I learned then that living life with visualization prepares you for the moment that is presented, so that you can take advantage of that moment and seize it when the opportunity arrives.

The only luck that may be involved is timing. However, the timing is irrelevant without the preparation to handle the moment when it does arrive.

Such as, I only discovered there was a television opening for a CBC summer sports spot because I had no food in my bachelor apartment. So I decided to make use of my media pass to eat at the Toronto Blue Jays game that night in June 1985.

Once there, someone mentioned to me about the TV auditions taking place.

I had no experience, but I seized the moment. You might call that luck, since I was in the right place at the right time because I was hungry. Fair enough. But I had already prepared through hard work, career versatility, and visualization to handle that moment, lucky or not, when it arrived.

It means the world to me that I have a story to tell. And that is what excites me.

The preparation for every game enthuses me, too. I love doing the research and being able to convey what I find to the viewer; it energizes me.

If I'm excited by the story, that's what matters to me. I then hope you will enjoy what you hear.

It's with great gratitude that you let me share it with you.

Jamie meets Patrick Kane of the Chicago Blackhawks in their dressing room on March 2, 2016. The fact I captured Jonathan Toews in the background earned me big points.

With son, Jamie, and daughter, Arlyn, in the Red Wings dressing room in 2013.

CHAPTER 1
GO TO BED

I had a dream from a young age . . .

Voices in My Head

Beginning in 1966, all *Hockey Night in Canada* televised games were broadcast in color. That didn't matter to me. We didn't get a color television until the early seventies. My world was black and white—in more ways than one. I was either watching hockey or thinking about hockey. That was it. I was a pretty simple kid. Math class in fifth grade was all about calculating the goals against average of an NHL goaltender, not about how long it would take one train on a parallel track to catch another train, leaving later but going faster.

But there was a bigger problem to solve in little Kenny's life. When I first started watching games in the mid-'60s, *HNIC* would join the game from Maple Leaf Gardens in Toronto already in progress. The game would show up in our family living room around 8:30 PM, late in the first period. Here's the issue. I was seven. By the time the third period rolled around, tiring perhaps of my early play-by-play years, my parents or much older siblings, either Linda, John, or Gary, would say it was time for bed. I must not have let the game breathe or mistakenly said Keon when it was Kelly!

Once upstairs, Foster Hewitt took over. Foster was the legendary voice of the Toronto Maple Leafs. Foster was the gold standard when it came to hockey play-by-play. His goal call "He shoots, he scores" was copied by almost everyone who followed him into the booth. He started calling games in the 1920s, and when he was hired full-time by the Leafs in the early 1930s to call their games coast to coast on radio, it helped turn the team and Foster into national icons.

As strange as this may sound, Foster and I shared a passionate love affair—with the game, that is. Foster would later say,

"It's hard to explain why hockey meant so much to me, but it had always been the epitome of everything." I knew that feeling. All those nights I was sent to bed with a radio tucked under my pillow, play-by-play must have come to me through osmosis. I literally dreamed the game.

So 23 years later, that dream came true. I called my first-ever hockey game from that same arena Foster did, Maple Leaf Gardens, on the same station, 1430 AM, that Foster used to own. Also 56′ above the ice, but directly across from his old gondola, which Leafs owner Harold Ballard foolishly had destroyed.

Foster's gondola, to this day, was the perfect place from which to call a game. It was five floors up, designed specifically because Foster and an architect went to a downtown Toronto building on Bay Street, and looked down. From there, he felt he could accurately describe minute details of people walking beneath them. The gondola got its name from an advertising executive who suggested the broadcast spot resembled a gondola of an airship. First time Foster ventured out onto his perch, he did so on his hands and knees on a metal plank that led from the fan room to the top of the gray seats at Maple Leaf Gardens. Then he'd walk up a stairway, to a catwalk that was 80 feet high. Once he'd hit the middle of that, there was a 90-degree ladder to one end of the gondola. He got used to it. Many others, I hear, wouldn't try. But Foster always sounded comfortable, and so did all hockey fans listening to him.

When the Leafs weren't playing, I could scroll down the dial and find Dan Kelly out of KMOX in St. Louis, calling Blues games. I loved Dan Kelly's booming voice, his cadence, and immaculate inflection, and Foster's calming, reassuring, almost grandfatherly sound. I guess from listening to Dan Kelly, that's in part why I became a bit of a Blues fan. Once in a while I would get 760 WJR-AM from Detroit and pull in Bruce Martyn calling the Red Wings games. It didn't matter who was on the call. I fell in love with the sounds of the game.

By the age of 10, I had been playing hockey for a year or so and picked up the skating part fairly quickly. I wasn't on skates at the age of three like the kids today. I was always fascinated with the speed and the sound of the game. It just stuck with me. And, as my mother Sylvia pointed out to me years later, I was destined to do this job because I was born on March 18. And on March 18, 1892, Lord Stanley of Preston donated the Stanley Cup. Somewhere there's kismet there, right?

Toronto Goal Scored By . . .

Maple Leaf Gardens was a place I could only dream of seeing as a kid. That is until my brother John hooked up with a girl whose dad had season tickets. We sat in the north end blues. It was the Leafs against the Buffalo Sabres. I don't recall much about the game, but I do vividly remember Gerry Meehan playing for the Sabres. He was a former Leafs draft pick who would go on to become GM of the Sabres, succeeding Scotty Bowman.

A few years later, a friend of mine, Benjy Walderman, had corner blue mezzanine season tickets right by Paul Morris' booth, and that fascinated me, too. Everyone in Toronto was familiar with Paul's steady, monotone, nasal voice over the public address system at Maple Leaf Gardens. He had a one-of-a-kind sound. And now, here I am looking at Paul Morris talking into the microphone and hearing his voice.

Twelve years later at CBC, I interviewed Paul for a TV sports item, imitating his voice. We would share the goal call. I'd say, "Toronto goal scored by No. 17 Wendel Clark." And he'd say, "Assisted by No. 10 Vincent Damphousse." Then I'd say, "The time 11:11." And then we'd repeat it. To this day, it's the best impression I do. That and the voice of Bill Hewitt, Foster's son.

Paul was a really good sport about it. I got the feeling that he'd heard plenty of imitations of himself over the years. I asked him how come he never sounds excited when he calls a goal. He said, "I am excited. It just doesn't come across that way." Paul was the Gardens' electrician. He only got the job as PA announcer because the guy before him had screwed up announcing the Canadian prime minister's name at the time, as Lester Boo Person, instead of Lester B. Pearson. Leafs co-owner Stafford Smythe, the son of Conn Smythe, who founded the Leafs back in 1927, told Harold Ballard to "Fire that guy." Paul was standing nearby and was told he was the new P.A. announcer. Ballard's reasoning was sound, you could say. "If your microphone breaks Paul, you know how to fix it." Harold could always find a way to get things done cheaply.

During intermissions Benjy and I would make the long trek down from the north end blues to go stand outside the Leafs dressing room. Back then we could stand right outside the door, with that big Leafs logo on it. I'd watch as Leafs goalie Bruce Gamble would come out with that huge scar underneath his right cheek. Bruce didn't wear a mask back then to cover it up. Not even his pork-chop sideburns could hide it. I'd see Toronto captain Dave Keon up close. Just to see them for a few seconds as they took the ice to start the period was well worth the walk and the jostling through the intermission crowd while navigating the tight MLG corridors. I knew the Gardens backwards and forwards long before I ever got there as a reporter.

Limited Time Offer

Growing up middle class in the Toronto suburb of Forest Hill, I knew hockey was going to be my life. I devoured everything I could about the game. I listened to and watched all the sportscasts and would religiously read cover to cover the sports sections in the newspapers, back when we were reading those. The *Toronto Star* would be delivered to our home around four each afternoon, and if the Leafs had played the night before, I could finally get the scoring summary. There was no Internet and immediate access back then, children. And there it was. The ad! The ad that would change my life. The National Institute of Broadcasting. This was better than sneaking a *Playboy* magazine upstairs. It offered the complete course of how to become a broadcaster. Are you kidding me? Thirty-six recorded lessons on 12" long-playing vinyl records. Kids, ask your parents what those are. And for younger parents, ask your parents.

The ad implied you listened to the lesson on your record player, then you did it yourself on your tape recorder. Your NIB instructor corrected your work, and then you attended in-station practice lessons. There were apparently 500 NIB graduates on the air all over North America. I was only 13, but I wanted to be the 501st. Just one problem—cost. I didn't care. I would have done it at any cost. My dad, Marvin, not so much.

I can't recall how much it was exactly back in the early '70s, but it may have been upwards of $1,000 dollars. My favorite pop band, Hall and Oates, later wrote a song, "I Can't Go For That (No Can Do)." That was my dad's motto long before. So I enlisted my trusty brother-in-law Shelly's help. He married my sister, Linda, when I was only 11. Linda was 13 years older than me. The fact that my brother-in-law Shelly is still alive is a miracle in itself. He is the "luckiest unlucky" person in the world. In 2006, he had his lymph nodes removed due to melanoma. Four years later, due to melanoma, he went through a liver resection. And if that wasn't enough for the "ill-lottery" survival victory, in 2014, not even a flesh-eating disease could stop the most patient patient any doctor had ever met. Shelly needed a facial reconstruction, and has had six plastic surgeries since. He even still has sight in the left eye, where the disease first attached itself. By comparison, hopefully you have little to complain about.

So, back to the rest of the story.

Shelly took me downtown, and we sat in the class together. I read a news article into the microphone, and the instructor thought I was great. I bet he did. He heard nothing but saw the money. Actually, I thought I did okay, too. So did Shelly. Dad didn't need to hear me. He only heard the cost and said no. I was really angry. But deep down I understood, and it wouldn't deter my passion. My dad would smile and say to me, "At 13 it's amazing how little you think I know, but when you're 22 you'll be amazed how much I've learned in the last nine years!" As a 13-year-old kid I didn't get it, but at 22 I realized how right he was. Again.

7

Bernie, Bernie, Bernie

One of my heroes growing up was Leafs goalie Bernie Parent, who, curiously enough, they got in a trade for Bruce Gamble, the goalie I liked to watch lumber to the ice from the Leafs dressing room. Outside the Gardens after games on Wood Street I'd wait for that garage door to open, and the players would come out. There was Bernie. Program in hand, I'd get his autograph. He also had a cigar in his hand. I wanted that, too. Why, I don't know. To this day, I only have the odd cigar on the golf course, but for some reason I had in mind that Bernie's cigar would make a wonderful keepsake. Smartly, Bernie declined the invitation to hand an 11-year-old his stogie, despite me following him to his car, asking persistently.

I started keeping scrapbooks on Bernie. And then I found out years later talking to Detroit general manager Kenny Holland that he also kept scrapbooks of Bernie. He was Ken's idol, too. Unlike Mr. Holland though, who went on to stop pucks in the NHL like Bernie, I was only a street hockey goalie. I only played goal on ice once, and it hurt like hell because back in those days the padding was minimal compared with today's standard. But I was a pretty decent street hockey goalie. I'd try to do the Bernie Parent kick save while flaring out the pad, before we were doing the butterfly style. I'd be tapping the posts like Bernie did and slapping the stick into the glove like Bernie did.

We played ball hockey almost every day after school. We kept the goalie nets and the sticks at my house. I made a stick rack in wood shop class in eighth grade and still have it. But today that rack is home to sticks from Hockey Hall of Famers like Bobby Orr and Bobby Hull, rather than Rich Caplan, Randy Lebow, and Jeff Stanton.

Hall of Fame goaltender Bernie Parent and me, in Mike Keenan's office in 1986. "I got really close, and still no cigar."

We'd go play at the church yard across the street from my house. I had the Bernie Parent white mask, and I would put two Philadelphia Flyers stickers up there just like Bernie had. I remember when he went to the Philadelphia Blazers in the WHA, I took the mask and painted the Philadelphia Blazers logo on there. That was in art class. See, I always found a way to tie hockey in with my schooling. That Blazers stop didn't go very well for Bernie, and he was back in the NHL a year later, winning back-to-back Stanley Cups and back-to-back Conn Smythe Trophy awards with the Flyers in 1973–74 and 1974–75.

Years later, because of my relationship with Mike Keenan, I actually got to spend some time with Bernie. When Keenan was coaching the Philadelphia Flyers I went to the Philly Fling in 1986, which is a big party for their players and staff. Mike performed with

9

Nick and The Nice Guys, his band from St. Lawrence University. Mike was the singer. He was okay, a solid third-line singer.

I was staying at Mike's house, and really as much as I appreciated being around Mike and the rest of the team, I only wanted to meet Bernie Parent. Mike brought him down to his office the next day to see me. Getting a picture with Bernie then was awesome. Twenty-five years later, when we were both much older, I got another with him while working with the Wings at a game in Philadelphia. This time, I had him sign it.

Iron Mike

I played high school hockey for Mike Keenan at Forest Hill Collegiate in Toronto, years before Mike coached the New York Rangers to the 1994 Stanley Cup, took the Philadelphia Flyers to the Cup final in 1985 and 1987 and the Chicago Blackhawks there in 1992, and nearly became coach of the Wings in the mid-1990s.

I was hardly a hockey superstar. I was probably a middle-range player. I killed a lot of penalties and played point on the power play for Keenan. I learned the fine details of the game from him, long before he was telling Dave Poulin to "take his line" as coach of the Flyers. That was Mike's signature line change call. Whomever was center was told to "Daniels...take your line." He still begins a telephone conversation with that very phrase.

Forest Hill Collegiate was a predominantly Jewish high school. Mike's first wife, Rita, was Jewish. I remember Mike walked into our dressing room before the first game of the twelfth-grade 1976 season and said, "We've got some high skill on this team. We're smart. If we play hard, we can win a lot. The chances of any of you guys making the National Hockey League? Zero. The chances of one of you owning a National Hockey League team? Eighty per cent." We just cracked up.

Mike was a phys-ed and history teacher at Forest Hill, along with his head coaching duties. He was also coaching Oshawa Jr. B Legionaires at the time and was playing-coach of the Whitby Warriors OHA Senior A team. He took me aside one day and said, "You want to see what it's like? Come on out." He brought me from the high school team to play for his Oshawa Junior B team in a preseason game, and I quickly realized how much different it was.

I went to hit some guy and just missed him in the corner and when I came back to the bench, Keenan said, "You're going to get yourself killed. I wouldn't be trying to hit somebody like that." I played that one game, but I came to understand that they were so much better and tougher than I was.

That was Mike's message in a roundabout way. Stick to broad-casting. Mike and I would often sit in his phys-ed office and dis-cuss what jobs might be coming up in the NHL. I wanted to broadcast one day; he was closer to coaching. Remember he was only in his midtwenties then, but like me, he knew visualization is the key. That, and he and I shared the same thought that Sir Laurence Olivier had when a reporter asked him what it takes to be a great actor. The four-time Academy Award winner and five-time Emmy winner said, "What it takes to be a great actor is the humil-ity to prepare and the confidence to pull it off."

Mike's passion was second to none...well, except maybe for mine. Mike's hockey practice drills were so far ahead of what most kids were learning at that stage. We had one called the Philly drill that he'd taken from Flyers coach Fred Shero. This is where I first really learned about the game. We even had a high school

11

Hosting *Hockey Night in Canada* at Joe Louis Arena in 1992 with Chicago coach (and my high school coach at Forest Hill Toronto, 16 years earlier) Mike Keenan.

playbook we studied. Mike was tough. We'd often run in the morning before practice, and if you didn't beat your previous time, you were likely a healthy scratch for the next game. One Monday morning, Danny Gellman, a defenseman, had been running the night before! He'd been out drinking Sunday night, and the next morning came all too quickly. We only had an on-ice practice that day and Mike decided to sit it out, watching from the stands. Danny curled up in the fetal position on the near boards where he was sure that Mike couldn't see him. We went through practice skating around him, laughing. As we're leaving the ice, Danny slips in with the group and Mike comes over and says, "Good practice, good practice. Gellman—see you in a while. Fifty laps." Danny thought he was pulling one over on him, but Mike didn't miss it. He knew something was up, and Danny was about to

12

throw up. Over and over. After about 20 laps Mike felt it was enough. Oh God, it was funny.

Mike was always on the go. Coaching us, and others, and playing. A group of guys from our high school team decided to go watch him play one night in Whitby, about a 40-minute drive outside of Toronto. Senior hockey was still a bit of a big deal back then. Howie Menard, who'd played in the NHL with the Red Wings, Los Angeles Kings, Chicago, and the Oakland Seals, was playing for Whitby with Mike, and even Eddie Shack, The Entertainer himself, who'd won four Stanley Cups with the Leafs in the 1960s, was there for a few games one season.

Anyway, Blake Papsin and David Greenberg, who was our goalie, Bob Seldon, Jeff Stanton, and I, we went out to watch Mike play in Whitby. We were leaving the parking lot after the game and Blake's car broke down, so we needed a ride back to Toronto. Mike and his wife, Rita, shoved five kids into their vehicle. We stopped at McDonald's on the way back, and Mike treated us all to a late dinner. I will never forget that night. Out of something bad comes something great. My buddies and I also went to watch him coach in Rochester (of the AHL). He got us tickets. We had to be a couple of rows behind his bench, and he must have looked at us five times but never acknowledged us. Honest to God after the game he asked us where we were sitting. To this day, I think he's full of crap, but for some reason because of his coaching focus, he claimed he had no idea where we were. On the other hand, Scotty Bowman, when he was coaching the Wings, would look at Gordie Howe's seat at the Joe and say, "Where's Gordie? He's not in his seat?" while the game was going on. Mike Keenan and Scotty Bowman are often compared. Keenan was born in Bowmanville,

Ontario, ironically enough, and then Scotty hired him to coach the farm team in Rochester when Scotty was GM of the Sabres. Like Bowman, he probably thought no one would ever be able to figure him out. That was Keenan's mantra. They were so much alike.

Mike got a lot of what he did and how he treated people—and not always necessarily the right way—from Scotty. Some players loved him and many didn't. Mike had his ways, but for me to be able to access that information at a young age was such an invaluable experience.

I Call Shotgun

Another one of Mike Keenan's teammates with the Whitby senior team was Shotgun Tom Simpson. He was also one of my heroes growing up. I couldn't get into many Leaf games, so we'd go see the WHA Toronto Toros, and Shotgun Tom Simpson was my favorite. He was a cult hero in the city, Toronto's first 50-goal scorer when he fired home 52 goals for the Toros in 1974–75 with that blazing slapshot off that big right-hand curve of his, the reason behind his nickname. I used to go down to Toros games, and even though the team had stars like former Detroit Red Wings Paul Henderson and Frank Mahovlich, I'd wait for Tom to come out after games and meet him.

While I was in high school at Forest Hill Collegiate, I asked Mike for a summer job, and I wound up being a counsellor at Mike's Blades Hockey School in Pickering, Ontario, and Tom Simpson was there as an instructor. After the kids had gone home for the day, I'm skating with Tom Simpson. We'd play pick-up hockey, but one game we only had one goalie, so for a shot to count at the other end, you'd have to hit the iron. Shotgun would come across center and snap a shot...crossbar. Another shot...post. I couldn't friggin' believe it. Here he was, shooting from center ice and putting it right where he wanted to put it.

Leo The Lip

The first time I actually did any radio would have been in high school at Forest Hill, and I was doing it as Leo Cahill, the former Argos football coach, who was working at CHUM Radio. Leo was a local legend in Toronto—he'd taken the Canadian Football League's Argonauts to the Grey Cup in 1971, the first time they'd played for the league title since 1952. Joe Theismann was the quarterback on that team before he went to the NFL and won the Super Bowl with the Washington Redskins. Theismann and Joe Kapp, who did it with the Calgary Stampeders and Minnesota Vikings, are the only quarterbacks to start a Grey Cup and a Super Bowl.

I've kept all my handwritten Leo Cahill reports. Leo had this harsh-sounding staccato voice that really got your attention. That's how he talked, and I'd imitate his voice.

Being on the high school hockey team, playing for Mike Keenan, I would do the game report the next morning from the PA in the vice principal's office. Even if I had scored (rarely) I'd say, "Ken Daniels scored for the Falcons to give his team a 2–1 lead midway through the third..." because it wasn't me doing the sports, it was Leo Cahill.

That was my first foray into the broadcast world. I'd do that for three minutes at a time twice a week. A lot of good people came out of Forest Hill Collegiate. Lorne Michaels, the creator of *Saturday Night Live*, graduated from there. Rap star Drake also attended FHCI.

My First TV Gig

In Grade 13 (when Canada had that many grades) I did a Metro Toronto Hockey League weekly show for Willow Downs Cable in North Toronto. It was my first time on television, and I only did a couple of shows. On one I had John Gardner, who was the president of the MTHL, the largest local youth hockey organization in Canada, and I did another one with a local referee. I thought I was going to get former Maple Leafs star Frank Mahovlich to come on, but he never made it. Frank, the former Red Wing traded to the Montreal Canadiens for Mickey Redmond on January 13, 1971, owned a travel agency in North Toronto. Funny that both he and Mick dabbled in the travel world for a while. I wish I had the recording of my first time on TV. But this was before the time of VCRs. It's pretty amazing when you think back on it that they'd let a kid host a TV show, even a cable-access show, back in the mid-'70s. What a great way to learn.

Whistle Blower

I started refereeing house league hockey games in my early teens, for the Forest Hill Hockey Association in midtown Toronto. It was just another way to get on the ice and earn some bucks. We were making four dollars and change a game. I'd get up at 5:30 on a Saturday morning and referee the mites, the atoms, and the minor peewees. I'd come out of there with maybe fifteen bucks.

After gaining some experience, I started working in the MTHL. That's how I got to know John Gardner. Supervisors would grade my work just like they do in the National Hockey League. Reports would tell me to improve skating or that I wasn't quick enough at times, or my blue line positioning was not correct. They were really careful on that stuff.

I'd be working Monday-Thursday night some weeks and then do tournaments on weekends. It was fun. It kept me in shape, kept me skating. I just loved being around the rink, and it was another way to be part of the game.

It gave me a method to earn cash so I wasn't bugging my parents for spending money. My work at the MTHL helped put me through college, along with my dad chipping in. I was making $3,000-$4,000 per year, cash, refereeing when I was 18, 19, and 20. There was so much hockey in the Toronto area.

I was refereeing a game one Friday night, and I said to my girlfriend, "Do you want to come to the rink?" And she said, "So I'm going to come to the rink while all the other girlfriends are there to watch their boyfriends play and they are going to say, 'Who are you here to see?' and I'm going to say, 'The referee?'" It wasn't necessarily an attraction for women to come watch me. But she didn't mind the dinner afterward because we could afford to eat!

Watching hockey, I always knew who the referees were. Once I got into broadcasting, I got to be pals with Bruce Hood and Bryan Lewis, who were two of the top NHL officials at the time. I've always respected the guys in the stripes, and in later years came to know Bill McCreary, who's now in the Hockey Hall of Fame, and Dan O'Halloran and Wes McCauley, whose late dad, John, was one of the best ever—and Wes is skating right in his steps. And now with the microphone on while making calls, Wes has taken to being demonstrative. I hope he never stops. It gives the guys some personality that the game has taken away from them over the years.

17

Those Dulcet Tones

I was relentless in my pursuit of this dream job I have today. I listened to everyone I could do the sports, whether it be on radio or television, and tried to learn how it was done so that when my chance came, I would do it right.

The first time I heard Dave Hodge, who'd later be the host of *Hockey Night in Canada*, was on CFRB Radio 1010 in Toronto. Dave would come on at 11:15 at night during the *World Tonight*, doing an in-depth sportscast. I'd have my yellow Panasonic toot-a-loop twist radio beneath my pillow hanging on Dave's every word. Hodge's voice even to this day is probably the most perfect I have heard. He rarely made a mistake. He was so professional. He could find 10 words to sum up a story, when others might use 25.

Dave is a stickler for getting it right, especially with those around him. I think I've got a lot of that in me. I'm not saying that I don't make mistakes, but now that mistake is on me. What I don't want is someone else's mistake coming back to haunt me. If we're going to say a hockey player's name, find out the correct pronunciation and get it right. The easiest way to do that is to ask the player how he wants it said. If there is a question about that, I seek out an answer before each game.

In the summertime CFRB would hire a boat reporter. Names who went on to very successful Canadian sportscasting careers include Michael Landsberg and Suneel Joshi, both of whom started on the water as the CFRB boat reporter. I thought, "Why can't I be a boat reporter?" The job entailed being out on Lake Ontario. I could swim, if necessary, and talk. How hard can that be? I wrote CFRB, but they told me I had to be enrolled in some course to know the boating safety laws and regulations. They also said, nicely, "Don't call us, we'll call you." They never did. I'm still waiting. I have the rejection letter. In fact, I got rejected twice.

Radio fascinated me. My mother listened to 590-CKEY (now the FAN), and Jim "Shaky" Hunt was their sportscaster. I met him years later, and what an off-the-wall character he was. He had life in his sound like no other. The other voices I admired growing up in Toronto, dreaming I could be like them, were Dave Wright (from 1972 to 1976) and Brian Henderson on CHUM, and John Hinnen at CFTR Radio. While in college, I got the chance to meet John Hinnen through Jeff Ansell, a CHUM-FM news anchor. Now try to follow this. Jeff was the brother-in-law to my closest friend Sharon. Sharon and I are still best friends to this day. I used to go to CHUM-FM in my teens to watch Jeff read the news. Jeff said, "Here's John Hinnen's phone number. See if he has any leads." John did indeed have a lead. It was to call a news director at a radio station that was a 60-minute drive north of Toronto. Rayfield White was his name. Ray had nothing for me but did give me the number and contact of his friend Mark Orton at an AM/FM radio station east of Toronto, in Oshawa, where my hero Bobby Orr played junior hockey. Voila! Synergy. More on that later.

The Letter

First, the letter. When I was 17, I wrote to Brian Williams—not the fellow who does the news for MSNBC, but Canada's Brian Williams, who was the dean of Canadian television sports broadcasters from the 1980s onward.

As it turned out, Brian and Dave Hodge were best friends. I didn't know that, but here I'd picked out the two icons of Toronto broadcasting. I listened to Dave a lot as I mentioned, and Brian was the guy I watched on TV.

After getting my letter, Brian wrote me and later called me, and I'll never forget that day. I was sitting with my family in the den and my mom comes in and says, "Brian Williams is on the phone." I ran to the kitchen (days of home phones only). There was a little broom closet off the kitchen. I went in there to speak

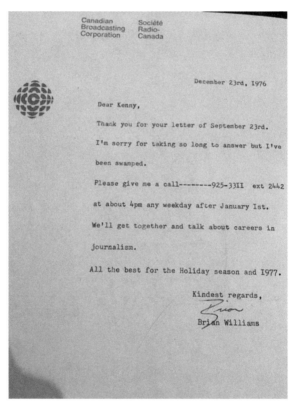

I was 17 years old, still dreaming of a career in broadcasting, when CBC's Brian Williams replied to a letter I wrote him three months earlier.

with Brian, so my mother wouldn't hear. I was damn proud coming out of that broom closet!

Brian had said, "Come on down and watch me do the suppertime sports," so the next month, in early 1977, I took the subway to downtown Toronto and to the CBC studios. He introduced me to his executive producer. After that I probably called Brian once a month, which was probably a little more than he would have preferred. In reality, what was he going to do for a 17-year-old kid? But he took my call pretty much every time. I'd go down and watch him a few more times, and he'd say, "Give me a call next month." Today, I have kids coming to me when I speak at schools asking me how to get into the business. That's why I always try to take the time to talk with people who want to get into this world. I can't help them get a job—that's going to be up to them—but if I can lead them in any way, I will.

Door to Door

Brian Williams had always told me to get a degree. "Let a radio station see that you'd put in the time," he'd say. So, I got a bachelor of arts degree in sociology, while also taking some political science and English courses at York University in Toronto. I wanted to do broadcasting at York University while I was there, but the radio station was bankrupt. So it was either go to York University and get a degree in something or go to Ryerson, which was the polytechnic institute for radio and TV. I chose York. Meanwhile, immediately after college I've got a job coming through my good high school friend Denise. Her dad's successful business was Amram's Distributing. They sold Russ Berrie plush toys, rattan furniture, and housewares. I was going to be their Northern Ontario sales rep. What do I know about (a) wicker furniture, (b) stuffed toys, and (c) selling, except selling myself? So I studied the business at Amram's office for a couple of weeks, but I hadn't yet signed the contract to work there.

While all this was taking place, I had just gone to see Mark Orton in Oshawa. Remember I mentioned a name that Rayfield White had given me to call. I did. I met with Mark. I now feel like I'm cheating on the Amrams. Jewish guilt.

Before going to see Mark in Oshawa about a radio job, my wonderful brother John said to me, "Sell yourself and tell them you'd work for free. Just show Mark how much you want this. That's where the passion comes from. If you truly want something from the heart, then it's authentic. Be yourself. Just tell him how much you want this."

A week passed after my interview with Oshawa, and wouldn't you know it, Mark called me at the Amram offices the day that I signed my contract with Amram. This is 1980. There are no cell phones. I was stunned. Apparently, I'd done what my brother sent me to Oshawa to do.

"I want to tell you something," Mark Orton explained. "I've never seen someone sell themselves or have the passion to want it, as you did." They hired me about three weeks out of college.

My brother said, "Did you tell them you'd work for free?" Absolutely I did. One hundred percent.

In truth, I didn't tell him that. I probably would have worked for free, but I was a little smarter than that, so I didn't offer it up. My mom and dad wanted me out of their condo. So I went to Oshawa and sold myself to the news director, and it worked. I got the job I'd wanted since the age of 10.

As happy as I was, the situation presented a whole new series of problems for me. I had to go in and quit working for my friend's father. I've been a friend with his daughter Denise to this day. "My dad's gonna kill you," she said at the time. I walked into her brother Roger's office and told him I was quitting. I would have been making $20,000 plus commissions in 1980. If I knew how to sell, and that remained to be seen, I could have made $60,000 to $80,000 annually, if not more.

Instead, I was working in Oshawa for $9,500. I didn't care. It didn't matter to me. I was getting to live my dream, to do what my heart told me I should be doing. Roger said, "You're making a huge mistake." And I said, "No, I'm not!"

It was my passion. That's why I always say to people, if you have a passion for something, do it. Money doesn't matter. Just do it.

The Amrams eventually were okay with it, and we've remained family friends. I still see Roger, and he told me years later, "I guess you didn't make a mistake. You had to follow your dream." That's how I got to Oshawa and my first on-air job.

I was covering local City Hall. I worked with Mike Inglis, who was doing the sports in Oshawa. He's now the radio play-by-play guy for the NBA's Miami Heat. That just goes to show you where talent and dedication and hard work can take you in the long run. Two guys who started at a tiny radio station east of Toronto in Oshawa, Ontario, end up going on to do play-by-play for major league championship sports teams.

There was a Red Wings connection to Oshawa as well. In the early 1950s before the NHL entry draft existed, NHL teams sponsored junior teams, and Detroit had two teams in the OHA Junior A series, the Windsor Spitfires and the Oshawa Generals.

The Generals were coached by Larry Aurie, who was a Detroit legend in the 1920s and 1930s and was part of the Red Wings' first two Stanley Cup championship teams in 1935–36 and 1936–37.

Aurie also produced another Red Wings legend while in Oshawa and that was Alex Delvecchio, who'd play more than two decades with the team; work as Gordie Howe's center longer than any player in the team's history; and become captain, coach, and GM of the Wings. "Fats," as Delvecchio was known, was also my broadcast partner Mickey Redmond's center when Mick became Detroit's first 50-goal scorer in 1972–73.

Cut That Out

Like Delvecchio, my road to Hockeytown began in Oshawa as I set out to learn the business. It was back when reel-to-reel tapes were used to edit conversations, and I had to splice the tapes together. I'd leave reports for the next day, and they'd be used by the newscasters. On a few occasions the tape snapped on the air. So I came in one afternoon, and Paul Rellinger, who was the traffic reporter, has the two reel-to-reels pinned up to the bulletin board with the sign, "Ken Daniels editing machine" and in the middle he'd tied a knot with the two pieces of tape. I guess I wasn't very good at it. Lesson learned.

My boss at CKAR-AM in Oshawa was station manager George Grant. That's right, just like Mary Richards on the *Mary Tyler Moore Show*, my boss was Mr. Grant. One day, I was doing a news report on General Motors, the company that was the No. 1 employer in the city of Oshawa. Like Detroit, it was a motor city. Anyway, I'm reading my story and I refer to the president of GM as Joe Rinehart. The next thing I hear is Mr. Grant's booming voice from the other side of the studio door bellowing, "It's Jim, not Joe." Not a good idea to get the name wrong of the guy in charge of the biggest company in town. I'm sure the folks in advertising were cringing.

I know being in radio early on, I screwed up a lot. After moving from Oshawa to Toronto and CJCL, my news director Scott Metcalfe, a great guy who is now in charge of 680 News in Toronto, said to me when I left there, "Nobody ever asked more questions than you did." That was how I learned, and I still ask questions today.

That comes from something my dad said to me. "There's no such thing as a stupid question. There are only stupid people who are going to think that your question is stupid." Now, there may be a little gray area in there where there could be some stupid questions, but his point was if you don't know something, ask. And to this day, I'm always asking questions.

Oshawa, Ontario, 1980. My first job in broadcasting, CKAR-AM / CKQT-FM, and a look made for radio—or the adult film industry.

I'll ask Ken Holland questions. I was always asking Scotty Bowman questions, just learning as much as I could about the game. I don't know it all, and those guys will forget more than I'll ever know. I ask Mickey Redmond questions all the time. That's how I learn.

Stu Billett, whose company in partnership with game-show legend Ralph Edwards did the *People's Court*, which debuted in 1981, was my first-ever interview on Oshawa radio. *People's Court* was just coming on the air with Judge Wapner. (Judge Wapner passed away at age 97, as I was writing this on February 26, 2017.) *People's Court* was really the first reality television when you think about it, and now look where we are today in that realm of TV.

Radio is great background training for television. There's nothing better because you learn to ad lib. You can feel comfortable, and, believe me, during my early years in radio I was pretty bad, but the stations put up with my mistakes. I did overnights, and I could make mistakes when few were listening. I learned how to incorporate sound into my broadcast and be more inventive because I was on my own. I'd write my own copy, which taught me how to write and put things in point form, more or less, as we speak.

It's really a shame that opportunities on overnight radio for graduates don't exist much anymore. The bottom line has become the bottom line. Syndicated programming has taken over the overnight airwaves.

The Graveyard Shift

About a year after starting my career in Oshawa, the next big break came my way. I applied for and then got a job at a newly formatted news station in Toronto. Larry Silver, who was an offbeat news guy I had grown up listening to at CFTR, was now the news director at Metro-1430 in Toronto, the old CKFH, the station Foster Hewitt founded. The station also owned the Maple Leafs radio rights.

I was doing three nights a week news anchoring/reporting in Oshawa and the weekend mornings news and sports. Larry said, "I'd like to offer you a job in Toronto, but it's overnights." I didn't have to think for very long. The pay was $11,000. I was up two grand and working overnights in Toronto from 10:00 PM. to 7:00 AM.

After a few months of being there, sarcastic Larry posted this note above my work station:

"Procrastination is my sin, it brings me endless sorrow. I really must stop doing it. In fact, I'll start tomorrow."

I loved that. And to this day I obviously still remember it well.

I was still living in my parents' condo (the procrastination part from my dad's perspective) while I was doing the overnight news, and one Christmas I decided to throw a station party. My parents went to Florida for the winter. Thus, the party.

They would leave me money when they departed for three months for the "other" land of the Jewish people, so I was a kid living on a per diem. But there wasn't much in the way of food left behind at the "home hotel." On one cold winter afternoon in December of 1980, what could be better than a hot bowl of Campbell's soup? My friend Ron Sherkin grabbed one of the few tins in that pantry, heated it up, and began to dig in, when Ron looked over at me and said, "Is this soup still good?"

I replied with the ol' "a tin of soup doesn't go bad!" And back then, labels for "best before dates" weren't a prerequisite. But, to appease Ron, I said I'd check the label. There was no "use before date," but there was a contest we could enter, with a deadline of December 1974. We were late for that contest, but right on time for "stop eating!"

So, back to the party. My boss Larry and his wife were the first to arrive. I greeted them and asked if I could get them anything. Larry looked around and without missing a beat said, "Some company would be great."

Larry always put his own slant on the news. I think I picked up a little of his writing style too, although not quite as pointed. On a hot spring day while reading the weather, Larry would say, "A beautiful sunny April day. It's 60 degrees in the big smoke. Ladies, it's time to drop your linen and men start your grinnin'." Try getting away with that in today's PC world.

I also remember looking on as a traffic girl came in to audition for Larry. He was sitting at his typewriter while she was kneeling on the floor next to him. I'm looking over at the two of them. She begins to take off her sweater, because it was hot in the newsroom. Larry looks at her and says, "Oh no sweetie, that won't be necessary. You already have the job."

My Parents: Life Givers—and Life Savers

So while working overnights and 23 years old and living at home, I wouldn't be here today if not for Mom's capabilities at charades and my parent's 40-plus years together that they could finish each other's sentences. I'd be sleeping all day and wake around 7:00 at night to join my parents for their dinner and my breakfast. My mom and I would discuss things at breakfast/dinner but we always knew my dad was "out to lunch," as we called it. He was physically present at the table, but somewhere along the way, take-out food had been ordered. His mind was elsewhere. We can all be like that at times. Marv was like that a lot.

So during their breakfast/my dinner, my mom and I had talked for about five minutes. I kid you not, my dad then decided he'd heard voices and asked me the very question my mom and I had been answering for that entire time lapse. I looked at my mother, and she burst out laughing. She had a wonderful cackle. As I began to join her in making fun of the obvious, a piece of steak I hadn't finished chewing lodged in my wind pipe.

I felt this could be it. I was doing the Fred Sanford. Dancing around frantically, arms waving, my mom starts yelling at my dad, with her arms making the "Heimlich motion." My dad looked at her and all I heard her scream was, "do that German thing."

My dad got behind me, and as he did, I collapsed, and I swear to you the last thing I remember thinking was, they won't be able to save me, and I saw that "white light." It was bright and round and white coming toward me. The next thing I saw going toward my mother was that huge chunk of steak. I looked up, saw the relief on my mother's face, and then the gasp, with the words that any son would expect to hear, as their mother just saw her husband save my life. "I just had the carpets cleaned!"

Leaving the Beaver

I had a lot of fun in the radio business, especially working the overnight shift. I was partnered with John Oakley, a very bright and funny guy, while I was doing the graveyard shift at CJCL Radio in Toronto in 1982. It was all news talk then. John has since gone on to become a main voice at 640 AM in Toronto.

John got Tony Dow on the phone one night, and he invited me in for the conversation. Unbeknownst to Tony, he got Jerry Mathers on at the same time.

Now we all knew then that Tony and Jerry were not close. That is an understatement, by the way. John didn't give a damn. He was just thinking that this could make for some great live overnight radio.

Tony Dow was talking and the conversation was going well. I was a huge *Leave It To Beaver* fan as a kid. It was an iconic television show in the late 1950s and early 1960s, as we were all watching Mathers and Dow grow up on the screen as their fictional characters, Theodore (Beaver) Cleaver and his older brother Wally, doing the same silly things and making similar mistakes and bad decisions that all young boys were making in real life.

Even today, a half century later, some hockey coaches will use the term, "He's like Eddie Haskell," referring to the Cleavers' troublemaking slacker friend. It just became part of our lexicon.

We're talking and the conversation is going fine until John says, "Tony, I've got a friend I want to get on the phone." At this point, Jerry doesn't even know who's on the other end. So he introduces Jerry Mathers and says, "Jerry, Tony Dow's on the line. Say hello to Tony Dow." And all you hear is "click." Tony's gone. He didn't even talk to him. Jerry wasn't happy about it either, and within a minute Jerry was gone, too. John thought he'd get fireworks, but all he ended up with was dead air. That was too funny.

Living the Dream

People say, "You're really lucky." I always say, 'Yes, I'm very lucky.' I never go a day without knowing how blessed I am to do what I'm doing. However, I think we always put ourselves in a position to be lucky.

"Luck is what happens when preparation meets opportunity."

If I have a passion for something, which I did from the age of 10, then I strive to put myself in a position that when the time is right, everything I've done up to that time will allow me to be successful. Thus the phrase, "timing is everything." Passion and hard work will lead you to the right place and time. We can meet someone out of the blue, and we may be fortunate to get a contact number through that person. But what we do with it is up to us. Everything we have done to that point in our life leads us to be prepared for that moment and to seize that moment if we have the passion. There's a little bit of everything that comes together, and it did for me. I'm still living the dream.

Another "Lucky" Guy

Dan Shulman was voted by *Sports Illustrated* as the top announcer in the United States for the decade of 2000–10. Dan is mentioned in this book because he has been a very good friend to me, and I was there when he was breaking into the radio business in the early '90s. Dan gave up a career as an actuary to try radio. Great idea! Dan was *ESPN Sunday Night Baseball*'s lead play-by-play man and is still ESPN's top voice for college basketball.

And here I plan to prove my point once again, as to why there is no luck, but "luck is what happens when preparation meets opportunity."

Here's how Dan Shulman tells his story of his big break in the business.

"I was hosting a talk show from 8:00 to midnight at CJCL 1430 in Toronto. I finished the show and as I walk into the newsroom, the phone is ringing. I answer, and I hear someone say, 'My name is Al Jaffe, I work for ESPN, and I would like to talk to you about coming down to Connecticut to audition for ESPN Radio.' So this being 1993, and me being from Canada, I was not even aware that ESPN Radio existed at that time, and I thought it was my college roommate, Rob, punking me. So I say something smart-alecky like, 'That's pretty good Rob, you even gave yourself a New York accent,' and I hear nothing but silence on the other end of the phone. Then I hear this: 'I'm going to say this one more time. My name is Al Jaffe, I work for ESPN.' So now I'm terrified I've screwed this up, but also still not completely convinced this is real, so I asked 'Al' for his phone number and tell him I will call him right back as soon as I finish up some things I need to do in the newsroom. He gives me his number with a Connecticut area code. I call it back, and sure enough, this is real. It turns out Al had been told there was a young radio host he should have a listen to, from Albany or Rochester or somewhere on an AM station at 1420 on the dial. And when he looked for him, he accidentally found me, at 1430. Remember, this is pre-Internet. Al had to turn the dial to find a station, and by sheer luck, Al found me. He also found the phone number to the station and offered me an audition. And that's how my career at ESPN started. Without question, one of the biggest breaks I've ever gotten. But the opportunity of working at CJCL helped prepare me for so many things that would come my way, including the chance to work at ESPN."

CHAPTER 2
GETTING THE CALL

A move to Toronto radio led me into play-by-play and eventually to Hockey Night in Canada

Moving on Up

At CJCL, I went from overnight news and sports to the City Hall beat. At least it was daylight hours. I swore I'd never be back at City Hall after I fought a parking ticket there and then spent three hours trying to remember where I parked my car in that maze of a lot. That *Seinfeld* episode could have been based on me. But that's another story for another book.

I had never voted before, so at least I was going to City Hall with a totally unbiased opinion of any politician that I had never met. There I was with an office right in Toronto City Hall filing reports on council meetings and the daily goings-on of the municipal government.

I have to admit my attention span for these argumentative legislators was limited at best. And these were days long before Jimmy Kimmel star Rob Ford was around. Had Rob been Toronto mayor at that time, I wouldn't have missed a second. But back in 1982, my give-a-crap meter had the E laughing at the F. I would often duck out, and when I returned I would get the gist of the meeting from a colleague, grab a clip from a decision maker into my trusted tape recorder (yes cassette tape), and use that sound bite in a 50-second audio report.

Noted Canadian TV host Steve Paikin was cutting his teeth in the political world at that time, too, but has gone on to grow wisdom teeth in that regard. Back then he would say to me, "I was driving home listening to your report on the car radio, and it was better than mine, and you weren't even there for most of it. How do you do that?" Well, the key is that less is more. I was truly a voice of the people. The listener likely knew as little as I did, so I tried to explain things that even I could understand—layman's terms.

To give you an example, a "hot-button" Toronto City Hall debate back in the early '90s (long after I was gone) was whether or not Mayor June Rowlands would allow a Toronto band named Barenaked Ladies to perform live at a City Hall event. The mayor didn't think their name was appropriate. June Rowlands lasted one term. The Barenaked Ladies sold more than 15 million records and in 2007 wrote the theme song for the hit TV sitcom *The Big Bang Theory*.

For me, the bottom line was and still is versatility. The news people at CJCL knew they could depend on me for whatever they needed. I was always doing a mix of news and sports through all the format changes.

There were plenty of different styles of radio employed during my days at CJCL. I started there in February 1982 at age 22 when it was called Metro 1430 (Metro for Metro Toronto) and at 1430 on the dial. Its previous call letters were CKFH (CK-Foster Hewitt). Metro 1430 was referred to as the "radio station for the city," and since the signal was so poor, you had to be in the heart of the city to actually hear it. Then there was "The Music of your Life"—well, music of your grandmother's life. So, as a City Hall and general reporter, the station gave me a vehicle to use. That was a perk! The con: emblazoned on the side of the white Chevy was THE MUSIC OF YOUR LIFE. I could get picked up in that car by a woman 60 or older. In my early twenties however, I wasn't looking for Mrs. Robinson. But that didn't stop my buddies from wanting to cruise in it, thinking it was so cool. I was thinking it was a chick repellent. Seemed to be the latter. So as I was saving on gas, I could afford to buy girls drinks in the bar. That I did. Then we took a taxi home, avoiding the Benny Goodman mobile.

After I left the radio station for the first time in 1985, it went to all talk and all news and eventually all sports. The Blue Jays and Maple Leafs radio rights helped the ratings significantly in the evenings.

Palling Around with Pal Hal

I had been at CJCL for about 18 months when the news came across the wire on September 1, 1983, that a Soviet fighter jet had shot down Korean Airlines Flight 007, killing all 269 passengers and crew aboard. A few weeks later, 80-year-old Harold Ballard, owner of the Toronto Maple Leafs, announced that he was canceling the appearance of the Moscow Circus at Maple Leaf Gardens because of the incident.

I was a young reporter, full of idealism and hungry to make a name for myself, so I decided to jump on the story. I called Maple Leaf Gardens just to get a comment, and Maple Leafs owner Harold Ballard answered the phone. It was 7:00 at night, and I was doing the evening shift. I just called the Gardens and this man said "Hello." I said I was looking for Harold Ballard. "This is," he answered. "Who's this?" So I explained and said that I wanted to talk to him about canceling the Moscow Circus. "What do you need?" Ballard asked. I told him I'd love to get an interview with him and he said, "Well, come on over." I asked how to get to him. He said, "Just walk into the Hot Stove Club (which was the restaurant in Maple Leaf Gardens). Someone will direct you. I'm upstairs in my apartment."

On a side note, if you are unfamiliar with Harold Ballard, he was bombastic. His teams were constantly in turmoil due to his petulant tirades. In the early 1970s he was convicted on 47 charges of fraud and tax evasion. He was sentenced to nine years in a federal

Neither Harold Ballard's politics nor grammar were spot on. He was a lousy owner. But he was a great quote, and character of the game.

prison. He served around a third of that, finishing in a Toronto halfway house. Once paroled he likened prison to a motel, with color television. But while Harold was doing time, the Leafs took the opportunity to sign their best defenseman of the 1970s and early '80s, Borje Salming. Borje began the Swedish invasion and finished his career as a Red Wing. Harold didn't like European players, but Borje was hard to resist. In the end, Harold's protection of Borje would not sit well with others.

When I arrived at Maple Leaf Gardens and asked about speaking with Mr. Ballard, someone immediately directed me up a staircase to Harold's apartment. And there he was in all his splendid glory—in his boxer shorts and T-shirt. If I only had my camera.

On his circular bed was a leopard-print duvet. He was also owner of the CFL's Hamilton Tiger-Cats at that time. Right next to his bed was an opulent desk and farther down the hall, a kitchen. I can't imagine he used it that much, with the restaurant and staff at his command at the bottom of the staircase.

I sat down at Harold's desk and turned on my cassette tape recorder. Harold held nothing back. He spoke of how he felt the Russians were murderers and they couldn't be trusted and, of course, he'd have none of them ever play on his Maple Leafs team. I left copious clips for the morning show from my exclusive interview with Harold. It was a major scoop, but the best thing for me was that he signed two posters of the Moscow Circus to me. The following is exactly how he wrote it—spelling mistakes and all:

"To Ken. There arn't any good Russian.There all muraders. Never trust the Ruskies. Remember KAL007. THIS SHOW CANCELLED DUE TO MURDER."

This young reporter who called and got lucky that Harold Ballard answered the phone was suddenly a big deal. And my favorite NHL players would later be Igor Larionov and Pavel Datsyuk. Sorry Harold, but thanks for the posters.

A Hunger for Television

The late great Ernie Harwell said "a man is lucky if God gives him a job he enjoys."

But having said that, was I lucky or just hungry? And in a position to have to eat?

It was early summer of 1985, and I was 26 years old leading the bachelor life. Which meant I had limited food in my fridge and Twinkies in my cupboard, nothing of substance to be found.

It was a Friday night. No food and no date. But the Blue Jays were playing at Exhibition Stadium, aka Excruciation Stadium, aka the mistake by the lake. I had nothing to eat, but I had a media pass, which would get me something to fill my 145 pounds. Free meal? Ken's on it. By the way, they now charge the media to eat.

I ran into sportscaster Don Martin from the CBC. I'd met him a couple of times at different news conferences. This time, Don said, "I'm going to work the Canada Summer Games for the network. Did you want to fill in for me?" And I said, "You're kidding me, right?" He said, "No, they're looking for a replacement." "At the CBC?" "Yeah." He told me to call Howard Bernstein, the executive producer. I said I've called CBC before, I've asked for Howard Bernstein. I've left messages, and he hasn't called me back. I just wanted a meeting with him. I was in radio looking to get into television. No face-made-for-radio jokes please.

Don said, "Call him Monday. He'll take your call." I did. And he did. I don't even think Don told him that I would be calling. Bernstein said, "Yeah we're holding auditions. Why don't you come down and meet me?" So I did. We talked for a while, and I found out there was another young man who'd be coming in from Montreal, also with no television experience, and would be auditioning on nights that I wasn't. We'd hang around the newsroom during the week and then on Saturday and Sunday nights, we'd audition. Live. The first night I was on, the CBC had a Canadian Football League game from Vancouver. By the time the football game ended in the east, it was after 1:30 AM.

By the time they got to me and the sports report it was nearly two in the morning. I had roughly a 10-minute sportscast prepared, and as nervous as I was (and you could tell) it was going okay. It was all written on the teleprompter (the words come up in the camera lens). I had about a minute left in the sportscast, and I had jotted down on the script on the teleprompter underneath my last item, "Ad lib." As we came out of the final taped item I looked up at the camera and all I saw was "ad lib" and I said "ad libbing now." It was awful!

What seemed like five minutes was probably only 20 seconds of ad libbing. The only person who saw it because it was so late was the brother of a friend of mine. He called me the next day and said, "That was pretty good, and funny at the end." It was bad, but I figured if I can get through that, I can get through anything. I went at it again the next night. It was better. And by midweek, the best news came. I was the one they selected. I was the summer replacement on CBC local television, and my life would change forever.

Meeting Mr. Hockey

Years before I became the voice of the Red Wings, I got to play hockey against the face of the Red Wings, the greatest Detroit player of them all, none other than Mr. Hockey himself, Gordie Howe.

It was November 1985. It was five years after the "Miracle on Ice," the gold medal Lake Placid win by Team USA in the 1980 Winter Olympics. So Lake Placid, New York, was still the place to play hockey. Paul Crowley, who would become a Red Wings scout in the 1990s, was running hockey schools and fantasy camps, and he decided the Olympic Center Arena (later known as Herb Brooks Arena) was the perfect venue. He invited Gordie to take part for the Red Wings along with former Wings defenseman Bill

Fantasy camp: chasing Mr. Hockey around in Lake Placid, New York, in 1985. Catching him would have been my miracle on ice.

Gadsby. Wayne Cashman and Don Marcotte were there from the Boston Bruins; Stan Mikita from the Chicago Blackhawks; and Eddie Shack, Frank Mahovlich, and Johnny Bower from the Toronto Maple Leafs. I convinced the folks at CJCL to allow me to go, and I would file reports to later be used during intermissions of the Maple Leafs radio games on the station. Talk about an ideal working vacation. But that's when Gordie worked me over.

The fantasy Wings were on a power play. I was penalty killing, playing for the fantasy Maple Leafs. Gordie was bringing the puck through the middle of his zone, and I angled him back to his left. He spun and went the other way, and I followed. I angled him back again, and that's where Gordie had a different angle. Cutting back, he knew I'd be waiting, and he turned

41

Rubbing elbows, sort of, with Gordie Howe in Lake Placid in 1985.

with an elbow high right to my head. Down I went. I just got elbowed by Gordie Howe. I couldn't have been happier.

We later played them in the semifinals, and I was skating up the left-wing boards with Gordie back checking. That's when I felt the blade of his stick come across the right side of my neck. Welt to prove it. I turned to him while skating, and I'm pissed. I said, "What did you do that for?"

He replied, "You were there." Gordie was 57 at the time, my age now. So 31 years later I can speak from experience. He was in great shape.

That's when I really got to meet the stars I grew up idolizing (besides Bobby Orr and Bernie Parent) like Gadsby and Howe and Bower and Mahovlich for the first time. Later when I came to Detroit, Gordie and Bill already knew of me just from the time I had with them at that fantasy camp. There I was, a 26-year-old, having drinks with Gordie and Bill. Along with one of the finest gentlemen you could ever meet, Johnny Bower. I talked to Bill Gadsby's wife, Edna, after Bill had passed in 2016 and we talked about those fantasy camps because she was down there with him. We had a great time. I remember meeting Gordie in Detroit about a year after I got the job here, and my beautiful daughter, Arlyn, was with me. Gordie was typical Gordie. Elbow first along with a smile, all the while holding his little dog Rocket, who was named after Rocket Richard. Within moments, he had handed off Rocket to Arlyn.

Eddie Shack and me, comparing nose size, at Paul Crowley's Lake Placid Fantasy Camp in 1985. That welt on my neck's right side is courtesy of Gordie's high stick.

If guys weren't playing well and you were talking with Gordie, he could be pretty honest off the record. I learned a lot about the game from talking with Gordie, first in Lake Placid and later in Detroit.

A Hall (and Oates) of a Time

Hall and Oates was my favorite band from the 1970s.

As I made my way driving into downtown Lake Placid for the fantasy camp, another fantasy appeared. On the Olympic billboard, there it was: "Tomorrow. 7 PM. Hall and Oates in Concert."

Tickets were my first stop. The next day I went downstairs at the hotel. I went out toward the tennis courts and John Oates is standing there. There were two tennis racquets with him. We got talking and I told him I was down for a fantasy hockey camp. And he said, "You want to hit some balls until one of our band members gets here?" I said no. ARE YOU KIDDING? Of course, I said yes. "Say It Isn't So." "You Make My Dreams Come True." "One on One." Those are all their song titles, but it fits the story now, so I couldn't resist. I got to play about five minutes of tennis with John Oates.

Later in the day, I was waiting in the lobby and here come Hall and Oates getting ready to go to the arena. I had my camera with me, and it was not an automatic. I gave it to one of the other hockey players to take the picture. It was back in the days when you couldn't see the picture until you had it developed—at a store. He took the picture all right, but either he was blind or he didn't understand how to focus a camera. You can tell from the picture it's me with John and Daryl out by the bus, but the bus was apparently the main point of focus. Thankfully, the picture with me and

John Oates and me in 1985, Lake Placid, on the tennis courts.

John Oates on the tennis court is great. I would have loved for the one with Daryl and John and me to have turned out. Besides the Beatles, Hall and Oates were my favorites. The top-selling pop duo of all time.

Dave Hodge Flips Out

I was working at the CBC the night of the fateful Dave Hodge pencil flip, the pencil flip heard around the hockey world. It was Saturday, March 14, 1987, and when the Leafs game ended *Hockey Night in Canada* switched the CBC national network over to catch the end of the game between the Philadelphia Flyers and Montreal Canadiens.

We're waiting to do the late sports at around 11:40, and I'm in my office with my feet up watching the game. It's close to

11:00. The game ends tied through regulation time, and Hodge, who is the *Hockey Night in Canada* host, comes back on air to announce that only viewers in Quebec will see the overtime and the rest of Canada would be going to the national CBC news.

Here I am happy that they're not going back for the overtime because frankly, I wanted to get out of there. I was just waiting for the game to end. I used to write generic scripts because I had to voice the highlights live anyway. I never gave away the score in the beginning just in case a viewer watching me hadn't seen the game. Why lead with the end? That's like putting the final pages of a book in the beginning. I'd let the highlights play out and tell the story.

Hodge wasn't done talking, though. He continued, "That's the way things go these days in sports and at this network. We'll leave you in suspense. And find out who's in charge of the way we do things around here. Good night from *Hockey Night in Canada*." And then he flipped his pencil in the air in disgust as they went off air and switched to the national news, rather than the end of the Canadiens and Flyers.

When Dave flipped his pencil, I knew he was toast. I also knew there was a job opening, but knew I wasn't ready for it. I couldn't be *that* lucky because I wasn't prepared enough. This was only my second year in television.

So, in came Ron MacLean, the former weatherman from Red Deer, Alberta, to take over as host of *Hockey Night*. He was a couple of years younger than me but light years ahead in terms of handling the heat of the No. 1 stage in the country.

I remember walking into the newsroom that night saying, "Did you see that?" There was a collective, "Oh hell yeah. This isn't good." The next day—and for that matter all week—it was all Dave Hodge stories. It took over the news. In Canada, hockey is religion. And I was right. Hodge was gone, but he left as the best.

Brophy

Among my regular reporting duties for the CBC was daily coverage of the NHL's Toronto Maple Leafs. That wonderment I had as a youth, pondering what it would be like to get on the inside of the door to the Leafs dressing room, was no longer a fantasy, it was reality.

The Leafs of the mid-1980s were not what you'd call a power-house club. Winning seasons were out of the question, but thanks to a 21-team NHL where 16 teams qualified for the playoffs, a postseason berth was attainable.

The Leafs made the playoffs in 1986–87 despite a 32–42–6 regular-season mark. Toronto then upset the St. Louis Blues in the first round of the playoffs and grabbed a 3–1 second-round series edge on the Detroit Red Wings. Suddenly, the Leafs were one win away from a conference final appearance.

Detroit posted 3–0 and 4–2 victories to pull even in the series. Game 7 was slated for Joe Louis Arena, and Toronto's once-bright hopes were quickly dimming.

Toronto was coached that season by minor league legend John Brophy. To Broph, *Slap Shot* wasn't a movie, it was a documentary about his career. Brophy spent his entire 21-season pro career in the low minor leagues, including 17 seasons in the Eastern Hockey League. The EHL could have been called the Jules Verne League, because it was about 20,000 leagues below the NHL.

As tough as nails, they called Broph "The Godfather of Goonery." Brophy accumulated 3,848 penalty minutes in 1,064 games. He led his league in penalty minutes seven times during his career. With his shock of white hair, menacing stare, and penchant for unleashing F-bomb-laced tirades, Brophy could put the fear of God into even a seasoned journalist. Considering their dismal regular-season mark and the loudmouthed approach often taken by Leafs owner Harold Ballard, my CBC partner Don Martin figured it was fair game to ask Brophy if he was worried about losing his job if the Leafs lost Game 7.

"Am I worrying about my job?" Brophy snarled. "Am I worrying about my job." And here come the F-bombs, one after another after another. Don uses the story on the air, plays the entire clip of Brophy's explosion—with bleeps, of course—and comes out of the clip and says, "I'll take that as a no." Don had a great sense of humor, but he also had enough guts to ask John Brophy that question. We all knew how scary Brophy was. And the Leafs did lose Game 7 to the Wings by a 3–0 count. As badly as that season ended for Brophy and the Leafs, the next season didn't begin well.

It was early October 1987 and I was doing color on Leafs radio for a one-goal loss at the Met Center in Bloomington, Minnesota, the place everyone recalls for the multicolored seats. Back then we weren't chartering flights after games, so we made our way to the team hotel right across the street. Some of the players ordered pizza to be delivered. We were on the main floor of the hotel, with doors opening to the parking lot. I heard a lot of noise coming from Borje Salming's room, and as I looked out my window, a streaking Leaf was passing by at a much quicker pace than he had on the ice two hours before in full gear. Other guys in Borje's room were playing a loud game of Nerf basketball and locked the door, leaving their teammate outside in the cold. Hotel security called head coach Brophy, but he suggested that they deal with it themselves. That was a mistake. Borje Salming and Al Iafrate were given hotel misconducts and ejected.

Salming, a 15-year Leaf, was sent home the next day by Brophy. John felt his 36-year-old assistant captain lost a lot of respect that night. But Brophy's public humiliation of the Swedish blueliner backfired, after the hotel later admitted it blew things out of proportion. Harold Ballard issued a public apology to Borje for the way he was treated by his coach. Brophy was fired the next season. In 1989, after 16 years as a Leaf, Salming signed as a free agent in Detroit, on a $425,000 one-year deal, playing the final season of his career as a Red Wing.

Don't Get Boxed In

What I loved about covering the Leafs for CBC Television was in those days things were a little looser and more relaxed. I didn't have to go through public relations to set up an interview for a story idea. Times have changed with players today. They're more protected by the teams than they were back then. At that time, I just went right to Leafs forward Wendel Clark and told him I'd love to do a skating session with him. I raced him. I was a pretty good skater at the time and a decent, but not great, hockey player. Wendel beat me, but not by much.

Toronto defenseman Al Iafrate, who was a local guy from Dearborn, Michigan, was one of the faster skaters in the league so I decided to race him, too. I don't think Al was going full bore and he still ended up beating me pretty easily. I was responsible for doing a daily item to run on the CBC local evening news, so I tried to think outside the box. Even after the Leafs got kicked out of their Bloomington hotel, I did a story on how many of them knew what they had ordered on the pizza that was to be delivered as they got kicked out. They had fun with it. Today, they'd have none of that sort of thing.

Getting to know the players, getting to know the personalities, I think helps. I got myself in a position with the players where they were willing to do pretty much anything I suggested.

I did a piece with Leafs captain Rick Vaive for Christmas at his house with his wife, Joyce. I did a piece at Eddie Olczyk's place with his wife, Diana. Edzo is now a TV analyst with Chicago and NBC. We knew back then that Eddie could talk, and now he's doing it for a living. I just tried to get the players out of their element. I always thought that helped the fans to get to know them. I wish we could do more of that today. I love Trevor Thompson's pieces when he goes "one on one" on the ice with Red Wing players. There's so much out there now, and fans have so much choice of what they can watch, that I think if they knew the personalities more, they might be more inclined to watch the game.

Seoul Man

My opportunity at CBC Television was quickly expanding beyond regular sports reporting duties and weekend sports anchor. Early in 1988, I was given a huge opportunity when I learned I'd be part of our CBC network coverage of the Summer Olympics in Seoul, South Korea.

My Seoul experience was the first time I'd ever be on the world stage, and I remember that time to be the most nerve-wracking experience of my life. The executive producer for the CBC Olympics was Bob Moir. He spent more than 40 years at the network and passed away just prior to Christmas 2016 at age 87.

Bob gave me the chance to cover canoeing and kayaking, and it was going to be my first crack at play-by-play in my broadcast career. I always thought I'd be doing play-by-play on frozen water—not this—but you have to start somewhere. Why not the Olympics?

My analyst on the canoeing and kayaking events was Sue Holloway. Sue competed in both Winter and Summer Olympics and won two medals for Canada in sprint canoeing in Los Angeles in 1984. Let's just say she competed a lot harder while on the water than she did in talking about it. A lot of analysts come in and think because they played the sport they can waltz through talking about

My first Olympic assignment in Seoul in 1988, with my mentor the past 12 years, Brian Williams.

it without much in the way of preparation. That's not the case at all. You've got to work at it. And now, in my first Olympics I was doing the work of two people while I should have just been worrying about me. I've seen it in hockey, too. It takes preparation to be good at this line of work.

Many fans at home think they could easily be a color analyst. But to be put on the spot and dissect a play moments after it happened in succinct fashion is an art. I always tell analysts who are new to the TV game, get used to the "how and why." People are watching you on TV. Don't tell them what happened. They can see that. Tell them how and why it happened. And be ready to say the same thing three different ways, over three different replay angles. And do it in 20 seconds or less. And by the way, here's a shot of a player so talk about his attributes, and don't sound like an idiot while you're doing it. And if play is going on, wrap up your thought before you talk right over a significant moment.

Moir wanted to throw some other things at me in Seoul. He wanted me to do basketball. I didn't feel I knew basketball well enough. It was an important game involving the Canadian team (Canada is where basketball was invented after all), so I decided to own it. I said to Bob, "To tell you the truth, I don't want to disappoint you or our viewers if I'm not comfortable." Bob understood and appreciated my honesty. "Well, we've got tennis," he said. "Chris Evert is playing tomorrow, and we'll come to you at different points during the sets." So he sends me to tennis, and I'm there alone. I know tennis well enough since I'd played it a little bit. Chris Evert is playing her first match. It's against Italy's Sandra Cecchini. Tennis was just coming back into the Olympics as a full-medal sport in 1988. It was a demonstration sport at Los Angeles four years earlier, the first time tennis had been part of a Summer Olympiad since 1924.

As I said, I knew tennis, albeit not to the level of expert, but I knew Bud Collins. He was the guru of tennis commentators, the best in the business. When I arrived at the venue, CBC was positioned in the row right behind where Bud Collins of NBC was going live with the Evert match. They didn't come to us until the second set, so I knew I had a first set to grab all the information I could. I wasn't even on headset. I listened, and I took notes of everything Bud Collins was saying about Chris Evert. When CBC came to me for live inserts, maybe four or five minutes at a time during the match, I was basically talking all about Chris Evert and her opponent, paraphrasing from things Bud Collins was saying earlier.

Tennis arrived for the Seoul Olympics in 1988. I arrived on the court where I shouldn't have been. But I got an interview with legend Chris Evert.

Tennis play-by-play isn't like other sports. You're not saying, "She hits the ball over the net." I knew it was a sport that was more conversational without overtalking it. I must have sounded like I knew what I was talking about, because one of our great script producers, Natalie Tedesco, told me later that Bob said, "Boy, for a guy who was doing his first tennis match, he did okay." See kids, it's not who you know but who you know to sit behind.

After Evert won, I was with CBC's Fausto Bellamy, who was one of those guys who did everything for everybody and who knew everyone. He was kind of like a "fixer" and had a way of bringing all the pieces together and making them fit properly.

The match is over and Fausto is sitting with me. I said, "Boy, Chris Evert, her first-ever Olympic match. I'd love to get an interview with her." And Fausto said, "Come with me. We can get it. I know Chris." I pointed out to Fausto that we're not allowed out on the court. We didn't have on-court credentials. As if that would stop him! We went right into the zone where we weren't supposed to be. It didn't matter. I was going on Fausto's coattails, God bless him. Sure enough, we get an interview with Chris Evert right after the match. I had mentioned to Fausto earlier, "I'd love to get a picture with Chris." Sure enough, Fausto says, "Chris please, will you pose with Kenny for a picture?" And Fausto snapped it. This was long before camera phones. You had to come prepared. I would have never asked, but I have a picture with Chris Evert.

I get back to the studio, and Doug Sellars, one of the CBC producers, laughs, "We're sitting here watching the tennis on the monitors and there you are with Fausto walking on the court. And we're all saying, 'Oh my God, they're not supposed to be there. But we knew Fausto went where no man could go.'" The people

I worked with at CBC were just wonderful, and they made it so easy for me. Doug Sellars would later be my boss at Fox in Los Angeles. Everybody loved working for Doug. We lost him way too early to a heart attack while he was playing pickup hockey at age 50 in December 2011.

You'd think the Olympics would be the most well-planned, well-organized event you'd ever attend, but this isn't the case at all. The fact of the matter is that the Olympics have grown so vast, with so many sports being contested, no matter how much staff you bring to cover the Games, there's always going to be something that comes out of nowhere and catches you by surprise, or some event that slips through the cracks.

That was the case with judo. Bob Moir said, "I need you to go to judo." I didn't know anything about judo. He said, "Here's a handbook, and when you get to the venue find yourself an analyst." Okay. When I got there, I set out looking for someone in a white bathrobe with a black belt. It was going to have to be someone whose country wasn't involved in the match I was calling.

I can't remember the fellow's name, or even who was in the match for Canada. I learned from the handbook on the way over in the taxi that how you pin someone is called an ippon. I went over to a couple of venue tables and found a guy from Germany. I said, "Are you doing your match or are you available to work with us?" So he came over and did the match with me. He gave me some pointers to ask him, because I didn't know anything about judo.

Before we went on air I said, "Do me a favor. If one of the guys throws the other guy down and it's a pin and the match is over, just say 'Ken, it's over.'" And he did. The Canadian judoka threw his opponent, and my imported analyst said, "Ken, it's over." And I said, (So-and-so) wins. Canada moves on." And again when I got back, Natalie said, "Bob thought you did well," which meant a lot to me because if your tie wasn't tied correctly, Bob would let you know.

Ben's Ban

The 1988 Summer Olympics will always be remembered for one thing—when Canadian sprinter Ben Johnson lost his gold medal and world record in the men's 100 meters after he tested positive for steroids. I wasn't directly involved in that story, but it impacted my life and my work nonetheless.

The phone call came to my room in Seoul at what had to be 2:00 in the morning. The canoeing and kayaking venue was a long drive from where I was staying. I get a call, "You're going to have to leave a little bit earlier because all of our programming has changed because of Ben Johnson." I'm still kind of wiping the sleep from my eyes, and they tell me about Ben's positive test. Now I'm wide awake, and my roommate, swimming analyst Byron MacDonald, was up, too. We start looking out the window, and we're seeing all the lights come on in all the rooms in press village. Everybody is getting the phone call at the same time, and it was lit up like a Christmas tree.

I vividly remember leaving to get to the canoeing venue that morning. We get in the cab and the driver sees the Canadian flag on the CBC logo and he says, "Ben Johnson, Canada." And we said, "No. Ben Johnson, Jamaica." We wanted no ownership of that. We returned Ben to his birthplace.

Filling in for My Idol

One of the perks that evolved from my national work with CBC was the opportunity to occasionally serve as host for *CBC Sports Weekend*. Brian Williams was the host of the show, which featured all sorts of sports from around the globe, everything from darts (network time filler), to skiing, to Formula One racing, to figure skating. As you'll remember, when I was 17, I wrote to Brian, who offered me advice on getting into the business. He really gave me the impetus to pursue my dream and make it happen.

Terry Leibel was Brian's backup on *Sports Weekend*, but it just so happened that in 1988, she was on maternity leave, so I was offered plenty of chances to fill in for Brian when he was off on

Hosting CBC's national *Sports Weekend*, Canada's version of ABC's *Wide World of Sports*, in 1987. This is black and white, but those jackets were melon in color, and instantly identifiable, until discarded in 1988.

another assignment. It presented me the time to really hone my skills as a studio host. My first appearance on *CBC Sports Weekend* came a year earlier in 1987. Brian wrote me another letter. This one was handwritten, congratulating me on the opportunity.

It would have been about that same time, back in the local CBLT Sports office, that I was hosting on occasion the 6:00 sportscast. Around 4:30 one afternoon a young man called and asked me for some advice about getting into the business. I spoke with him for five minutes, and I told him to give me a call next month. I shared an office with one of the kindest men on the face of the earth, Bill Lawrence. Bill did the weather at the CBC, and since 1957, he was the host of a television show out of Hamilton, Ontario, called *Tiny Talent Time*, a variety show for kids 12 and under to perform. Bill left the show in 1992. It's still on the air. Anyway, when I hung up the phone with the young man, Bill said, "Brian used to have kids calling him all the time. He would tell them just what you told him." I said, "Bill, I was one of those kids."

The Call Comes

I didn't realize it at the time, but going to Seoul and working the Olympics would lead to the biggest break of my broadcast career, a chance to call play-by-play for the Toronto Maple Leafs games on the radio. I was home from Seoul for about three weeks when my apartment got robbed. I knew who it was. It was the superintendent of my building. He saw me leave, and there was no break-in. It was a key entry, and I didn't double lock the door. I'd gone to the dentist, and all my things from Seoul were stolen, all the collectibles I had from there. I had a state-of-the-art VCR, a nice expensive Panasonic model. It really threw me, so I wanted to get out of there. I needed to own my own home, so within two months of the October 1988 robbery I bought a house.

I moved in January 1989. I bought the 1,100 square foot two-bedroom home in midtown Toronto for $215,000. Today, 28 years later, it's worth $1.1 million. I closed on the house and moved in on January 25, 1989. On January 24, Allan Davis, who was the sports director at the Telemedia Network and CJCL, called and asked me if I could call the Leafs-Bruins game the next night on radio from Maple Leaf Gardens. You know, that place I dreamed of since I was 10 years old. Allan helped hire Joe Bowen in the early '80s as Leafs play-by-play man (and he still is, 3,000 games later), and now Joe was also doing occasional TV games on Global Television. When Joe was calling a TV game, Paul Romanuk, who's now with *Hockey Night in Canada*, was doing maybe 15 games a season on radio filling in for Joe.

In this instance, Paul had to be in Jamaica on assignment for TSN Television. So again, versatility creates opportunity.

That's the key to any business. Be as versatile as you can and you become irreplaceable, even though you may not be the greatest at everything.

I had no experience at hockey play-by-play, but when I came back from Seoul in 1988, I sat down with Allan. He wasn't my direct boss at the radio station but close enough that I respected his opinion a lot. He said, "I listened to your call in Seoul. It was good, but you were so revved up"—and to this day I still remember that. It's the inflection. You've got to leave yourself somewhere to go. I was calling canoeing and kayaking. Can you imagine being too revved up for that? I was doing all sorts of different sports in Seoul. I remember Allan saying, "You have nowhere to go. You're up here at the start (pointing to the ceiling) but where are you finishing? You have to have a level of range. You need to let your inflection have a space to go to."

That's a key part of play-by-play broadcasting. You need to bring the viewers along with you for the ride as you bring it to a crescendo. Bob Cole is maybe the best at doing it among today's hockey broadcasters. Danny Gallivan and Dan Kelly were artists at that. I started so high, likely because I was so nervous since I had never done play-by-play before Seoul in 1988. I knew I wasn't very good and readily acknowledged it.

When Allan called and asked, I actually said no to doing the Leafs game because it was to be my moving day. Think about that for a second. Here's Allan, offering me the NHL, the gold standard of play-by-play to the Canadian broadcaster, and I'm more worried about getting my ottoman up the stairs. He said, "You mean to tell me I'm offering to let you do play-by-play of the Toronto Maple Leafs, and you're worried about moving?" And I told him it was my first house purchase. "I hear what you're saying," Allan said. "But you're doing the damn game."

Maybe somebody should have told me the Rocket Richard story. On December 28, 1944, in the midst of the season that would see him become the NHL's first 50-goal scorer, Montreal Canadiens superstar Maurice (Rocket) Richard helped his family move their belongings from one apartment to another within the Montreal city limits. When he got to the rink that night, Richard was sore and worn out and told coach Dick Irvin he was tired and maybe someone else should suit up for the game in his place. Irvin would hear none of it, and Richard donned his familiar No. 9 sweater for the game against the Detroit Red Wings. By the finish of the game, Richard was really moving. He had scored five goals and assisted on three others as the Habs whipped the Wings 9–1. His eight-point night stood as the NHL single-game record until 1976.

Like the Rocket, I got the move done. I got some friends and family to help with the movers. And I prepared like crazy for the game. Andy Brickley scored the winning goal in overtime as Boston beat Toronto 2–1. I would later call games with Andy for NBC Sports.

I never listened to that game on radio until I got the job in Detroit. I discovered then, eight years later, that I did a decent job. The radio station must have thought so, too, because that game led me to do 15 games the next season at $850 bucks a pop, and 20 each year after that, until John Shannon brought me to TV play-by-play in 1994 on *Hockey Night in Canada*. Not long after I left, in 1995, the FAN radio station lost the Leafs rights for a short time to Toronto FM station Q-107.

A Hair-Raising Experience

When I first started doing Leafs radio, I would meet with Toronto coach John Brophy before every game and ask him, "Who are your starters tonight? What are your lines?" And before one game, he said on his own—I didn't even ask the question—he just blurted out, "I'd love to start Al Iafrate, but I can't get the guy to start because he won't take his helmet off for the national anthem. That's how f-upped our team is."

I said, "What are you talking about?" And he said, "Al's got a hair issue." Al didn't want anybody to see that he was going bald. (Author's note: it was fairly evident.) One game at Madison

Square Garden I remember Al got hit so hard his helmet went flying, and yet he was scrambling on the ice trying to put his lid back on so no one could see he was follically challenged.

Al has since shaved his head, and now he couldn't care less. But back then Brophy couldn't start him. Al would go down the tunnel and stand there during the anthems where fans couldn't see him. But Al wasn't disrespectful. He always took his helmet off— in private.

You Don't Want to Eat Here

For a Toronto kid to be calling games at Maple Leaf Gardens was a dream come true. The Gardens was the Taj Mahal of hockey, and yet, the food they served in the press room wasn't what you would classify as gourmet fare.

The Leafs served these sandwiches that were so hard and crusty you'd have thought they were first made during Toronto's last Stanley Cup win in 1967. I often wondered if Harold Ballard brought the leftover food from a recent baby shower or bar mitzvah he may have attended around town.

It was really disappointing, but that was how Harold operated. He sure wasn't going to spend any money on stuff like that, especially if it was for the enemy—the media.

They Got It on Tape

Long before anyone had heard of EA Sports or *Madden Football*, I was the original voice of sports video games. If you ever played the VCR *Hockey Night in Canada* game with your friends, that was my voice calling the play-by-play.

I was asked to voice the game in the summer of 1989. It was very nice of *Hockey Night* to ask me to do the game, and that tells you something because I hadn't done a lot of play-by-play yet. My first game was in 1989 and here they hired me to do this. Mark Askin, who was *Hockey Night in Canada's* producer, also produced the video game along with Ron Harrison.

The game involved a board and dice and a VCR tape. You would move around the board and when your piece landed on a square that said "VCR action," you would play the VHS tape and you'd have to guess the outcome of the play from an actual sequence from an NHL game, with me calling the play-by-play. It was the predecessor to today's computer video games. You think of all the play-by-play guys who've voiced the NHL video game for EA Sports, from Doc Emrick to Jim Hughson, and I was really the first to do it. I just didn't get paid like them.

Repaying Bill

I was calling a game between the Minnesota North Stars and the Toronto Maple Leafs, and I hadn't been doing radio play-by-play very long. I said, "Along the near boards Churla shoots it down the ice for Minnesota." And as the play stops, Bill Watters said, "Ken, I don't think Shane Churla is in the game tonight." That was one of those heart-in-your-mouth moments. We were pretty close to the action in Toronto with the press box in the old Maple Leaf Gardens looking right down on the bench, and I'm thinking to myself, *Why would Bill say that on the air?* I didn't appreciate it. I think as an analyst you wait till the commercial break if you'd like to mention to your "partner" that you think he made a mistake. On radio you can make some mistakes without really anybody knowing unless they are listening live while watching at the game. And with delay, even that takes some work.

I thought Bill should have waited, but he didn't, and much to my pleasure as I looked down at the bench, they made the line change and Churla came off. I said, "Well Bill, if Shane Churla isn't playing tonight, you tell me who is wearing number 27 for Minnesota?" He then apologized. I would hope another analyst would never embarrass a play-by-play guy like that on the air.

A Learning Kurvers

A few years later, Bill Watters and I were doing a game at the old Chicago Stadium. The Leafs had previously made a trade for Tom Kurvers, the deal with New Jersey in 1989 that saw the Devils get Toronto's 1991 first-round draft pick, third overall, which the Devils turned into Hall of Fame defenseman Scott Niedermayer.

It was a wild high-scoring game, and Kurvers had coughed up the puck late in the game on the play that resulted in Chicago's winning goal. Bill Watters said after that, "Ken, I'll tell you this. If Tom Kurvers is on the ice for the Toronto Maple Leafs in the final minute of a game again, I'm going to upchuck my cookies."

First of all, I couldn't believe he said it, but Bill took no prisoners. The next day I get a phone call from Bill. "Ken, we've been called into Floyd Smith's office." Floyd, a pretty nice guy, was general manager of the Leafs, and you didn't get an audience with him unless you'd crossed a line during the broadcast. I said to Bill, "I'm not being called in on the carpet. You are." I knew he was the one in hot water for what he'd said on the air about Kurvers. And he said, "Yeah, I know. You're right. Not to worry. I'll get us out of this one." Somehow he worked it and wound up being the assistant general manager of the Leafs, so he obviously got himself out of the jam. Could you imagine that being said today on the air? Not a chance.

What's Cooking?

I was working at the CBC during the day and hosting the 6:00 sportscast. I was doing Leaf radio one night every couple of weeks, and Monday to Friday I'd be up at 4:45 in the morning to do the sports at the FAN after it became Canada's first all-sports station on September 4, 1992. A year earlier I had moved right next door to the radio station. CJCL was in midtown Toronto at 40 Holly Street, and I was at 60 Holly. My apartment was on the seventh floor and looked directly across into the 7th-floor radio station. When dinner time rolled around after work, I would barbecue on my balcony.

Dan Shulman had been hired by Allan Davis to do evening sports talk at the station in March 1992, prior to it actually becoming the FAN. Dan was just breaking into the business. Today, as detailed earlier, Dan is the voice of *Sunday Night Baseball* on ESPN and college basketball. Dan is truly one of the best play callers in the world. Dan would be waving to me from the CJCL newsroom. Then the call would come. "What are we having for dinner?"

Joe Bowen was the original morning sports guy when the FAN turned on its lights. But a year or so into his gig, his son, Sean, was diagnosed with leukemia. Thankfully, today he is thriving with a clean bill of health. But often at a moment's notice, Joe would call in the early morning for me to take over if he had to make a hospital run. I could be at work in an instant—I'd literally walk 50 steps and I'd be there. Eventually I took over Joe's sports gig, and I'd be on from 5:30 to

9:00 AM, but later when I became the full-time morning sports guy, I took a pay cut and I switched the hours from 7:00 to 10:00 AM and four days a week because I'd be exhausted after doing a Leafs game or the late night sports at CBC, or traveling on Fridays for *Hockey Night in Canada*'s Saturday game on the West Coast or in Montreal.

When my morning shift was over at the radio station, I'd take the short walk home and shower and then go do a sports profile story during the day for CBC local TV and perhaps from there go to Maple Leaf Gardens to call a radio game if Joe Bowen was doing television. I'd get home at 11:30-12:00 in the evening and I'd be waking up less than five hours later.

Living so close to the radio station was convenient, but they were long, long days. I followed that job ritual until I got laid off by CBC local TV in December 1996. My contract with the local TV station was pretty good. I got two months off a year, so I would use some of those days if I was on the road with the Leafs. And the TV station liked it because it was good exposure for all of us. Even after the CBC local TV station let me go, I was still employed by the CBC network and *HNIC*.

Shoutout—Shutout

There are enough superstitions around pro sports to fill a book, but I've never been one to buy into that sort of thinking. When you are calling a baseball game, you're never supposed to mention it if the starting pitcher is working on a no-hitter. Likewise, in the hockey booth, if the goalie has a shutout going, we are unlikely to mention it. Otherwise, you'll jinx him.

But there was a night the Leafs were playing the Minnesota North Stars. Toronto goalie Felix Potvin had a shutout going, and it was in the third period. And Gord Stellick, my analyst, did the old, "We can't mention it," when we were talking during a commercial break. I didn't buy it for a minute, and I still believe that to be the case today. But the Twitter world will let you know otherwise, so you're best off avoiding it. So now I go along with it just to avoid the subject if a goalie has a shutout going.

But at that time with Gord, I hadn't done play-by-play for long, and Potvin is working on a shutout, and Gord said late in the game, "Just one more thing to be decided now." To which I replied, "Gord, you really believe in a superstition like saying a shutout will jinx the goalie?" And I blurted out, "Shutout, shutout, shutout." And I barely had the words out when Minnesota's Stew Gavin came right down the wing and scored on the next shot.

I was stunned. Gord looked at me, and then we're laughing. We said nothing. It was literally the next shot within five seconds after I said, "Shutout, shutout, shutout...scores! There goes the shutout." Thank God that was before social media. I would have been crucified.

Toughing It Out

I've been fortunate through the majority of my career—knock wood—to have not been sick. I've lost my voice at times, even delaying my debut on *Hockey Night in Canada*, but the only game where I was really sick was a Blues-Leafs game at Maple Leaf Gardens. I was at CBC that afternoon, and I didn't want to go home, but I begged off the 6:00 sports. We were right next door to MLG, so normally I would do the 6:20 sports and then go to Maple Leaf Gardens.

My car was out in the parking lot. I went to get something out of it, and I threw up in the parking lot. At that point, I was worried. I didn't think I'd get through the game. It was scary, but there was no one else to do play-by-play. You had to get through it.

I had the garbage can sitting next to me through the whole broadcast. I got through the first two periods okay, and then in the third period a brawl broke out. This was the last thing I needed. They were really going at it. I was able to get through the game and the drive home. But as soon as I got through my front door, I was ill for the next four hours. Somehow, I willed myself from being ill before the game and to get through and call the game, but that was as close as I came to saying, "I can't do this."

I missed two games when my father passed at the age of 96 in December 2011, and I missed three games when my beautiful son, Jamie, passed in December 2016, but I've never missed a game through illness.

The Ballad of Ballard Buffoonery

You couldn't cover the Leafs in the 1980s and early 1990s without gathering your fair share of Harold Ballard stories. We've already talked earlier about my first encounter with the cantankerous owner of the Leafs, but there is so much more to say.

Interviewing Harold in the mid-1980s about the state of the Leafs, I pointed out to him that many teams employed more scouts than the bare-bones staff of bird dogs who worked for the Leafs. "Who has more scouts than us," he demanded to know. I pointed out that, for example, the Edmonton Oilers did, and Ballard scoffed. "What have they done?" he growled. I pointed out that the Oilers had won Stanley Cups and were in first place. "I don't care," Ballard bellowed. "I wouldn't want any of their scouts." Sure, because what did they ever do? Oh yeah, they found Mark Messier, Kevin Lowe, Jari Kurri, Grant Fuhr, and Paul Coffey. And they won five Stanley Cups in seven years from 1984 to 1990.

Another time the Leafs were playing the Quebec Nordiques at Le Colisée. There was no washroom in the press box. You had to go out on the concourse to go to the washroom, and Harold wanted no part of that.

Bob Stellick, who was the public relations director for the Leafs at the time, was sitting next to Harold. I walked by and Bob gives me one of those looks where he's trying not to laugh. I looked down and all you see off the copper-colored radiator under the table is the urine bouncing off the heating vent. Harold just opened up and was taking a leak right there, right underneath his seat. Later I asked Bob if Ballard knew there was a bathroom in the concourse. "Oh, he wasn't going there," Bob said.

It's My (Hockey) Night

I was sent by CBLT (Toronto local TV) to cover the play-off series between the Leafs and St. Louis Blues in the spring of 1990. I was going to provide updates and some profile pieces. After arriving back in my hotel room from dinner the night before Game 1, the light was flashing on the hotel room phone. This was before cell phones. The producer for *Hockey Night in Canada*, Mark Askin, left a message. "Ron (MacLean) had to go home for a family matter. He's left his blue jacket for you. We'll roll up the sleeves and you're going to host *Hockey Night in Canada* tomorrow." Once again, Mark had faith in me—more than I had in myself.

Hosting *Coach's Corner* in February 1992 with Don Cherry. A thrill for a kid who grew up watching him with Dave Hodge and then Ron MacLean.

I did not sleep that night as you might imagine. It was the opening night of the Stanley Cup playoffs and here I am doing *Coach's Corner* with Don Cherry. With Don we would pre-tape because there would be different regions with different game time starts. We would pretape at 4:30 or 5:00 PM, and Don on this night was making his Stanley Cup playoff predictions. I got through that taped part okay, and then then it dawned on me. I had to go out and open the live show. I was really nervous as I was heading to the ice. As soon as I was in position by the old St. Louis Arena boards, with Mark Askin counting me down in my ear to start speaking and the players on their way out, I realized there is no greater thrill. I'm revved up and ready to go. Even the Maple Leaf players knew I was pretty nervous. As he came out, Leafs defenseman Todd Gill, who'd later play for the Red Wings, patted me on the head and the moment was caught on camera as he went by. That seemed to relax me.

I got through the opening just fine, and I was happy about that. I was feeling much more calm, until about halfway through the period. I'm sitting in one of the rooms with Don watching the game and waiting for the intermission, and Don says, "We're going to have to do *Coach's Corner* live." I said to him, what are you talking about? And he said, "The Leafs didn't come out like I thought they would. I thought they'd be much better in here and they weren't, so we're gonna do it live. I've gotta do it again." That portion would be going into the Leafs region of the country live. I told Don that I was nervous the first time and now he wanted me to do it again? He said, "Don't worry. I was great the first time. I'll be better the second." He didn't really care about me, so we did it. We did the Leafs region live, and the rest of the country saw the piece we had on tape.

It was a great experience for me, and sure enough when the Olympics were in Albertville, France, a couple of years later, I was slated to do ski jumping for the CBC. They came to me and said that Ron was going to be over at the Olympics, and asked if I'd like to not go to France and host *Hockey Night in Canada* for a month instead. I said hell yeah. When Ron was asked about missing a month with Don he said, "It's a reprieve for me." Then he added, "Ken asked me for some advice and I told him, just endure it." But Don was always wonderful to me.

Coach Talk

It was actually during that Olympic month when we started to—at Mark Askin's insistence—ask coaches for interviews during the game. The first night, I got Toronto Maple Leafs coach Pat Burns at the end of the first period. We were really the first ones to do that. Pat would come off at the end of the first and he did an interview with me. I remember Edmonton Oilers coach John Muckler doing an interview with me, and I had to stand on a box with him because he was so darn tall.

Mike Keenan was coaching the Chicago Blackhawks but didn't want to do an in-game interview. He relented, realizing it was me he'd be speaking with and because of our prior relationship as teacher and student in Toronto.

Today, it's commonplace for coaches to be interviewed in-game, but *Hockey Night in Canada* I think set the standard for coaches doing those interviews. Football may have already been doing it at the time, but for hockey it was something new and different.

Eric the Nord

Eric Lindros was labeled as the Next One when he was the top-rated player for the 1991 NHL entry draft. The Quebec Nordiques owned the first overall pick and used it to select Lindros from the Oshawa Generals, the same junior team that produced my idol, Bobby Orr.

There was just one problem—Lindros wanted no part of Quebec or the Nordiques. He refused to report, and eventually his NHL rights were traded to the Philadelphia Flyers. And even that was contested.

Before the latter part of that equation came to be, Eric was a head-table guest at the Toronto Jewish Community Centre's sports celebrity dinner, alongside Los Angeles Kings owner Bruce McNall and actor John Candy.

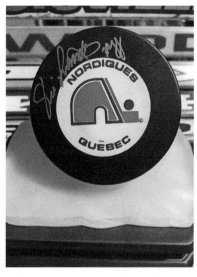

While Eric Lindros was still "technically" a Quebec Nordique in 1991, I had him sign this puck for me.

I was co-emcee of the event along with Toronto sportscaster Mark Hebscher, and naturally, with Lindros sharing a table with an NHL owner, there was plenty of playful suggestions that maybe McNall might make him an offer that he couldn't refuse. Before you knew it, watches, wallets, and credit cards were appearing on the table in front of Eric.

At the end of the night, I came up to Eric with a special request. I put a Quebec Nordiques puck in front of him and asked him to sign it. He wasn't happy about it and at first refused, but I would not take no for an answer, and eventually he relented and gave me the autograph.

I still have the puck and for a time thought I was the owner of a unique piece of hockey memorabilia. But apparently, time does heal all wounds. I've since learned that Lindros is now readily signing Nordiques items.

With Eric Lindros and great actor/Toronto Argonaut owner John Candy. John sadly left us too early.

Having Their Cake

Another job I worked at with the CBC in the early 1990s was as host of Toronto Blue Jays baseball games. Labatt's Brewery was a sponsor of the Blue Jays in that era, when the Jays won back-to-back World Series in 1992 and 1993. Being a host, our producer would give me a wad of cash at the start of every game, and I'd line up player interviews and give them what the players called "The Cake." It would be $50 a player.

Obviously, I was accountable for the money. They would know how many interviews I did, so there was no theft going on (other than by the players). This practice no longer exists.

Toronto outfielder George Bell loved me because I was shorter, and he called me the "friggin' midget." But as cantankerous as he could be, I never had a problem with George. George was always wonderful to me. A lot of the Blue Jays were, but in general they were a tough group with which to deal. The visiting players were, too.

That's the one difference I find about hockey. The players in this game are much different than those in baseball. Whether it's hockey players being small fish in that huge pond of pro sports and they're not really sought after by agents at 12 and 13 (although that's changing a little more today), I can't explain it. Maybe it's the parents and the time spent with their kids with the travel involved. Maybe it's the money invested in the sport. The kids truly appreciate the extensive sacrifices many parents make so their children can play an expensive sport such as hockey. Whatever the

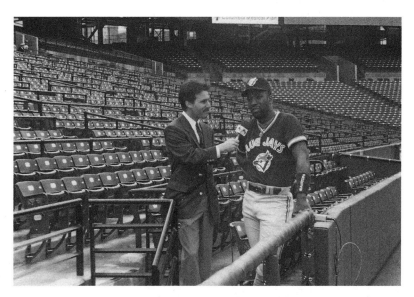

I hosted Blue Jays Baseball on CBC in both 1992 and 1993 and they won the World Series each year. And this man, Joe Carter, belted the walk-off three-run homer off Mitch Williams to beat Philadelphia in Game 6 at SkyDome in 1993.

case, hockey players just seem to be different. And from what I've found after the fact, you find the same disparity between hockey and football and basketball players, too.

I think that's why our producers just found it easier to pay baseball players for interviews. We were in Texas when I went up to Jose Canseco. It was a hot day and the afternoon of a doubleheader, back when they used to play doubleheaders. Jose wouldn't know me, but I walked up to him at the batting cage and said, "Here's your cake, can I get you for an interview?" He said, "I've got batting practice. I'll come over after." So while I waited, I went to three other players for chats at a cost of $150.00.

It's about a half an hour later, and I don't see Jose at the batting cage anymore. I went to look for him, and I got down into the Texas Rangers dugout and see Dean Palmer come out. I had met

My life was the pits at CBC. I spent many years as Indy pit reporter for our Toronto and Vancouver races from the late '80s through the mid-90s.

Dean before. I said, "Where's Jose?" And Dean said, "He's in there playing poker. You'll never get him now."

I walked into the clubhouse—unlike hockey, you can go right into the room before the game. Sure enough, there's Jose playing poker at the table with some of his teammates. I walked up behind him. He looks over his shoulder and does a double take when he sees me. I said, "I think I've got you for an interview." He said, "Oh yeah. Right." And I said, "If you're in the middle of your game, either give me the fifty back or come do the interview." And he stood up and said, "Boys, I'm out." He threw down the cards, and he was done. And out he came to do the interview. Even then, fifty bucks meant more to these guys than a poker hand.

Rickeyisms

One of the true characters who played with the Blue Jays during their run to the 1993 World Series title was outfielder Rickey Henderson. Rickey held the single-season and career Major League Baseball records for stolen bases, but let's just say he wasn't so quick off the diamond.

The Blue Jays acquired Rickey from the Oakland Athletics during that 1993 campaign, and when he got on the bus for the trip to the ballpark for his first game with Toronto, Rickey was perplexed. The rookies were sitting at the front of the bus. With all of his previous teams, the rookies were seated at the back of the bus.

Looking around, Rickey finally asked aloud, "Where does Rickey sit?" Henderson always referred to himself in the third person. Blue Jays manager Cito Gaston told Rickey to go to the back. "It goes by tenure," Gaston said.

"Tenure," Rickey questioned. "Rickey's got 15 years." To that Dick Enberg would have said, "Oh my."

The Blue Jays also had John Olerud at first base. Olerud wore a batting helmet in the field as a precautionary measure because he'd undergone surgery for a brain aneurysm and a piece of his skull was removed during the operation.

Years later, Henderson was acquired by the New York Mets, who had previously added Olerud to play first base. One day, Henderson asked Olerud why he wore the batting helmet in the field, and Olerud explained to him about the aneurysm and the brain surgery.

"Man," Rickey said. "I played with a guy in Toronto who had the same damn thing."

"Yeah, Rickey," Olerud said with a shrug. "It was me."

Draft Schmaft

There was a strong rumor going around the league on trade deadline day about a deal that I knew had been on the table for Leafs captain Wendel Clark. Cliff Fletcher, a wonderful man, was the Leafs GM at the time. In the Leafs dressing room, I was the one who asked him the question if it would be possible to get a first-round selection and other draft picks from Pittsburgh for Wendel.

The Leafs were going nowhere, and that's when Cliff uttered the famous phrase, "Draft Schmaft," insisting he had no need for high draft picks, and assuring everyone that Wendel wasn't going anywhere. As the Leafs floundered, Cliff took a lot of heat over the years for that comment, because it made it sound like he didn't value the draft, which, when you study his career and team-building skills, the exact opposite proves to be the case.

I have a lot of respect for Cliff. Working in Toronto to have Cliff Fletcher there when I was there and Pat Gillick of the Blue Jays, you couldn't ask for two better guys to deal with on a daily basis. They are two of the smartest men in their fields.

When I look at the guys I've been able to learn from over the years, it's an impressive list. I start with Mike Keenan during my high school days, and when I'm covering and then working for the Leafs, there's Cliff Fletcher and Pat Burns. Then I come to Detroit, and there's Scotty Bowman and Kenny Holland and then Mike Babcock. What an education in hockey life.

Big Deal, Bigger Number

The Leafs and Calgary Flames, the old team of Toronto GM Cliff Fletcher, engineered what was at the time the largest trade in NHL history on January 2, 1992. The Leafs sent forwards Gary Leeman and Craig Berube, goalie Jeff Reese, and defensemen Michel Petit and Alexander Godynyuk to the Flames for goalie Rick Wamsley; defensemen Jamie Macoun, who'd later join the Red Wings for the 1997–98 Stanley Cup win and Ric Nattress; and forwards Kent Manderville and Doug Gilmour.

Gilmour was the key to the deal, the catalyst who would turn the Leafs into Stanley Cup contenders for a couple of seasons, including the 1992–93 campaign when Toronto beat Detroit in that epic first-round playoff series on Nikolai Borschevsky's Game 7 overtime winner at Joe Louis Arena. Doug Gilmour became the savior of that franchise.

Interestingly, the Joe would also be where Doug made his Maple Leafs debut. The Leafs were playing the Wings on January 3, 1993. We're at the rink for the morning skate, and I'm standing with Toronto coach Tom Watt because I'm doing the Leafs play-by-play that night in Detroit. Tom's out in the hallway, and I already knew that Tom was a traditionalist and he wanted nothing to do with high numbers. He hated them with a passion, and Dougie was wearing No. 39 in Calgary, the same number he had worn with St. Louis, his previous NHL team.

Tom said to me, "He's not wearing a friggin' high number here, I'll tell you that." Dougie's first appearance as a Leaf was at the morning skate that day at Joe Louis Arena, and the media was gathered, awaiting his arrival. He finally comes down the hallway to the visitors' dressing room. I introduced myself to Doug. I said, "What number are you going to take?" And before Doug could say anything, Tom interjects, smugly saying, "Thirty-nine's not available." Doug answered without missing a beat, "Okay, I'll take 93."

That was the end of the discussion, and that's how Doug came to wear No. 93 in Toronto. I just looked at Tom, and he didn't say anything. I just thought, *You're screwed on this one baby.* That was pretty funny.

Murphy's Law

The Leafs reached the Stanley Cup final four in 1992–93 and 1993–94, and the belief was that they were a player or two away from going all the way, so when they added two-time Stanley Cup champion Larry Murphy from Pittsburgh, he was viewed as the final piece of the puzzle. But the Leafs went south just as Larry arrived in town, and he became a lightning rod for abuse, booed mercilessly by the Toronto fans.

Larry got a lot of abuse in Toronto, and his father, Ed, until his passing, probably never forgave me or Gord Stellick. We probably said some things on the air about Murph. We always loved Larry, but the crowd was on him. He came to the team at a bad time and he didn't have a lot of help around him, so it wasn't his fault, but for some reason the fans just gave Larry heck all the time.

It was trade deadline day in 1997, and my birthday on March 18th. I was talking with Leafs equipment manager Brian Papineau in his office. He didn't say anything to me about a deal, but I walked out and walked back in because I had forgot to ask him something, and in the interim he had grabbed a bunch of Larry Murphy's sticks and was taping them up in a bundle. I didn't say anything to Pappy, knowing he wouldn't say anything to me, and I walked out of the office. Gare Joyce, who was with the *Globe and Mail*, saw me, and Gare said, "It's five minutes to three now" and 3:00 PM was the trade deadline. Gare said that the Leafs are not going to do anything. I said, "I think they're going to trade Larry Murphy." He said, "Not a chance. They're not going to trade anybody." And I said, "I'll bet you dinner." "Okay, they're not making a move," Gare said.

Sure enough, about 10 minutes later, we found out that Larry Murphy was traded to the Red Wings. Which leads to something all young reporters out there should know—always go to the trainers, the equipment guys. They know what's going on first. They'll get the call before anybody else.

Paired with Nicklas Lidstrom in Detroit, Larry won two more Cups in 1996–97 and 1997–98. And you know what? When he got traded, I was a winner, too. Larry would become a future broadcast partner and is still a good friend. But I never did collect on that dinner from Gare.

Hockey Night (The Sequel)

While I was doing radio play-by-play for the Leafs, John Shannon was producing games for the North Stars and Dave Hodge, who was doing play-by-play for Minnesota after he was let go by *Hockey Night in Canada*. We went for a drink at the Marriott bar near the old Met Center in Bloomington, Minnesota, where the North Stars played. I had never met John before.

Obviously, he took a liking to me. It wasn't in-depth conversation by any stretch that night. But I also met him a few times after that night.

John listens to everything and is so well-versed in the business, and I guess he liked my call. In 1994, John took over as executive producer at *Hockey Night in Canada*. I can remember exactly where I was in my home when the phone rang. John said, "I hear you're up for the Vancouver Canucks job." I said, "Well, I'm up for it, but I think Jim Hughson is going to take it." If Jim didn't take it, I would be next in line. Ultimately, Jim took the job. But John said on the phone, "Don't take it. I'm coming to *Hockey Night in Canada*. I'd like to move you from radio to TV. But you've got to give up the radio. I want no bad habits."

I understood exactly what he meant by that. He didn't want too much play-by-play description on television. You can look at what you're seeing on TV, so you don't need someone describing it from player to player to player. We still can overtalk on TV. We are guilty of that sometimes. But for the most part, pictures tell their own story. As for leaving radio, it turned out to be no big deal. The FAN lost the Leafs rights for a short time the following season anyway, so it all turned out for the best, except for the fact my *Hockey Night in Canada* debut was delayed, first by an owners' lockout to start 1994 and later by laryngitis.

You know how sometimes they say it's who you meet? Basically, that's what happened to initiate the process that led me to doing play-by-play for *Hockey Night in Canada*. Had I not been doing Leafs radio, I probably never meet John Shannon. I dreamt

The Sutton Place Hotel

FOR DANIELS, MR KEN
ROOM DLXK   MESSAGE NO   383

REG GUEST DANIELS, MR KEN		RECEIVED	03/10/95 10:08 406
ACCOUNT NO 1202 ARRIVE 03/10/95		CHANGED	
STATUS 3 DEPART 03/12/95		DELIVERED	

CALLER ALLEN CLARK		SOURCE		ACTION	
FROM		X PHONE		PLEASE CALL	RETURNED YOUR CALL
PHONE				WILL CALL BACK	URGENT
MESSAGE GOOD LUCK WITH THE GAME! THANK YOU.					

The Sutton Place Hotel

FOR DANIELS, MR KEN
ROOM DLXK   MESSAGE NO   791

REG GUEST DANIELS, MR KEN		RECEIVED	03/11/95 23:05 981
ACCOUNT NO 1202 ARRIVE 03/10/95		CHANGED	
STATUS 0 DEPART 03/12/95		DELIVERED	03/11/95 00:04 439

CALLER MR. SHANNON		SOURCE		ACTION	
FROM		X PHONE		PLEASE CALL	RETURNED YOUR CALL
PHONE				WILL CALL BACK	URGENT
MESSAGE CONGRATULATIONS!! GREAT FIRST NIGHT. I WILL TALK TO					
YOU IN TORONTO. THANK YOU.					

The telegrams sent to my Vancouver hotel on my first night of PXP for *Hockey Night in Canada*. Before the game from Alan Clark, head of CBC Sports, and after the game, from executive producer John Shannon (long before the ease of texting and email).

of hosting *Hockey Night* but until 1989, I didn't know if I could do play-by-play. So here I was, Saturday, March 11, 1995, getting ready to call my first game for *Hockey Night in Canada* from Vancouver.

I'd done play-by-play for five years, and for sure I was ready to make the transition when John called. The timing was perfect.

The first *Hockey Night in Canada* game I was supposed to do was in Montreal against Philadelphia, but I got laryngitis. I had lost my voice. It was Tuesday, and John Shannon said I sounded like Kermit the Frog. I don't know whether it was a total fluke or the stress of my first big game on *Hockey Night in Canada,* but my voice just disappeared. Philadelphia won that game 7–1 over Montreal. I debuted the following week, calling a Vancouver Canucks–Anaheim Ducks game from Vancouver. It was March 11, 1995. My first official play-by-play game for *HNIC,* working with former NHLer Jim Peplinki as my first analyst. Alan Clark, the head of CBC Television Sports, sent a telegram (that's right boy and girls—a telegram) to my Vancouver hotel wishing me luck in my debut. After the game, John Shannon sent another, congratulating me. A text today would be so much less complicated.

Tying One On

A couple of years later, Dick Irvin and I were doing a Hartford-Montreal game. I was playing ProLine in those days, the Canadian sports lottery where you pick games and try to cash in. It was opening night, and one thing I learned back then was take the visitors or ties on opening night. I took four ties that night of the six games I played. It was going to pay $4,400 on maybe a $40 play. I needed Hartford-Montreal to end in a tie to cash my ticket.

Dick knew I had four tie games on my ticket that night. I got really excited when Montreal's Vinny Damphousse came down the wing in a tie game in overtime and drilled one off the crossbar. I bellowed, "He hit the crossbar!" and I was really excited that he missed. To me it was just an exciting point in the game, but to Dick I was a little too excited. After it finished I said, "Boy I got that tie I needed," and Dick said, "I could tell that when Damphousse rattled that one off the bar." But I did buy after the game.

Political Football

The Quebec Referendum was two days away when we did the Canadiens–Chicago Blackhawks game for *Hockey Night* on October 28, 1995. With all the political upheaval in Quebec, as the province was about to vote on whether to remain part of Canada, there was a conference call in the morning to talk about it, and I wasn't part of it.

I was on that night with Dick Irvin. We'd gone to break during the national anthem because they didn't want to show any of that. The crowd was going crazy as we were about to come out of commercial. I hit my talk back button and said to my producer Ed Milliken, "Can we refer to this?" And he said, "Sure." So as we came out of break, the crowd is standing and I said something about all the political unrest going on. I referred to the crowd standing and representing both opposing sides in the issue. And then the game carried on. Dick chimed in, too.

We went down to the green room after the game and Ed Milliken hands me the phone and says that John Shannon wants to talk to me. I thought, *This can't be good.* Dick is standing there and Scott Russell is there, who was hosting that night, and John starts to scream at me for more than a minute. "We said there would be no talk of the referendum," he hollered loudly. I take the phone away from my ear, and I'm holding it out and I see Dick's eyes and Scott's eyes and I could see they were having one of those holy cow moments. Finally, I put the phone back to my ear and I hear John say, "Who told you that you could refer to the national anthem?" and I said, Ed Milliken. And John yells, "Put Ed on the phone."

John later apologized to me for that because I took the brunt of the abuse and it was Ed's call. I didn't know I wasn't supposed to talk about it because I wasn't on the conference call, but the producer did know because he was on the call. But when you come out of break and the crowd's going crazy before the game even starts, and people are seeing that on their screens, do we just ignore that? I was going to. I knew it was a "should we or shouldn't we" issue, so if in doubt, ask. I asked and was told okay, but Shannon just ripped me. He threatened to see that I never worked, for *Hockey Night in Canada* again if I disobeyed another order.

At the time, I was angry that Ed said yes. I like Ed, but he threw me under the bus. And then he backed up the bus and ran over me again by not acknowledging it. The main thing I've learned about this business is, if you screw up, own it. Own your stuff.

A Roy Deal

One of the big factors that made the Red Wings–Colorado Avalanche rivalry so intense and ultracompetitive during its heyday from 1996 to 2002 was the bravado and goaltending skill of Colorado's Patrick Roy. And it might just have been a Red Wing who put the bug in Roy's ear about getting out of Montreal.

Mike Vernon, who was Detroit's goalie from 1994 to 1997 and who won the Conn Smythe Trophy when the Wings captured the Stanley Cup in 1996–97, went for breakfast the morning of that fateful December 2, 1995, game at Montreal. He just happened to walk into a breakfast spot near the Forum, and Patrick Roy was there. They had breakfast together, and Patrick Roy was complaining to Verny about how things were not going so great in Montreal. So Verny said, "Why don't you ask for a trade? Why don't you get out if you're not happy?"

There was all kinds of speculation about trouble brewing at the time between Roy and Mario Tremblay, who'd been named Montreal's coach earlier that season. When Tremblay was a player with the Canadiens, the two had roomed together in Roy's early time with the Habs and they didn't get along. Tremblay allegedly mocked Roy's struggles to speak English when he first arrived in Montreal, and there were a couple of occasions when they almost came to blows.

Sure enough, right before Verny's eyes, the thing just blows up on Patrick. Roy gave up nine goals on 26 shots in Detroit's 11–1 victory that night before Tremblay finally replaced him with back-up Pat Jablonski in the second period. The Montreal fans were mocking Roy with taunting cheers even as he'd make a routine save, and there's no doubt he was embarrassed and felt that he'd been hung out to dry by Tremblay. As Roy went to the Canadiens bench after he was pulled, he walked past team president Ronald Corey, who always sat in the first row of seats behind the bench, and told him that he'd played his last game for Montreal.

Verny will tell you that he got dressed very quickly that night, out of his uniform and into street clothes and out of the Forum as fast as he could go, before reporters could ask his thoughts about what happened at the other end of the ice, and before he blurted out something he shouldn't. Verny said, "I never dressed so quickly after a game. I got the hell out of there."

Four days after that debacle, Montreal traded Roy and team captain Mike Keane to the Avalanche for goalie Jocelyn Thibault and forwards Martin Rucinsky and Andrei Kovalenko in one of the more lopsided deals in NHL history.

I was on the FAN in Toronto the morning the Roy trade was made. Bill Bird, who was at Global Television, called me that morning saying he knew someone who knew someone who had basically told him that Patrick Roy had been dealt. That was before the huge Internet explosion, so word of mouth from sources was the only way news got out back then. We broke the story of the trade that morning. We had Ron MacLean and Don Cherry from *Hockey Night in Canada* on talking about it. That was the great thing about morning radio back then. When you were telling people about something like that, they weren't going to hear it anywhere else.

It certainly was a blockbuster trade, and it led to plenty of great hockey over the next six years between the Wings and Avalanche, as all of the games in this heated rivalry became must-see TV. Plenty of memories—some happy and some sad—were forged for

Don Cherry and me, prior to *Hockey Night in Canada* playoff coverage in April of 1996. (Courtesy: CBC Sports)

Wings fans over the years, but when you think back on it, those Colorado-Detroit games wouldn't have been nearly as much fun if Roy hadn't been part of them, now would they?

Revisionist History

Those 10 morning sportscasts I was providing were about six or seven minutes long (no need for that today on radio in this world of immediacy), and it gave me a forum to commentate. I vividly recall, following the 1988 Winter Olympics in Calgary, that with the new NHL buildings that would be constructed over the next decade plus—and I hadn't much thought there would be 10 more teams—that all buildings should have the ability to go to wider ice, such as the Saddledome in Calgary. That building, and the new Little Caesars Arena, to the best of my knowledge as of today, are the only NHL buildings to have the ability to go to a wider ice surface.

I mentioned circa 1988–89, that players were getting bigger, and the new arenas should have the ability to get bigger too, as did the Calgary Saddledome, still using NHL standards, 200 by 85 feet. The international ice surface at 200 feet by 100 feet is too wide. There is too much room, and defenses change to adapt, and then little of consequence happens. My suggestion then and still today is to have the ice surfaces 90 feet wide, adding 2½ feet per side, and five feet total. Had they all done that in the early '90s before all 30 NHL cities had a new arena (and they all do except MSG, which was renovated at a cost of billions), do you think the game would be better today? Retro-fitting a building would now cost millions. And it has nothing to do with losing the first few rows of seats, since you'd actually be losing the last two rows, and the cheapest seats. Every row just moves back.

You're Out

Between *Hockey Night in Canada*, working for CBC Sports, serving as the sports anchor for CBLT (the local Toronto CBC affiliate), and doing the morning sports on radio for the FAN, I was a busy guy. Some days lasted 19 hours. But that was about to change.

There were cutbacks coming at CBC. Everyone knew the axe was going to fall on some of us. It was 9:30 AM on December 11, 1996. I was in the kitchen of my house, and I got a call from Marilyn Scott, who was the human resources director at CBC. It's never good when HR calls. "Can you come down to my office?" *Should I bring my playbook*, I wondered, remembering the infamous line that every football player hears when they get cut. There had been previous cutbacks at CBC. I was already down to four days a week, but as I said, I still had the FAN and *Hockey Night*, so I was working a lot of hours.

They wanted people to switch from being contract employees to staff employees. I don't know exactly what that meant, but I didn't want to become a staff employee because I was getting two months off as a contract employee, and it gave me the freedom to do my other work. I resisted all along, and when the call came I thought, *They're going to let me go.* I was still shocked that they would actually do it, but I honestly thought it was their loss.

I went down to Marilyn's office and she said, "Ken we're having cutbacks, and we've got to let some people go, and unfortunately you're one of them." And I looked at her and I said, "You've got one bullet in that gun aimed at the sports department and you're pointing it at me? That's a huge mistake." She said, "It's December, and you've got a contract until next September. You could stay until April, and we'll be making more decisions then and through attrition you could probably stay on." I said, "You're going to pay my contract until next September no matter what, right?" She said "Yes" and I said, "See ya."

I walked upstairs and put stuff in a box. I didn't say goodbye to anyone, and I was gone. I wasn't the only one who got whacked. Because there were nationwide cuts on a government-run station, a lot of good people lost their jobs. It was a sad day at CBC for a lot of people, not only me.

On to Hockeytown

When one door closes, another opens, right? Well, that's exactly what was about to happen for me.

I did the Ottawa Senators–Buffalo Sabres first-round playoff series in the spring of 1997 with Greg Millen as my analyst. Mark Askin was the game producer. I later asked John Shannon how come we got Askin, his top producer, to work that series, and he said, "So you and Greg wouldn't screw it up." But as it turns out getting that playoff series—it was a tremendous series that went to Game 7 overtime, as Derrick Plante's winner pushed Buffalo past Ottawa—was about to open the most significant door of my broadcasting career.

I did the next round between Buffalo and Philadelphia, so that really showed the trust that *Hockey Night* had in me. While I was in Buffalo, I ran into former Red Wings play-by-play man Dave Strader, who was working for ESPN International with Mickey Redmond doing that second round. Dave came to me and said, "They're letting the play-by-play guy go in Detroit." That was in late April 1997. I called my agent in New York, and I said, "I can get you a tape. How fast can you get it to Detroit?"

I was going back that night to Toronto to film a segment for the Tony Danza movie, *The Garbage Picking Field Goal Kicking Philadelphia Phenomenon*. Tony played a garbage man who makes the NFL's Philadelphia Eagles as a placekicker. If you look it up on the Internet Movie Database, you'll see that I am listed in the cast simply as "male reporter." I wasn't the only broadcaster in the movie. ESPN's Chris Berman and former NFL tackle Dan Dierdorf, who played his college ball at Michigan and later called games for CBS, both portrayed themselves.

On set at the SkyDome in Toronto on April 30, 1997, with Tony Danza, filming *The Philadelphia Phenomenon*.

Greg Millen and I drove back to Toronto after the game in Buffalo—Greg had a driver—and I was on set at the SkyDome at 7:00 AM. If you can, try to imagine all that was spinning through my mind. I just found out there's an opening with the Detroit Red Wings. I'm in the midst of doing the *Hockey Night* series, and I'm shooting a movie with Tony Danza. And all day I'm on the phone with someone at CBC trying to put a tape together of the previous series to get to the Wings. We got it done. Then it was just a matter of waiting.

In July, Ted Speers from the Red Wings called my agent, Maury Gostfrand, in New York. Losing my day job at CBLT was the reason I went out and got an agent.

I went down to Detroit and met downtown with Atanas Ilitch from the Red Wings, and with UPN-50 producer Toby Cunningham. Fox Sports Detroit was still in the midst of the changeover from PASS.

I went down again and met with them in late August with game analyst Mickey Redmond and Toby and John Tuohey from FSD. I felt I was on the verge of being hired. Then I didn't hear anything for a little while until they made me an offer in early September, one that I turned down because it was too short of a deal. I didn't want to move my family on a two-year contract, and I had told them originally I wouldn't move for a two-year deal.

Arthur Smith, my former boss at CBC, was now the head man at Fox in Los Angeles. Arthur wasn't pleased. "Do you know how hard I worked to get you to Detroit?" I said, "I understand that, but we're talking about my family moving and I need more security." To complicate matters further, since it was September and

I still hadn't heard anything firm from Hockeytown, I had agreed the night before to a new three-year handshake deal with John Shannon to stay with *Hockey Night in Canada*. The next day—it was a Thursday afternoon—another offer was made that included a third year from the Red Wings.

I then called John Shannon, who was with Greg Millen at his house, and I was in tears at the time because I was unsure. I'm moving family, wondering, *What do I do? What's the right decision?* Here I had just agreed to a deal with *Hockey Night in Canada*, and now I'm saying no to them?

John said, "The only way you're going to get really good at this job to where you can meet your expectations is to do more games. With *Hockey Night* I can probably give you 20 of 27 weeks and a playoff round, but you wouldn't be doing that many games." There

With the Hanson Brothers of '70s *Slap Shot* fame. We took part in a Dave Coulier Foundation celebrity hockey game at Joe Louis Arena in 1999. We played to a "full house."

were other benefits in the move to Detroit. It meant I wouldn't have to get up at 4:30 AM to do radio. John implored me. He said, "You've got to take this job. I'll handle Alan Clark." Alan Clark was the head of CBC Television Sports and wasn't happy I was leaving.

Wake-Up Call

I still had one last sports shift at the FAN, the morning after I had accepted the Red Wings offer. It was the only morning I slept in. To make matters worse, my impending departure was in the *Toronto Sun*. A Friday sports headline read: "Daniels heads to Motown."

The previous afternoon, I had the *Toronto Sun* and *Toronto Star* calling me because CBC had put it out there that I agreed to a new deal with *Hockey Night in Canada*—which I had. Sort of. I've got two newspaper guys on hold now, asking if I can call them back in 30 minutes. I was stickhandling like Sergei Fedorov. Once the deal was finalized, I called back Rob Longley at the *Toronto Sun* and Ken McKee at the *Toronto Star* and told them I was heading to Detroit.

Now it's in the paper the next morning, and I hadn't told John Derringer and Pat Marsden, who were hosting the morning show at the FAN. I had told my bosses at the FAN that I was leaving and going to Detroit. And then I slept in.

My shift started at 6:00 AM, and I was usually there by 5:00 AM I got a call from Derringer. He said, "Hey big shot. Are you coming into work or are you going right to Detroit?" It was one of those "oh shit" moments. I got in my car and was at the station at five minutes to six, ripped and read the wire for the 6:00 AM sports. Of course, on the air they're ripping me—congratulating me but ripping me for going to Detroit, calling it such a down-trodden city in their smug Toronto way. I said, "Yeah, but there's a hell of a hockey team that just won a Stanley Cup!"

I never came close to missing a radio shift except for that day. I've never regretted making the decision I made.

CHAPTER 3
WINGING IT

From Canada's Hockey Capital to Hockeytown

Number 4. . .Bobby Orr

Although I was all for the Toronto Maple Leafs as a kid and I loved (Darryl) Sittler and (Lanny) McDonald and Jim Dorey with the way he skated upright, when it came to ultimate hero worship, it was Bobby Orr. Whether it was the white tape with the No. 4 on his gloves, or the one strand of black tape on his Victoriaville stick, I did the same to my equipment. But I had to wear socks in my skates, even though Bobby didn't wear any.

My radio career began in Oshawa in 1981, where Bobby Orr's legend was first born as a junior star with the Oshawa Generals. With the Boston Bruins, he was the first and remains the only defenseman to lead the NHL in scoring, and he did it twice.

So you can imagine years later, while with the local CBC station in Toronto, it would finally be my opportunity to reach out to Robert Gordon Orr.

As a teenager, through the 1970s, I spent many late-night hours staying up and watching Tom Snyder's *Tomorrow* show on NBC. It came after the *Tonight Show* with Johnny Carson. Tom's one-on-one, long-form, no-nonsense interview approach, with cigarette smoke billowing and no studio audience, was classic television. I had that burning desire to do a similar style segment with Bobby. But being for the local news, it would have to be divided into four segments. Four for Orr, of course. And no cigarette smoke.

Through George Kaz, my great friend back then and still today, we contacted Bobby. In the early 1980s, George had produced a series for *Hockey Night in Canada* called "Bobby Orr Hockey Legends," where Bobby would gather a group of former greats like himself and he would interview them at a resort in

Jamaica. Bobby and I met at the Westbury Hotel by Maple Leaf Gardens, where Orr was staying while he hosted his annual Easter Seals Charity Skate-A-Thon. He gave me an hour of his time, probably 30 minutes more than he wanted, but was as gracious as he could be.

Fast-forward to 1997. It was early September that I agreed to join the Red Wings. Well, Bobby had a golf tournament around the same time of year in Oshawa, and the guy who was to host it had to cancel at the last minute. The day after I signed in Detroit, Bobby Orr calls me—and asks if I'd mind coming off the bench to host.

Are you kidding me?! Bobby Orr? So I said, for sure. And consider the synergy here. Back in Oshawa where my career began, working for my idol, who helped pique my interest in this game when I was eight—and my last official function out of Toronto would be helping out my childhood hero. Then Bobby said, "How much do you want?" And I said, "I've got a game-used Bobby Orr stick. I just want you to sign it. That's what I want." And he said, "Deal." It was pretty chewed up, and Bobby said, "I didn't change sticks every game. I'd use them for a while, especially if it was one that I liked."

I remember hitting off a par three, and I was shaking because Bobby was there. The way the tournament worked, Bobby would play that same hole with every group. He'd hit off the par three and you'd try to get closer than where Bobby's ball landed. It's not like I'm a great golfer today, but I rarely played back then. Here I am with my idol standing there watching me. It was about 160 yards, and whatever I hit, it was just off the green and Bobby said, "Great shot."

That was such a relief. In front of Bobby, I didn't want to look like a complete idiot. And today, I have those memories and his stick. Signed. It doesn't get any better than that.

Stevie Hi

When I arrived in Detroit for my first season in September 1997 I immediately headed to Joe Louis Arena. I was in my 1987 Honda Prelude—without air conditioning—and it was a hot day. I'd been to the Joe a few times but really didn't know my way around all that well. I still had a lot of my stuff packed in my car.

That was going to be our first year of training camp in Traverse City. It was probably two days before we'd be leaving for camp, and when I get out of my car, the first guy I see is Red Wings captain Steve Yzerman.

I didn't know Steve, but while working from Toronto I'd interviewed him for a piece about Joe Louis Arena in 1986. I interviewed Denise Ilitch for the story I was doing, since the Joe was still relatively new at that point, and because our CBC show went to Windsor Channel 9, so that gave it a local flavor. That was the first time I was ever at Joe Louis Arena. Steve was relatively new then, too, only three years into his NHL career.

Now, 11 years later, I walked over and introduced myself to him. He was very welcoming. We talked about me working for *Hockey Night in Canada,* and he said he knew that. I don't know if he really knew that or if he was just trying to be nice. We talked about Traverse City and what a beautiful spot it was and how it would really help the guys to bond getting away for camp like that. He basically said, "Good luck and we'll see you around."

Hart Failure

A few weeks after that, we'd been through training camp and we were back in Detroit, readying for the preseason. My Prelude had seen better days. My family had not yet moved to Detroit with me, so I was heading back to Toronto to see them for a few days. It was a rainy Sunday morning as I'm driving along Jefferson Avenue toward the Detroit-Windsor Tunnel to cross the border into Canada, and the car just shuts down.

I was still living in a downtown hotel, so I had more than a few items stuffed in my car. I was living out of suitcases, and I was going to get more clothes at home. Now I'm stuck on one of the busiest roads in downtown Detroit going nowhere fast.

This guy was nice enough to help push me to the side of the road. I gave him a 20, and he was looking for more. I thought 20 bucks was pretty good. I called my family, and said I wouldn't be coming in. I was just thankful it didn't break down in the tunnel, because another five minutes later...well, could you imagine that?

I often remember that because it was right in front of Hart Plaza. I had a much better memory of Hart Plaza later that spring, hosting a Stanley Cup parade in front of upwards of a million people.

Lost and All Alone

When the team headed out on a road trip, we used to leave out of Pontiac Airport. At the time, I was living at Drake and Maple in West Bloomfield in the Aldingbrooke Apartments. When I first moved here, I was renting until we found a house. I had no idea where I was going, and that was before you had a GPS or

103

could download the maps on your phone. Really in those days, you're going blind. You're writing down directions from someone.

We landed at Pontiac Airport coming back from our first road trip October 1997, and I have no idea where I'm going when it's pitch black. Luckily, I had a guardian angel in Red Wings forward Martin Lapointe. Marty says, "I'll guide you home." He was living over at Haggerty and Eight Mile. I said, "That would be awesome." I followed Marty all the way home. He didn't lose me. He got me home. And then he went on his way.

The next trip we land at the airport again, and I ask Marty if he's going to guide me, and he's just apoplectic. "Holy crap. You can't find your way yet?" I said, "No, not really." It was late at night again, so he got me to Haggerty Road and I told him I was good to go from there. Was I ever mistaken! I waved to him to be on his way. I made a left turn and somewhere along the line, I made a wrong turn. I was lost for an hour and a half. I didn't know where I was. I didn't know where my apartment was. I couldn't even find the street. The streets are not well lit in West Bloomfield, Michigan. I'm starting to panic. I didn't know who to call. I didn't want to call my wife, who was still in Toronto and wouldn't have a clue as to how to help. That, and I wasn't about to tell her I was a dummy and got lost and have her use that against me at a later date. Right ladies? We're now divorced, so it doesn't matter. This story can get in line with all the rest.

This is the first time I'm telling this story, actually. I found my way back to where Marty dropped me off, and I went into a gas station at Haggerty and Maple and asked the attendant if he knew how to get to Drake. It was only two miles down the road. I just had to go down to the light, make a left, and go up the hill. I must have gone by it and made a wrong turn somewhere and wound up who knows where. I was all discombobulated, as Mickey would say.

After all, this is no place for a nervous person.

Play-by-Play Isn't Brain Surgery

Tony Colucci, one of the Red Wings doctors, asked me to host a dinner for the DMC docs—brain surgeons and every other specialty medicine you could imagine. They honor the best and hand out awards. I was emcee for the evening. And before the dinner, everyone's coming up and asking me, "How do you do what you do? How do you follow this game? How do you follow that guy? How do you keep all the numbers straight?" I was amazed. That's how I started off my speech.

"You know, the most shocking thing about this evening is that I'm in a room full of brilliant minds. You operate on brains, and you're all asking me how I do what I do? Seriously?" And it just broke up the room. Think about it. They're opening up someone's skull and operating on a brain and they're coming to me saying, "I could never do what you do." It's play-by-play. You're brain surgeons. Let's put things into perspective here.

A Backward Law

I first learned it was truly Hockeytown fairly quickly after my move from Toronto to Detroit in 1997. We went for dinner in Royal Oak, Michigan, at a restaurant called Goodnite Gracie. I parked in the lot right across the street and backed into my spot. But when I returned to my car, there was a ticket for $25 on the windshield for backing in. Meter readers apparently don't like the extra walk.

In fairness, there was a sign that did say, DO NOT BACK INTO PARKING SPOT. Being from Toronto, where we have plates on both the front and back of vehicles, I would never have thought to have looked for a sign like that, nor had I ever seen one. However, my ignorance aside, I sent a letter of explanation with my ticket to the judge. I did not mention what I did for a living. Just that I was from Toronto and was unaware. A month later, the ticket was returned with the judge writing, "DISMISSED! GO RED WINGS." I felt very much at home.

Good Things Come to Those Who Wait

Since the deal to bring me aboard as Detroit's TV play-by-play voice wasn't finalized until September 6, 1997, my debut as the Red Wings television broadcaster was delayed by immigration issues. So the great Mike "Doc" Emrick, now the voice of the NHL on NBC, called the first two games from the Joe, while I got to stand there quietly between him and Mickey and watch and learn. There was a brief on-air introduction, although I couldn't say I had been "officially" hired.

My first game I worked for the Wings was September 20th, 1997, in my hometown of Toronto at Maple Leaf Gardens, where I had called Leaf radio games for five years. And being Canadian, that brought no border issues. A few weeks later, October 1, 1997, my first Red Wings regular-season game was in Calgary at the Saddledome, and it also hit home because my brother, Gary, has lived there since the 1970s.

Gary is a Flames fan and longtime season ticket holder, and even when I worked for *Hockey Night in Canada*, whenever I did a Calgary game, Gary would always accuse me of anti-Flames bias.

On this night, I didn't care if my brother thought I was being too partial to the Wings. That was my job now. I have no recollection of the specifics of the first goal I called, other than it was a power-play goal by Doug Brown just 1:54 after the opening faceoff. Calgary forward German Titov was in the penalty box for holding at the time.

The Wings went on to win that first game 3–1. Brendan Shanahan scored, Marty Lapointe collected a goal, and Chris Osgood blocked 25 shots for the win. Detroit opened the season 5–0–1, but far be it from me to suggest that the new play-by-play guy brought the team good luck. The Wings were the defending Stanley Cup champions after all.

Game Day—Game Ready

If there are 75 announcers in the NHL between network and local TV and radio play-by-play callers, I'd say 70 of us do our prep work differently. There is no right or wrong way. It's just a matter of preference. I keep files on every team in the National Hockey League. If I hear a story about someone that is repeat worthy, I will follow up on it when we next see that team. I may talk with the player personally about it in the morning and then use it on the air that night. As for game notes, I used to predominantly use a scan card system where I would keep computer notes, and then print and paste them onto labels and then onto 4"x4" index cards that I would put in order numerically into an open folder. It became so cumbersome to maintain for all 750 players or so in the NHL, that I use it for just Red Wing players now. I presently do lineup charts for the visiting team. I'll make note of recent superlatives and streaks they may be on, both good and bad.

I don't rely on Corsi or Fenwick stats. I do think there certainly is a place for analytics in the game. I just don't delve deeply into it because the majority of our audience won't benefit. If a guy is hot, he's hot, and if he has nine points in the last six games I will mention it. Maybe he continues to roll, or he gets shut down. If it becomes a storyline in a game, then it becomes a reference point for me.

Also, if a visiting player is from the area or played for Little Caesars, that becomes a noteworthy story. I try to tie things together locally from the visiting team. If I come up with three or four stories on the opposition, maybe one a period that I can use out of commercial breaks when I've got a little more time, I'm good to go. Other than that, the game takes over.

I've relied less and less on stats over the years because the game's become so much faster, but there is still a place for stories to be told at the right time.

I like to overprepare and try to get a lot of work done the night before. I obviously have the NHL Center Ice package. If an announcer doesn't watch a lot of games, then he isn't doing his job to the best of his ability. If we're playing Buffalo next and the Sabres are playing within a few days of our game, I'll be sure to watch it live or record it. I'll get game notes from the league online and pore over those. We have a conference call the morning of the game with the producer, director, and the talent. We get our storylines for the day. For the game, I will talk with my producer and suggest three or four stories that, if we get time, are the ones I'd really like to get to.

If we've got a high-scoring game, we don't need anything else. If we've got a low-scoring game or as we always joke, what if the glass breaks? That's when you need to fill. How are we going to fill that time? Well, for example, if Dallas was playing the Wings, the Stars' Jiri Hudler didn't have any shoes on when he went up to accept the Lady Byng Trophy in 2015. That's a story with video that would be great to show and tell. That's where our conference call comes in handy, and we've got the best tape/video guy in the business in Mike Johnson. M.J. can find just about anything on a moment's notice, but making everyone's life easier with preparation helps a lot.

Near the end of a game, if the Wings are winning at home by more than one, I love to let the crowd take it. I don't need to be talking over that. I try to let the pictures tell the story. I've done that in the playoffs where the sound of the crowd takes it for the entire final minute, if it's more than a one-goal lead. I love nothing better. Just get out of the way and let the emotions of the fans tell the story.

I Have Another Voice in My Head

As play-by-play guys we seem to always have a running clock. Our 90-second commercial timeouts to pay the bills, during a hockey period, are generally the first stoppage of play (non–power play) after the 14-, 10-, and six-minute marks. I personally can sense time without even thinking about it. I am always on time. It drives my wife and daughter batty—only because they're jealous. Even when I'm not working, I can watch a game, or any TV show for that matter, and flip to another channel during commercials, and that voice in my head will tell me to turn back to the game/show almost to the second of the commercial run being over. It's as though that voice is a producer living up there counting me down.

The Name and Blame Game

A key to morning skates the day of a game is to make sure we are familiar with a how a player pronounces his name. And with so many Europeans in today's NHL, it gets tricky. The league has been better lately with website audio from each team to help. I will ask the play-by-play guys from the other team how they say a name on their team if I need clarification, and sometimes I will ask the player himself. When Andreas Athanasiou came into the NHL, visiting announcers would shudder and say, "He either won't touch the puck tonight in our minds, or we will go with double-A." But when I mentioned to them, it's just like saying, "GLAD to SEE you," they immediately got it. Not so hard. That is until his father, Stan, met me on the father's trip in Dallas, and introduced himself as "Stan Ah-THON-a-see-you." I said, "No you're not. You're AH-than-a-SEE-you. Your son told me that, and it's too late to change." He laughed hysterically and said, "I totally get it. I say it the Greek old-fashioned way."

When Tomas Kopecky played for the Wings, he asked his name be pronounced Ko-PETS-skee. We even had him on our air saying his name. We still got letters (back then) saying we were wrong, and we should learn how to pronounce his name. I sometimes wish I could go to the workplace of people and critique their job on a daily basis! And then put it out on social media how they suck at what they do, even though I've likely never done their job.

And speaking of Europeans and the Tomas name, there was a day in Nashville, when three Wings all named Tomas (Jurco, Tatar, and Nosek) all decided they would prefer it be pronounced Taw-MAHSH. I said we could do that, but they had to stick with it. They agreed. Tatar loves when I call him Taw-MAHSH now. Getting the rest of the guys on the crew, including me, to consistently remember to do so is a game in itself. Mick had a tough time landing Jared's last name as CORE-oh and not core-OH. Sometimes, we just have to laugh.

A Refreshing Discovery

When I first came to Detroit, Sergei Fedorov sat right across from me. I was surprised by that. I didn't think one of the club's veteran superstars, the 1993–94 Hart Trophy winner, would find himself sitting by the play-by-play guy, but am I ever thankful he did. That's where I first learned about Vernors Ginger Ale. I had no idea because it was a Michigan company and it just wasn't prevalent in the Toronto area where I was raised. In terms of ginger ale, I only knew of Canada Dry.

On one of our first trips, Sergei said, "I'll have Vernors." "Vernors?" I asked. "Yeah," he said, "Ginger ale."

I tried it and I loved it instantly. Vernors ginger ale is awesome. But I don't think that's what Mickey is usually referring to.

And when it comes to my drinking, The Mick always has my best interests at heart. Our first road trip was to western Canada, and the night before my first game with the Wings in Calgary, we went out for a few pops (ginger ale). Okay. Alcohol. We were at the bar of the team hotel, and not being a beer drinker (that's why I had to leave Canada), I made the fatal error of ordering a peach schnapps. Mick's head snapped around as if Dave Schultz was going to lay the lumber on him. "Peach schnapps?" he inquired in ghastly fashion. "What the hell," he continued. "You can't drink that. What else can you drink?" I said I do have vodka from time

Sergei Fedorov giving me a champagne shower after the Cup win in Washington in 1998. Much more fulfilling than ginger ale. (Photo courtesy of the Detroit Red Wings)

to time. Mick said, "Well make it this time, and every time after this." And I have. Valentine is made in Ferndale Michigan, and happens to be the best Vodka I've ever had. Valentine rocks with lemon please. And a peach schnapps for the young lady.

We All Have Baggage

First class is the best way to describe Red Wings travel. Great seats, fantastic flight attendants and pilots, and outstanding food. A few years ago, someone wisely made the executive decision to pass on the dessert trays, such as cookies and rice crispy treats. That helped immensely, since I rarely passed on any of them.

Once we land, and players and staff depart Red Bird 3, often in the middle of the night somewhere, we wait on the tarmac for our bags to be unloaded, and put them ourselves in the large bus compartments. There is only one bus for the Red Wings, unless there are extenuating circumstances and two buses are needed for additional seating. Unlike MLB, and NBA teams, who have one bus for players, and another for the rest, we travel as one cohesive unit. And it usually goes like clockwork.

The toughest job belongs to the trainers, and specifically equipment manager Paul Boyer, who travel separately, heading to the arena where we play next, to hang wet equipment in the players' stall to dry for the next morning's skate. Their sleep during a season is limited. When the rest of us reach our hotel destination, the luggage is our responsibility. Not so for NBA, MLB, and NFL players, who will head directly to their rooms and hotel staff will either get their bags to them that evening or store them until needed the next morning. NHL players carry their own, and proceed to pick up room packets with keys that are laid out on a lobby table.

It used to be that a player had to play 400 NHL games before he could get his own room on the road. That changed with the last CBA, and all players now have their own rooms, if they so choose. But before they get there, there is a pecking order. Veterans first on the elevator, while rookies and young players wait until they get the go-ahead. If I beat the herd and no one is waiting, I will grab an elevator with others. If not, players first is the code.

And just in case you were wondering, Red Wings staff and broadcasters get their own rooms as well. Could you imagine Mickey and me sharing a room? Well, I'm sure you could for the hilarity of it all, but I can't. You'll see why in Chapter 5.

Studious Shanny

It's no surprise to me that former Wing Brendan Shanahan went on to work for the NHL and today is president of the Toronto Maple Leafs. As a player, Brendan always paid close attention to what was going on around him—even wardrobes. It was early in 1999, and I'm sitting at McNichols Arena in Denver for an off-day practice. Brendan walked past and turned to me and said, "Canadian tuxedo!" I had never heard that term before, then quickly realized I was wearing blue jeans and a blue jean jacket. I have never worn that tuxedo since.

With Brendan Shanahan after the Stanley Cup win in Washington in June 1998. Check out those thin shoulder pads Brendan wore. If players used those today, the NHL would have fewer head and boarding injuries, as players wouldn't run into the boards, feeling they may hurt themselves if they missed. (Photo courtesy of the Detroit Red Wings)

Brendan was like me in that he was always asking questions and a student of the game. When I say something on the air, I have to be accessible and accountable, but rarely do the players say anything to me about it.

But I'd made some comment about Brendan that I thought was pretty innocuous, and Brendan came to me at the next day's practice and said, "My brother said to me..." And I said, "Like you didn't see it yourself." "No, I didn't," Brendan insisted. "I don't have time to watch."

Brendan was a very cerebral player, and that came through in the way he played. He occasionally made a move that if he was cutting through the middle, and the pass came his way but he knew his teammate was open to his left, he would lift his foot and the puck would go across to the far side. A few games later, maybe two weeks after he'd spoken to me, he tried this move and the Red Wings scored a goal.

I made the point about that play by Brendan Shanahan going to the net and lifting up his foot and faking as if he was going to play it. The puck went right through his legs and the Red Wings scored a goal.

A few days later, Shanny comes up to me and says, "That was very astute on your part to be able to figure that out, why I was lifting up my leg." For a guy who watched nothing, he was pretty good at catching stuff like that.

It was Brendan's hockey summit during the lockout season of 2004 that helped change the game. He brought together players and executives, including from the TV industry, to spitball about how the game could be improved. Even today, if only the NHL and equipment manufacturers would take a cue from Brendan's shoulder pads. He wore little in the way of protection on his shoulders when he played, and Chris Chelios did the same. Same with Mickey. All knew that if they went to hit someone and missed, they'd be the one to get hurt. If the league limited that piece of equipment in size, there would be fewer injuries and bad hits. Seems so simple. Cap the shoulder pad size by just wearing shoulder caps.

The College Game

A weird thing about my evolution as a hockey play-by-play caller is that I started right at the top. There was no minor-league seasoning, nor junior action that I utilized to build my resume. I never rode the buses to small towns to work in tiny old arenas. In that sense, there is no question that I was very fortunate, although there would have been great memories!

Getting to call College hockey has meant a lot to me. My first year with Fox Sports Detroit, I worked 18 college games, so including the NHL and the Red Wings' two rounds of the playoffs we were broadcasting in those days, I worked 101 hockey games that 1997–98 season.

The next year, FSD's Detroit Tigers baseball guy, Josh Lewin, had it in his contract that he got first dibs on college hockey—much to my dismay. So my games went from 14 in the CCHA down to four in 1998, and I truly missed it.

I always loved spending time prior to games with head coaches like Red Berenson of Michigan and the late, great Ron Mason of Michigan State. Ron's death in the summer of 2016 floored me. He was so great to Jamie and me. Long after his retirement as the winningest coach in college hockey history, I'd be calling a game at the Munn Ice Arena press box at Michigan State and these thick hands would appear on my shoulders, and I just knew it was Ron standing right behind me. Ron and Red both loved Red Wings hockey and rarely missed a game. Ron watched every Red Wings game. So did Red. I learned so much from both men.

I saw Red at the Great Lakes Invitational in 2015, and I said, "You're coming back for another year, aren't you? You've got to come back for another year." He said, "You sound like my wife." I'd just love seeing Red. Prior to games, we'd chat for upwards of 30 minutes some nights, and not that much about his team. Red retired in April 2017.

After Ron Mason retired, there was Rick Comley and then Tom Anastos at Michigan State, and they loved to talk hockey, too. I learned so much just from sitting in their offices.

Another big reason why I enjoyed the college game so much was that it let me know the players and vice versa. Many of these guys would go on to NHL careers, and it gave me a recognition factor, and trust, walking into their pro dressing rooms and them knowing me. I never underestimate how much that means. Mike Cammalleri knows me. And Eric Nystrom. Marty Turco, too. All those guys, you meet them along the way, so when they come up to the National Hockey League, you're a familiar, friendly face.

I guess when you're a college player and you're getting your games on television, that's a big thing. I went to the Air Canada Centre when Mike Komisarek had signed with the Maple Leafs in 2009, and an usher came up to me before the game and said, "Mike Komisarek wants to say hello." It's pretty cool. It means a lot to me that the players give a crap to meet me. You can talk to them and maybe get a story that you can share about them on the air.

Eric Nystrom told me a wonderful story when he was playing for Nashville in 2015–16. I asked him how often he got back to see Red. He said, "I went back to Michigan to see him when we played the Wings a month ago, and my game turned around right after that. I went to talk to Red because Red always gave me the best advice. The smell of Yost Arena with the walnuts roasting when you walk in there, I miss that. And it just brought me back to my roots of hockey." I told that story on the air, and it ties Eric Nystrom back to Michigan and it may lead Mickey to talking about playing against the Islanders and Eric's dad, Bob.

It's the people you meet in the game that make for the best stories.

The challenge of calling college games was that I didn't have the same familiarity with the teams and the players that I did while working NHL games. Sometimes I'm thrown into the mix, and it's two college teams I've never seen. Preparation for those games involves short-term memorization. If I've seen Michigan or Michigan State once or twice, I know both teams' players.

I've often said the first period of a college game is the best period I've ever read. The puck goes down the ice, and I'm looking down checking to see who's wearing this number and who's wearing that number. I try to learn them driving to the game. If my son or my daughter came to the game, they'd have the roster and they'd ask "two green," "15 blue," "five green." And in about 20 minutes, I'd know them. I'd have both rosters down pat. It's about an hour's drive for me to East Lansing or Ann Arbor, so by the time I got there, I'd have them in my head. I may look down a few times, but for the most part, I've got it.

But if I'm doing the GLI and call four teams in one day—and I haven't seen Michigan Tech all year—to memorize four teams that fast is a challenge. And Michigan Tech's yellow numbers on white sweaters must go! From 120' away, your player recognition factor is limited at best.

A few years after I moved to Detroit, I had the chance in March 2000 to call the NCAA East Regionals in Albany, New York. My agent, Maury Gostfrand, hooked me up to call the NCAA broadcast with former WHA New England Whalers goaltender and then San Jose Sharks scout Cap Raeder. Cap had that great Boston accent going for him. Cap; Tommy Reid, the former Minnesota North Stars defenseman; and Fred Pletsch were all wonderful college analysts I worked with in the booth.

In a game I will never forget, since it was so damn long, St. Lawrence, Mike Keenan's alma mater, beat Boston University in the fourth overtime period. St. Lawrence's Robin Carruthers put his own rebound past Boston University goalie Rick DiPietro 3:53 into the fourth overtime period as the Saints won 3–2. At that time, the nearly 124-minute game that Cap and I called was the longest in NCAA history. It was eclipsed in 2010 by the five-overtime UMass victory over Notre Dame.

So that March day of 2000, instead of calling just two games, we called three and a bit. Maine beat Michigan 5–2 in the other game I finally called that afternoon/late evening.

The NCAA tournament is a true challenge to your skills of memorizing. I'm getting six teams and I'm just saying *holy cow*. I did a lot of prep for that, trying to make a good impression on the new people who just hired me.

That's what I miss now. Fox has basically done fewer and fewer college games each year.

Until 2017, I had done college hockey every season for Fox Sports Detroit. Today, with the Big Ten Network involvement and the CCHA no longer a league, FSD began taking fewer college hockey games. And with Red Wing conflicts, it's left me on the outs.

Familiar Faces

Even though I was new to Detroit in 1997, I already knew plenty of guys in the Red Wings dressing room.

Bob Rouse and Larry Murphy, who'd played for the Toronto Maple Leafs when I called their games, were key cogs in the Detroit defense, and when the Wings moved to bolster their blue-line depth for the Stanley Cup run, they made deals to add Jamie Macoun from the Leafs and former Leaf Dmitri Mironov from the Anaheim Mighty Ducks.

Murphy—who still holds the NHL record for assists and points by a rookie defenseman when he produced 60 assists and 76 points for the Los Angeles Kings in 1980–81—enjoyed a career revival with the Wings, teaming with Nicklas Lidstrom in Detroit's top defense pairing. He had the last laugh on Toronto fans who booed him out of town in 1997, winning the Cup with the Wings that spring, and he got the better of Washington, another team that sent him packing, in the 1998 Cup final.

During the two games of that series at the MCI Center, Washington fans taunted Murphy with chants of "whoop, whoop, whoop"—much like Curly of the Three Stooges used to say. After

Murphy scored in Game 4 to make it 3–1 Detroit, the crowd fell silent. There were no more "whoop, whoops" after that.

Murph, who'd later work with me in the booth as an analyst on Red Wings games, became just the fourth player in NHL history to win back-to-back Stanley Cups with different teams. He'd also won consecutive Cups with the Pittsburgh Penguins in 1990–91 and 1991–92, the latter with Scotty Bowman as his coach, so three of Larry's four Stanley Cup wins came under Scotty's tutelage. *Val Marie, SK.*

Dick Duff, Red Kelly, and Bryan Trottier were the other three players to twice win back-to-back Cups, in case you were wondering. Trottier was Murph's teammate for two Cups in Pittsburgh, while Kelly's first back-to-back titles came with the Wings in 1953–54 and 1954–55.

Macoun, who won a Stanley Cup with Calgary in 1988–89 to go with his 1997–98 win with Detroit, was one of the real characters of the game. A kid from the rural community of Newmarket, Ontario, he'd gone to play hockey at Ohio State and with a couple of his teammates, decided to go out and purchase motorcycles to get around.

They were out on their bikes one day in the countryside and spotted a bar with dozens of motorcycles parked outside and stopped for a visit. Being naive farm kids, they figured this was some sort of motorcycle club and didn't realize that it was actually a hangout for a biker gang.

The bikers took the keys to their motorcycles, refusing to believe that they were hockey players for Ohio State. They said they'd come to the next Buckeyes game, and if they were indeed playing, they'd return their keys. But if not, they'd come looking for them.

Sure enough, Macoun was playing that weekend and when he took a penalty early into the game, one of the bikers leaned over the glass by the sin bin and tossed in the keys to their motorcycles.

Ozzie's Odyssey

Chris Osgood is another former Wing who has since joined me in the booth as an analyst, but in 1997–98 he was Detroit's go-to goalie, and there were plenty of questions as to whether he was ready to ascend into that role for the Cup champs after Conn Smythe Trophy winner Mike Vernon was dealt to the San Jose Sharks in the summer of 1997.

I remember Detroit GM Ken Holland relaying to me why he so believed in Ozzie, and it was scoring with a ball, not stopping a puck, that helped pave Osgood's path to the Wings' net.

Holland was putting together a team to play in a summer ball hockey league in Medicine Hat, Alberta. One of the players he recruited was Osgood, then the goalie for the Western Hockey League's Medicine Hat Tigers.

"He was a forward," Holland remembered. "He had great hands and could score and had great drive and competitiveness. I got to know him as a person, better than you usually get to know these kids heading into draft."

Holland, Detroit's amateur scouting director at the time, strongly recommended that the Wings draft Osgood in 1991. Holland felt that insight into Osgood's character helped make it easier for him to trade Vernon after Detroit's Stanley Cup win, and he wasn't worried at all about placing the pressure to repeat on the shoulders of the boyish-looking Osgood.

The day the 1998 playoffs started, nobody in the league had the pressure or scrutiny that Osgood had. He was replacing the Conn Smythe Trophy winner in the hockey-crazy city of the defending Stanley Cup champs. His critics—of which Osgood had many—didn't think he had what it took to get the job done.

I was so happy for Ozzie when the Wings won the Cup. He had to put up with so much crap that year and was under the gun all season. No matter what he did, it was always, "Yeah, but can he do it in the playoffs?" There were so many questions, and he answered them all. He seemed to thrive on the adversity.

Victory for Vladi

Before every game of the Stanley Cup playoffs, Dave Lewis would scrawl an inspirational message on the blackboard in the Red Wings dressing room. Prior to Game 3 of the 1998 Stanley Cup final, the message was about faith. "Faith is to believe what you do not yet see. The reward for this is to see what you believe."

The belief system in the Detroit dressing room was emboldened by their desire to win for fallen teammate Vladimir Konstantinov, who along with team masseur Sergei Mnatsakanov had suffered debilitating brain injuries in a limousine crash six days after their 1997 Stanley Cup triumph on June 13, 1997. That's right, the tragic limousine crash took place on Friday the 13th.

Because the NHL had halted the season's play for the first time ever to participate in the 1998 Nagano Winter Olympics, everything was backed up further into the spring during the 1998 Stanley Cup playoffs and Game 3 of the final happened to fall on the anniversary of that terrible tragedy. Sergei Fedorov, Konstantinov's best friend on the team, scored the winner in that game, a 2–1 victory that gave the Wings a commanding 3–0 series lead over the Washington Capitals. It was his 10th tally of the playoffs, tying a Detroit club mark for goals set by Petr Klima in 1988. After the game, Fedorov scooped up the puck, planning to present it to Konstantinov and Mnatsakanov.

"I will take it and give it to them," Fedorov explained, "in honor of the memory of what they meant to this team. Two minutes before the game, I paused and thought about where I was last year, on my way from the golf course [where they'd enjoyed a team outing that day] to the hospital."

Playing on the anniversary of the day their hearts were so shattered seemed to fortify the Wings. "I think the memory kind of helped us to be a more united team, to play our best hockey," Igor Larionov said. "We thought about how tough those guys are and how tough we have to be."

Even Scotty Bowman, on the brink of his eighth Cup as coach, a win that would tie him with Toe Blake for the most Stanley Cups by a coach, saw something more important than victory attained by his team on that day.

"It's nice to win all those Cups, but this puts you in touch with reality," Bowman said. "Playing is important and winning is big, too, but what we have to face—winning one more game—is nothing compared to what those two warriors must face every day."

Defenseman Slava Fetisov was also injured in the limousine crash but recovered from his injuries and returned to playing. Most people thought that after he'd finally won his first Stanley Cup at the age of the 39 that Fetisov, who like Larionov had fought the old Communist system in the Soviet Union to gain permission for Russian players to come play in the NHL, would hang up his skates, but he felt that he must go on as a tribute to Konstantinov, his fallen defense partner.

Fetisov suffered bruises to his chest and lungs and cracked ribs and was left to wonder why he was spared.

It was not the first time he had pondered his fate. In 1985, Fetisov was involved in a car crash in Moscow in which his brother, Anatoly, was killed.

"I have to go through this," Fetisov said of the mental anguish he faced. "What I must deal with doesn't compare to the pain Vladimir and Sergei must go through."

Throughout that season, Konstantinov's locker in the Red Wings dressing room remained a shrine to the man they called the Vladinator. "That's the way he left it last," Brendan Shanahan said. "It's never been touched, except to add a few things."

His locker included a Curious George doll in a Red Wings sweater. That was Konstantinov's nickname because, just like the cartoon monkey, he was always sticking his nose in where it didn't belong. A pet rock winger Slava Kozlov received in the mail during the 1997 playoffs inscribed with the word "Believe" rested on the shelf.

The Konstantinov who patrolled the blue line for Detroit was a contradiction in terms. On the ice, unyielding, a warrior. A man who asked no quarter and gave none. Away from the rink, as warm and as friendly as a man could be.

"Vladi liked everybody," Detroit senior vice president Jimmy Devellano said. "And he had time for everyone."

"Great guy," Fetisov said, recalling his friend and teammate. "Big heart. Easygoing. Sometimes, I'd look at Vladi's locker and I'd want to cry. But you couldn't cry. You had to stand up and play your best again and again—like Vladimir did."

The biggest ovation of the playoffs was reserved for when Konstantinov and Mnatsakanov returned to Joe Louis Arena for Game 4 of the Western Conference final against the Dallas Stars.

When the Wings beat the Capitals 4–1 in Game 4 in Washington to clinch the title, Konstantinov, wearing his No. 16 Red Wings sweater, was wheeled out on the ice to join the party, the first time he'd been between the boards since the previous spring's Cup clincher against the Philadelphia Flyers. They toured him around the rink in a victory celebration, Fetisov and Larionov, his Russian countrymen, helping him carry the Stanley Cup.

"Win No. 16 is for No. 16," Fetisov said, his voice cracking with emotion. "Vladi's spirit was with us in the room all season."

"This is so emotional, it's great," Larionov said. "This is for Vladi and Sergei."

The players wore their hearts on the sleeves. A patch with both men's initials and the word "believe," in English and Russian, adorned each Detroit sweater.

The Red Wings believed. They hoped. And they've never forgotten.

"How could you ever forget a guy like Vladi?" asked goalie Chris Osgood.

No one ever has.

Captain MVP

The unquestioned leader of the Stanley Cup champion Wings was Steve Yzerman, even if he chose to question that himself. Stevie would insist that Scotty Bowman was the leader of the team, but on the ice, everyone bowed to Stevie.

For the majority of his career, Stevie had played in the shadow of Wayne Gretzky and Mario Lemieux on the NHL stage. They'd taken the vast majority of the individual honors and the many Stanley Cups until the Wings finally won in 1996–97 and 1997–98.

Winning is about sacrifice, and Stevie was about sacrifice. In 1988–89, he scored a club-record 65 goals for the Wings, a mark that still stands today. In 1997–98, he led the Wings in scoring with 69 points, the lowest total to top a Stanley Cup–winning team since captain Jean Beliveau had 68 points for the 1967–68 Montreal Canadiens, the first team that Mickey Redmond won the Stanley Cup with as a player. But you know what? Stevie didn't care about individual accomplishments by that time in his career.

He'd become one of the NHL's best two-way centers by then and along with Sergei Fedorov may have given the Wings the

My two captains: Steve and my son, Jamie, age five, on photo day after the Stanley Cup win in 1998. (Photo courtesy of the Detroit Red Wings)

best 1–2 punch of offense and defense down the middle. Stevie was only worried about competing, about winning. He didn't put much stock in his individual numbers. The only number that mattered to him was that the Wings be No. 1. But he was a big reason why they stayed on top. His 18 assists and 24 points in the playoffs in the spring of 1998 equaled club playoff records.

As is his style, Stevie preferred to place the credit for Detroit's success elsewhere. "This is a statement more so of the team as a whole," he said of the back-to-back Cup triumphs. "I think this team has gotten to a point where we don't care about stats."

I Love a Parade

There were upwards of a million people crowded along the parade route as the Wings celebrated their second straight Stanley

A thrill to experience Woodward Avenue in a Stanley Cup parade doing the queen's wave.

On stage at Hart Plaza with Mickey in front of an estimated 1 million people on June 18, 1998. (Photo courtesy of the Detroit Red Wings / photo by Action Image)

Cup victory. (Until the 2017 Penguins, it was the last occasion that a team successfully defended its Stanley Cup title.) It was an unbelievable spectacle to be part of that, for someone who had just completed his first season as the Wings' play-by-play broadcaster.

Being co-host with Mickey Redmond of three Stanley Cup parades and being down at Hart Plaza in Detroit, looking out and seeing nearly a million people there, and introducing your Stanley Cup champion Detroit Red Wings, that's pretty darn cool, too. Those moments—being in the Stanley Cup parade with my kids— are great moments that stand out for me more than just one game.

That entire first season was a very special time for me. I was making new friends, and winning the Cup was great. You can't top that. I always loved watching players like Steve Yzerman and Igor Larionov play, and now I was announcing them every night. That year was truly a highlight of my broadcasting career.

129

2002 Stanley Cup parade: son, Jamie, age nine, and daughter, Arlyn, age six.

I will never forget a famous line from Red Wings general manager and executive vice president Ken Holland. After the Wings won a fourth Stanley Cup in 11 seasons in 2008, and Kirk Maltby and Kris Draper were aging, Ken was asked, "What do those guys do for the Wings?" Ken's response was a classic. "I'm not sure what they do. But I do know that every four years or so they get in a car going down Woodward Avenue and wave to a million people!" If I had a microphone, I would have dropped it.

CHAPTER 4
THE VOICES I'VE HEARD, THE PLACES I'VE BEEN

Favorite sounds and least favorite sites

Dan's the Man

It's not a prerequisite for being an NHL analyst, but being a former goaltender at a college or professional level sure can't hurt. Just look around at how many ex-goalies are thriving in the occupation. We've got Darren Eliot and Chris Osgood on our broadcasts in Detroit. There's Tripp Tracy in Carolina, Darren Pang in St. Louis, Brian Hayward in Anaheim, and Daryl Reaugh in Dallas. In Canada, *Hockey Night in Canada* has employed Kelly Hrudey, Glenn Healy, and Greg Millen; Sportsnet has John Garrett; and TSN has Jamie McLennan.

Chico Resch was sensational and insightful for years working the New Jersey Devils broadcasts alongside Doc Emrick. Before he turned to running the fortunes of the Columbus Blue Jackets as their team president, ex–New York Rangers goalie John Davidson was the smoothest analyst in the business.

It's similar, I guess, to how many catchers become such wise baseball analysts. Maybe it's just how goalies see the game develop in front of them coming and going from their crease, that their perspective is prevalent.

My view from the crease growing up came as a goaltender in ball hockey. From there, not having to run, I practiced my play-by-play in my head. There's always one kid doing the play-by-play, loudly sometimes, and in our neighborhood, that was me.

And then I honed my skills at night listening on the radio to Dan Kelly call the St. Louis Blues games. Dan had that marvelous inflection, building to that fabulous moment. Like Bob Cole does. Like Danny Gallivan did. For me, Dan Kelly did that four and five decades ago better than anyone—even when Bobby Orr scored the goal to win the 1970 Stanley Cup in overtime, "Sanderson to Orr."

When Mario Lemieux's goal beat the Soviets in the final game of the 1987 Canada Cup, if you listen to Dan's call, that puck is in and out before Dan actually says, "He shoots. He scores. Mario Lemieux." It's just the pause. He sees it in and sees it coming out, but it didn't matter. Not that he missed it. He didn't want to miss it. It's timing. The call is amazing. Just like "Sanderson . . . to Orr . . . Bobby Orr." The puck's already in. He didn't need "he shoots, he scores." Dan just went straight to "and the Boston Bruins win the Stanley Cup." That was his cadence, his inflection. It was just perfect.

Another Dandy Dan

Growing up in Toronto, I didn't hear a lot of Danny Gallivan. I wasn't really accustomed to Danny and his totally different sound and style to that of Foster or Bill Hewitt, the voices I heard the most while they were calling the Maple Leafs games. The more I listened to Danny in later years, the more I appreciated him and the way he called the game.

All the great ones just pause at the right moment and build it. And Danny could build it and he could bring it.

A funny thing about Danny. During the game, Danny had all his stuff written down on a piece of cardboard, the thin flexible kind you'd get inside a folded shirt that you got back from the dry cleaners. And Danny couldn't call a game without holding a microphone in his hand. Even after they went to headsets, Danny would still hold a mic in his hand while calling the game, even though it wasn't turned on.

Bill of Rights

It took a long time for Bill Hewitt to get into the Hockey Hall of Fame, but Bill was a more-than-worthy inductee. His style was completely different to today's broadcast. If you live in Canada, you see a lot of the old Leafs games rebroadcast on Leafs TV, and Bill called the game as a loner, as if his analyst wasn't even in the booth with him. There was little in the way of conversation. Brian McFarlane, the analyst of the Leafs *Hockey Night in Canada* broadcasts with Bill, would occasionally step in and say something, but Bill wouldn't play off Brian. Brian could say anything, and Bill would say, "That's right Brian." During a Boston-Toronto game, Brian had mentioned that Bobby Orr was a unanimous selection for the All-Star team. And Bill not really understanding the term, or barely listening replied, "That's right Brian. Just about everybody voted for him."

Bill's call was pretty much spot on, though. It was just a quality sound. Again, it was inflection. It was excitement at the right moment. Bill wasn't a storyteller, just a classic play-by-play guy, a lot like his dad but more exciting, I think, than Foster.

Ol' King Cole

Bob Cole came on to replace Bill Hewitt on the *Hockey Night in Canada* Leafs games. You want to talk about involved in stories, Bob never is and never was. He learned from Foster on how to call a game, and he's stuck with that old-school formula throughout his storied career.

I didn't know Bob well, and we didn't get off to a good start. He caught me one time in Anaheim imitating his voice when I

With the legendary voice, Bob Cole, during the playoffs in April 2015, in Tampa Bay.

was hosting the game for *Hockey Night in Canada* and we were in a makeshift locker room as our studio. Producer Mark Askin was in the bathroom. He asked me a question, and I didn't know Bob Cole had come in another door. He heard me say, "That's right baby...oh baby" to Mark, and then I heard the door close and it was Bob. Mark came out and said, "You are so dead. Bob hates that." I'd heard the stories about Bob hating the impersonations.

On another occasion, I'm hosting a *Hockey Night in Canada* game and Bob and I hopped in a taxi to get from the hotel to the game. We're leaving the cab, and I've got my roller bag with me. Bob gets out, and he's got nothing with him. I said, "Did you leave something in the cab?" He said, "It's all up here, mister," and he pointed to his head.

Bob goes into a game and just calls the game. It's old-school, but that's how he's always done it. It's the storytelling that has changed most over the years. There's so many players in the league and for most of us, our hope is to get fans to know the players we are talking about. Maybe because of it, that fan becomes more engaged. Most play-by-play guys enjoy weaving stories into the games. It's our game within the game. But Bob is just one of those guys who has refused to bend. People just know with Bob Cole, that's what you're getting. When I go into a game and I have a story to tell, I'm excited about it. We told a story about Zach Redmond, who is no relation to Mickey, while he was in town playing defense with Montreal. Zach had a stroke when he was 15 and an artery in his leg lacerated all in a span of six years and thought his career was over. But he persevered. So to me, will that get people to remember the name Zach Redmond? Maybe. But if we didn't tell that story, would anyone remember him? With 30 teams in the National Hockey League, you only see some of the teams twice a year. We don't even know the non-high-profile young players in the league now. To me, if we can go into a game and have one or two or three good stories to tell about a player in game and it makes someone say, "Oh that's neat," then that's a good thing.

Those Analysts Should Shut Up

It really wasn't until the last few years, including the 2016 playoffs against Tampa Bay, that I got to know Bob Cole better. After the morning skate for Game 2 in Tampa, Mickey and I were going to our hotel and grabbed a cab. Bob was going to a different hotel, but we shared the cab and would drop him off. I asked Bob about meeting Foster for the first time. He told us the story of driving back through Toronto after seeing a baseball game in New York in the 1950s. He and three friends were in the car, and they were to wait for a moment so Bob could drop off a tape at CKFH just in case Foster would be so kind as to critique it for him. Not only did Foster listen to the tape, he gave Bob a sit-down in his office for two hours. Bob told me, "Oh my God. Can you imagine? My knees were shaking. And when I got back to the car, boy were my friends pissed."

And on another matter, Bob was pissed, too.

He said, "The game's the thing. You stick to the game. Boy, some of these analysts, they don't shut up." We all laughed, Mickey the hardest. Bob gets out of the taxi and Mickey says, "Appreciate those 15 minutes you just had right there."

That was my best 15-minute hockey cab ride ever.

A Harry Experience

Just prior to the 1998 Winter Olympics in Nagano, Japan, during my first season as the Red Wings' play-by-play voice, I was recalled back to Toronto to do one last Maple Leafs game for *Hockey Night in Canada* on January 31, 1998, with the Phoenix Coyotes visiting Maple Leaf Gardens.

My analyst on this night was Harry Neale, *Hockey Night in Canada*'s top guy at the time. He was slated to leave for Nagano the next day, but all their play-by-play guys were already in Nagano, preparing for the upcoming Olympiad, which would see the NHL take a break during its season for the first time to allow all of the world's best players to participate. Since the Red Wings game that day against the Pittsburgh Penguins was a national broadcast on Fox, I wasn't needed to call it.

Now Red Wings fans might not hold the fondest memories of Harry. He was the team's coach for the start of the forgettable 1985–86 season, when the Wings finished last overall in the

NHL. Harry lasted just 35 games behind the Detroit bench before he was fired from what would be his last coaching job—but what a break that proved to be for hockey fans.

Hired to work with *Hockey Night in Canada*, Harry and Bob Cole formed the network's No. 1 broadcast team for years. Harry was the template for a great analyst, combining a glib sense of humor with a distinct eye for the minutiae of the game, and he could break down a play in an instant. But what Harry is probably remembered most for are his stories and his one-liners.

He once said of his Vancouver Canucks team, "Last season we couldn't win at home. This season we can't win on the road. My failure as a coach is I can't think of any place else to play." Too bad for Harry that the NHL didn't play outdoor games during his era.

Another time, speaking of his team's woes, he cracked, "I know my players don't like my practices, but that's okay because I don't like their games."

Harry could spin a yarn with the best of them. He coached the cash-strapped Minnesota Fighting Saints in the wild west days of the World Hockey Association in the 1970s. The Fighting Saints were always on the verge of folding, staying one step ahead of their creditors. But this day, the players are at the airport, about to leave for a road trip. They haven't been paid for weeks, and they hold an impromptu meeting and announce to Harry and GM Glen Sonmor that unless they get paid, they aren't getting on the plane.

Well, Harry calls the team's owner in a panic and a short time later, a driver arrives at the airport with thousands of dollars stuffed into a paper bag. It's time to board the plane, so Harry takes the bag around and opens it to show the players the cash and says that they will get their back pay on the plane. The players agree to the offer and get on board.

Harry and Sonmor are sitting together on the plane and they are counting the cash into piles to give the players their salaries. One of the flight attendants spots these two men holding a paper bag filled with money and she notifies the pilot. They're thinking that somebody has knocked over a bank, and when the plane arrived at its destination, the FBI was waiting for Harry. Well, you better believe he had some explaining to do.

Harry coached Gordie Howe in the WHA with the New England Whalers. He also coached against Gordie and remembered a time when Dave Langevin, who was just a cocky kid at the time but who would later go on to be a solid stay-at-home defenseman for those great Stanley Cup–winning New York Islanders team, was prepping for his first game against Mr. Hockey. Harry advised those unfamiliar with Howe to be wary on the ice, but Langevin merely scoffed. "He's an old man," Langevin told Neale. "What's he gonna do to me?"

Langevin went over the boards for his first shift against Gordie and within moments, returned to the bench bleeding profusely from his head, off to the medical room for stitches.

Harry was also the first pro coach to experience the Carlson brothers and Dave Hanson, who'd go on to hockey immortality as the Hanson Brothers in the 1977 hockey cult film, *Slap Shot*. "We were trying to market the Fighting Saints to the general public, so we held these open tryout camps throughout the state of Minnesota, simply as a publicity ploy, never expecting to find any players," Harry explained. "Well we had this camp up in the Iron Range of Minnesota and they showed up and they looked just like they did in the first scene the movie, wearing their hockey jackets and their glasses, and Glen Sonmor and I looked at each other and said, 'Who the hell are these guys?' We got on the ice and they just beat the crap out of everybody."

That was the only time in my career I ever worked alongside Harry, and what a pleasure it was to call a game with one of the best.

Those Who Came Before Me

I had the pleasure to get to know two of the all-time play-by-play greats in Detroit, Budd Lynch and Bruce Martyn. They were both legends of the booth, each deservedly enshrined in the Hockey Hall of Fame.

Budd was the first to do what I do, call play-by-play of Red Wings games on television. He'd already been the radio voice of the Windsor Spitfires, at the time a junior affiliate of the Red Wings. Budd began calling games on TV during the 1949–50 season, and you know what? Just like me, in his first season, the Red Wings won the Stanley Cup.

Hit by a shell while serving in the Canadian Armed Forces during World War II, Budd lost his right arm, but his dulcet tones weren't affected in the least. He actually stayed in the military after losing his arm and did radio broadcasts of the war effort for the BBC in England.

Budd remained with the Red Wings organization for 63 years, right up until his death at the age of 95 in 2012, serving as director of publicity after leaving play-calling behind, and as most of the current generation will most fondly recall him, as the public address announcer at Joe Louis Arena. Budd called four Red

Wings Stanley Cup wins (1949–50, 1951–52, 1953–54, 1954–55) as a play-by-play man and four more (1996–97, 1997–98, 2001–02, 2007–08) as the public address voice.

Budd was a wonderful man who always had a smile on his face and had time for everyone. He did countless hours of work helping those who'd lost limbs adapt to their new lifestyle. His golf tournament raised over $1 million for at-risk children. He touched the lives of many.

He never looked upon his loss of an arm as a disability and actually made light of it. "Bruce always gave me a hand," Budd would say of Martyn, his longtime partner in the broadcast booth. "He needed one," Martyn would answer.

The banter between these two, who called Red Wings together from 1964 to 1975, was side-splitting. It was evident how much they cared for each other and they shared natural chemistry that I've found in the booth with Mickey Redmond.

"Far and away, I was the easiest one to get along with," Bruce jokingly suggested of Budd. "My biggest problem was shutting him up."

Bruce and Budd met in 1950 when the Wings had training camp in Sault Ste. Marie, where Bruce was working in radio at the time. Budd would bring Red Wings players to Bruce's station for live interviews. From that point on, they became friends.

Bruce retired in 1995, but Red Wings radio play-by-play man Ken Kal did a wonderful thing when he brought Bruce back to the booth and let him call the second period of Detroit's Game 4 win over the Philadelphia Flyers during the 1997 Stanley Cup final, the game that gave the Wings their first Stanley Cup triumph since 1955.

When I was first starting out in Detroit in 1997, it was interesting to talk to Bruce and Budd about their philosophy of calling a team's games over such a long period of time. You always feel like you're part of the team you are working for, they told me. "You travel with them, you live with them on the road," Budd would say. "And you never bury a guy when he makes a bad play or a costly mistake."

"'He'd like to have that one back,' is a good way to do it," Bruce offered.

Catching Irvin's Ire

God bless him, I love Dick Irvin. He's a great man. Most of the games I did for *Hockey Night in Canada* when I first started doing play-by-play were in Montreal. At first it was just me with Dick as analyst and then with Dick and Greg Millen, sometimes all three of us in the booth.

Often, Dick would leave with a minute or two to go in the period because he was doing the interviews during the intermission. His family owned a legendary link to the game. Dick Irvin Sr. had played in the NHL and later coached both the Toronto Maple Leafs and Montreal Canadiens to the Stanley Cup. He still holds the NHL record of coaching 26 consecutive seasons in the league. Dick Jr. grew up in and around the game and knew more about the lore of the NHL than anyone. When Scotty Bowman became the winningest coach in NHL history, it was Dick Irvin Sr.'s record that he surpassed.

I learned pretty early on not to go too deep into stories when I was in the booth working with Dick. I guess there was a story about a Canadiens player that I told during one game, and it was the same story Dick had the intention of telling. I looked over and there's Dick with his pen, scratching angrily across the page and he then threw his pen in the air. He didn't even look at me. I knew right then to be careful with the stories I use, or at the very least steal a peek at his notes before the game, so as not to replicate. I'm glad Mickey Redmond doesn't use notes.

Dick also has a wicked sense of humor, a really dry wit. He's written many hockey books, and I've read most of them. The latest he had was of great coaches in the league, and when I asked him if I could get one, he shot back, "It's $19.95 at Cole's down the street."

What's Up Doc ?

You want to talk about storytellers, NBC's Doc Emrick is the best at weaving one into a game.

Mike—Doc's given name—has a Ph.D in communications from Bowling Green University, hence his nickname. A lot of people don't realize that Doc got his play-by-play start right here in Michigan, doing International Hockey League games for the Port Huron Flags from 1973 to 1977.

His work on the national NHL games has done a world of good for selling the game in the United States. Among the numerous honors that have come his way was the Lester Patrick Award in 2004 for service to hockey in the United States. Doc was the first member of the media to be so honored. And in 2011, he was the first member of the media inducted into the United States Hockey Hall of Fame. Doc was already presented the Foster Hewitt Award and enshrined in the Hockey Hall of Fame in 2008. He truly is the voice of hockey in America.

Spotty Behavior

Some broadcast locations are a problem. Many are a long way from the ice. And then there are booths that are a challenge to get to. The old Pacific Coliseum in Vancouver, that place scared the crap out of me. We could only get to the broadcast booth from one side of the building by going across a rickety, old, circular, wood walkway. You went across one side and on to the other.

Gord Stellick, my analyst on Leafs radio, is up on the roof walkway shaking it as I'm heading across. He's waiting for me to get to the middle and then he starts shifting his weight back and forth so that the whole thing is rocking to and fro. I'm grabbing on to the railing, screaming obscenities at him and it just kept moving more and more. I got down on all fours and crawled the rest of the way. Once I got over I realized the restroom was on the other side, so I would have to go back during intermission if I needed it. I wouldn't. I'd rather wait.

The Calgary Saddledome has a ramp you have to go down to get to the broadcast location. I just don't look down and make a sprint for the booth.

The restrooms at the old Rexall Place in Edmonton were on the concourse and inconvenient. Plus, I often couldn't risk it because with the men lining up I might not make it back to the booth before the end of the intermission. We had a double overtime game there with the Oilers in the 2006 playoffs. I had to go, so I just grabbed a big popcorn box. I wasn't about to leave the booth.

The press box area at Joe Louis Arena offered a small restroom and cramped areas to call the game. The visitors had it worse than us. The entire thing was an afterthought, after builders in

144

1979 realized they forgot about it. They later took out the last few rows of seats at the Joe to build the press area. But as far as Little Caesars Arena is concerned they didn't overlook a thing. It sets the standard. The Ilitch family asked our input for the broadcast gondola location long before a shovel was ever in the ground. They wanted the broadcast amenities and location to be the best in the NHL, as close to the ice as possible, and be a large comfortable spot for everyone to work. They succeeded. And they included large restrooms nearby, too!

Rat Patrol

I was in the coach's room at old Boston Garden before a game, and out of the corner of my eye I catch something scurrying past. It was the biggest rat I'd ever seen, as they chased it out of the room and into the hall. The trainer for the Quebec Nordiques told me they would take coat hangers and hang the hockey bags over the pipes in the ceiling during the game. Otherwise, the rats would get into the bags.

Beantown was also a very hostile place if you were the visiting team. After the game one night in Boston—I was hosting it for *Hockey Night* and we had to do a postgame interview after the Maple Leafs–Bruins game to send it back to the studio so that they could use it later in the broadcast; I didn't want to do it in the hall, so I asked Toronto coach Pat Burns, "Can we go out on the bench?" He tersely replied, "I'm not going on the frickin' bench to the interview." I asked him why not and he said, "Because they throw stuff at you here. I'm going nowhere near that bench. I'll get pummeled. I'm not going on the bench. We're doing the interview right here."

National News

I've done maybe a dozen games for NBC over the years. They've got a lot of guys they can use.

Calling a network game, as compared to calling a Wings game, is a totally different experience. It's about finding that comfort zone. When I was working with *Hockey Night in Canada*, I would do a lot of games from western Canada. My brother lived in Calgary, and even he thought I was biased toward the Vancouver Canucks. My own brother.

On a regional broadcast, I think there are different levels of excitement. Some regional broadcasters don't get excited if the other team scores. If a visiting team scores on Detroit, am I getting really excited? Heck no. But I don't think you want to do the goal an injustice. It's a hockey game. You're still calling the game. If there's a Red Wings level of excitement for a winning goal, trust me it will be noticeably higher than where it would be if the visiting team scores.

Calling a regional game, do I want the Red Wings to win? Absolutely. Are we homers? To a certain extent. And others from another city may think we're the biggest homers in the league. You ask somebody else and they'll say their local broadcasters are the biggest homers in the league. There's no reality. There's only perception.

I challenge you to listen to the 1979 Challenge Cup between the NHL and the Soviet Union, in a year the series replaced the NHL All-Star Game.

It was a best-of-three that the Soviets dominated. They won the series two games to one and galloped 6–0 in the final. Find it on YouTube, and catch the excitement in the voices of Danny

Gallivan and Dan Kelly when the Soviets scored. Mr. Gallivan even called a Sergei Makarov goal, "Holy Makarov." Today, they'd be called Russian spies, and then some, by Twitter standards. But they were just being professional.

Bobby Orr, in an interview, inadvertently called the NHL All-Star team, that included three Swedish players, including former Red Wing Borje Salming, "Team Canada."

If I'm perceived to be more of a Detroit homer, that's okay. I work for the Detroit Red Wings. I can live with that. If I'm doing a national game and I'm doing Detroit, which I have—I called the NBC Detroit game when the Wings won their 22nd game in a row at home in 2012 beating San Jose. Was I happy Detroit beat San Jose? Sure. But I was very cognizant of the fact that the game was going back to San Jose and I made certain to bring down the Detroit level to equal that for the Sharks.

Talking with Legends

This line of work brings you wonderful opportunities, especially working with such a tradition-rich, Original Six franchise like the Red Wings. One of those opportunities came in 2008, when the NHL asked me to host a town hall–type show with six players who'd won four Stanley Cups each with the Red Wings in the 1950s—Gordie Howe, Ted Lindsay, Marcel Pronovost, Red Kelly, Alex Delvecchio, and Marty Pavelich.

In my mind, there's a symmetry between the Wings of that era and the Wings who won four Stanley Cups from 1997 to 2008. When you think of Steve Yzerman, you think of Gordie Howe. When you think of Nick Lidstrom, you think of Red Kelly.

Just to hear their stories of that glorious Red Wings era in the 1950s was an unforgettable experience in itself. I think Joe Falls, the great writer for the *Detroit News*, best expressed what those legends meant to Red Wings fans and the city of Detroit as a whole.

Falls wrote of those teams that dominated in the 1950s, winning four Stanley Cups in six years from 1950 to 1955 and capturing an unprecedented seven successive first-place finishes from 1949 to 1955, "This is where Hockeytown really was born, where it took its roots. They brought such joy to Detroit. They were seen everywhere, and not only became part of the fabric of the city, they truly represented the city. Good guys and hard workers, they became us, and we became them."

NHL commissioner Gary Bettman was on hand to present special miniature Stanley Cups to each of them, but it was this sensational sextet that stole the show.

Lindsay relayed the story of how in a fit of petulant emotion, he scooped up the Stanley Cup after a Detroit victory and carried it around the ice, something no one had ever done before. Up until then, the Stanley Cup was placed on a table at center ice. None of the players touched it, except to maybe put a hand on it in reverence. But as Lindsay told me, he unwittingly changed all that.

"I was very aware of who paid my salary," Lindsay explained. "It wasn't Red Wings owner Mr. [James] Norris, it was the fans who sat in the seats. I saw all these fans after they presented the Cup to [Detroit GM] Mr. [Jack] Adams and they were all along the boards. I saw the Cup sitting there and nobody was around it and I just picked it up and went over to the boards to let the fans see it. I just went all the way around the boards to let them see it.

"I wanted to respect the people who paid my salary, and that's why I did it. I was not starting any kind of tradition. I didn't think I was starting a tradition, but as it turned out, I guess I did. Very innocently I did it. Most importantly, no individual wins the Stanley Cup. It's a team effort."

Lindsay also fondly recalled the night he shot Toronto down in the 1956 Stanley Cup playoffs. "Larry Hillman hurt Tod Sloan, Toronto's top center, in the second game of the series at Detroit," Lindsay explained. Some kook contacted Maple Leaf Gardens and said that if Howe and Lindsay showed up for Game 3 in Toronto they would be shot.

"Well, we had this French-Canadian forward by the name of Marcel Bonin, who couldn't speak English when he got to Detroit. The only words he could say were ham and eggs, so he had ham and eggs for breakfast, lunch, and dinner.

"We're getting dressed for the game and Gordie said to Marcel, 'Here, put my sweater on.' Well, Marcel knew enough English to understand what was going on, and he wanted no part of being a target. 'Oh no Gordie,' Marcel said. 'I know what you're thinking.'

"During warm-up, the guys were saying, 'Don't skate too close to us. He's liable to be a bad shot.'

"Of course, nobody shot at us. I was lucky enough that I got the tying goal in the third period and I got the overtime game winner. After the game, I go to center ice. I took my stick, turned it around and went into the circle at center ice, turned and circled the entire rink, and went rat-a-tat-tat like I was shooting a machine gun.

"When the game ended, there was 14,500 people booing, but when I did that with my stick, about 5,000 stopped booing, figuring, 'Hey Lindsay has a sense of humor.'"

Pronovost was a Hall of Fame defenseman who operated in Kelly's shadow but was an All-Star in his own right and like Lindsay, an unwitting part of another long-standing Red Wings tradition.

When Detroit was poised to sweep the Stanley Cup in the minimum eight games during the spring of 1952, local fishmongers Pete and Jerry Cusumano hatched an idea. They would bring an octopus to Game 4 of the series and throw it on to the Olympia Stadium ice when the Wings scored their first goal of the game, its eight tentacles representing the eight wins it took to capture Lord Stanley's mug. And so on April 15, 1952, when Metro Prystai zipped a shot past Montreal Canadiens goalie Gerry McNeil, out came the first flying mollusk in Red Wings history.

No one wanted to touch it as it lay there on the ice, but Pronovost was from a family of 12 kids—nine of them boys—so he knew not to let food sit anywhere for long and he scooped up the octopus.

"I took a look at it and nobody wanted to pick it up," Pronovost remembered. "I had gloves on, so I went and grabbed it and threw it in the penalty box. I didn't know what the eight tentacles meant, but I soon found out when we won eight straight."

The memory of becoming the first team to go 8–0 in the Stanley Cup playoffs stuck with those players. Wings goalie Terry Sawchuk posted four shutouts and an 0.85 goals-against average during the 1952 playoffs.

"They never scored a goal on Detroit's ice," Pronovost said. "They called us Terry and the Pirates."

Remembering the two sides of Sawchuk, they marveled at his puckstopping abilities, calling him the best ever, insisting he might not allow a goal if he were wearing today's bulky goalie equipment. But they worried about his troublesome life away from hockey.

"He was a very moody type of goaltender," Pavelich recalled. "Every goaltender I ever knew, they were a different breed of cat."

Pavelich was also fondly enamored with that 1951–52 team. "I think we could have played all summer and never lost," Pavelich said. "If we lost two games in a row, I felt sorry for the team we played next because we were going to kick the living hell out of them."

Like Pronovost, Delvecchio was probably overlooked by some, skating in the shadows of Howe and Lindsay. But it should never be forgotten what a playmaker the guy they called "Fats" was on the ice. He played more games as Howe's center than anyone. He was Howe's center when Gordie became the first NHLer to record 700 career goals, and he was Mickey Redmond's center when he became the first 50-goal scorer in Red Wings history.

"They treated me real well," the understated Delvecchio said. "I stayed around for 23 years."

His teammates supplied the superlatives. "We used to marvel at what he could do with the puck," Lindsay said of Delvecchio. "He was a magician. This is [Pavel] Datsyuk's forerunner."

The players also recalled their longtime coach and GM Jack Adams, who, like Sawchuk, was prone to mood swings, especially if his team wasn't playing well. During intermissions, the team would fuel up for the next period on tea and oranges—if they were still there.

"Jack would throw the teapot and the oranges when he was mad," Delvecchio said. They felt especially bad for defenseman Benny Woit, who sat in the corner stall, which was generally where Adams would aim the oranges when he was overcome with a fit of pique.

Most of all, the players fondly recollected the kinship and camaraderie of those championship teams of the 1950s.

"It was a group of players that played as well off the ice as we did on the ice," Kelly said. "We played for the team with the same objective in mind. It didn't matter who scored as long as we scored. Winning the Cup was it. That's what you wanted to do, what you set out every year to do."

Away from the rink, the team was seldom apart. They had a bowling league. "We even had our own shirts," Pavelich said. "We were competing off the ice."

Howe was the most impressive bowler. "Gordie Howe threw what we called the Torpedo Ball," Pavelich explained. "We used to feel bad for the pin setters down at the other end every time Gordie fired that ball right down the middle."

They planned outings as a group. "We had Mondays off, so we would go to different homes twice a month with our families," Howe said.

"We just felt very strongly we should be a team," Lindsay said, adding that attendance at these team functions was mandatory. "We didn't want any excuses. Everybody had to get there."

There was extra incentive to ensure 100 percent attendance at these team functions.

"If you didn't show up, you paid your share anyway," Pavelich noted.

Red Wing through and through, Lindsay grew up a fan of the team and still fondly recalled the day he became part of the organization.

"Carson Cooper was a scout for the Wings," Lindsay said, "I was playing at the old Barton Street Arena in Hamilton, Ontario.

I came out of the rink and this white-haired man came up and asked me if I was Ted Lindsay. And then he said, 'Ever think of playing pro?' Detroit was my favorite team. I grew up in Kirkland Lake, Ontario, which is about a 400-mile straight line north from Detroit, and on a clear night, you could get WJR on the radio and the Red Wings games. The Wings had these two heavy-hitting defensemen, Jack Stewart and Jimmy Orlando, and that was my kind of hockey. Run over top of them."

The Wings traded Lindsay to Chicago in 1957, where he played until calling it a day in 1960, but Lindsay was also proud that he was able to end a four-year retirement to finish his NHL career with Detroit in 1964–65.

"I ended up a Red Wing, and that meant a lot to me," he said.

Is Detroit Hockeytown?

Growing up in Toronto, where it's been since 1967 without a Stanley Cup, "Leafs Nation" is Cup-starved. And yet, the Leafs will always rule that town. I saw it in the early 1990s when the Toronto Blue Jays won those back-to-back World Series. There were people in Toronto actually asking, "Is this a hockey town or a baseball town?" Really? Seriously? Yes, baseball matters a lot, but hockey matters a lot more if you had to choose between winners.

Yet you never see a dropoff in attendance at the Air Canada Centre. Leafs tickets are the hardest tickets to get in town. People will line up at the box office at the crack of dawn on Saturday morning in sub-zero temperatures, hoping against hope that there are a few returns for that night's game. Toronto and Detroit both love their hockey teams. Here's the difference and the part of the equation that makes Detroit Hockeytown—as much as Toronto loves the Leafs, the city could care less about the other hockey around town. The AHL Marlies, the OHL Mississauga Steelheads, college hockey, none of it draws much in terms of attendance. As a hockey team, Toronto is really Leafs town.

In Detroit, you get beyond the passion for the Red Wings and there's the excitement generated by Michigan fans at Yost Arena and by Michigan State fans at Munn Arena. Outside the city limits, Western Michigan draws huge crowds, and there's a strong following in Grand Rapids for the Griffins, the Red Wings' American Hockey League affiliate.

In my mind, it all adds up to make Detroit Hockeytown.

CHAPTER 5
STOP IT RIGHT THERE GANG

Working in the booth with the The Mick

Uncle Jed

With his flannel shirts, homespun down-to-earth logic, and vast array of commonsense sayings, Mickey Redmond is my Jed Clampett. The way Mickey delivers his sage advice and words of wisdom, we don't necessarily value it until the game/episode ends. At the conclusion of an episode of the *Beverly Hillbillies*, Jed Clampett is actually the smartest person in the room.

So this has me wondering about my place in all of this, but I am way too small to be Jethro.

October 1998. Celebrating with the Stanley Cup at Mickey's house with my son, Jamie, age five, and daughter, Arlyn, age two and a half.

Working with a Star

As of September 2017, Mickey Redmond and I began our 21st season together with the Red Wings. That makes us the longest-tenured current TV duo in the National Hockey league.

We grew up with *Hockey Night in Canada*. The play-by-play guy talked 80 percent of the time, and the analyst added color usually when play stopped. When I joined the Red Wings in 1997, my style had to adapt. With Mickey I realized immediately this was going to be a 60–40 split and play stopping doesn't matter. While play-by-play is paramount, more conversation and storytelling is where the game has evolved, especially with the additional voice between the benches.

When I came from *Hockey Night*, I knew Mickey was the man. He was the star in Detroit. Long before he became the face of the team in the booth, he was an NHL All-Star, winning two Stanley Cups with the Montreal Canadiens in 1967–68 and 1968–69 and becoming the first player in Red Wings history to post a 50-goal season, doing it in consecutive seasons in 1972–73 and 1973–74.

Mickey likes to say he gained a Harvard education in hockey playing for two Original Six franchises and learning the ways of the game from the likes of legends such as Jean Beliveau, Henri Richard, Gordie Howe, and Alex Delvecchio. Then when he launched his post-playing career with *Hockey Night in Canada*, he gained a Harvard education in broadcasting working alongside such booth legends as Danny Gallivan, Dick Irvin, and Bob Cole.

Working with those *Hockey Night in Canada* guys Mickey had to fit in, being the new kid on the block. Now it was my turn to fit in with him. It took a few years of learning one another's cadence, and finishing each other's sentences, and some give-and-take, but this marriage has lasted 20 years and is still going strong.

And as in a marriage, you can't fake chemistry. Laughter and enjoying the other person's company are key. When Mick walks into the booth and says, "Kenny boy," that's my "Hi honey, I'm home."

It All Started Where I Finished

Due to those 1997 visa issues when I first arrived in Detroit, Doc Emrick called the first two preseason games in my spot at Joe Louis Arena.

So, as fate would have it, my first call for the Red Wings, albeit during an exhibition game, came where I called my first NHL game for Toronto—at Maple Leaf Gardens. The Gardens is still

October 1997. First game with Mickey in the "new TV gondola" at Maple Leaf Gardens. Great view. Harold Ballard had Foster's original gondola destroyed.

"We're not worthy!" Mickey and me rockin' and rollin' at a Coyotes game in 2001 with Detroit native and Phoenix resident Alice Cooper.

standing with a grocery store on the main floor and an arena on the fifth floor. If you ever get to Church Street and Carlton to visit, make sure you pick up some groceries at Loblaws, and go to the big red dot in the middle of the store. That's where the puck was dropped at center ice in Toronto until the Leafs moved into the Air Canada Centre in 1999. The only TV game I called from the Gardens, other than with Detroit, was when I returned in 1998, to work that *Hockey Night in Canada* game with Harry Neale. I moved my family from Toronto to Detroit during that Olympic break. The timing was perfect.

Gluten-Free Birthday Wishes

My first regular-season Leafs–Red Wings game at the Gardens came in my first season, and it just so happened it would also be

December 27, 1997. My first few months with the Red Wings, aboard Red Bird. We ordered a gluten-free cake for Mickey's 50th, and shared it with the team on the way home from Toronto.

Mickey Redmond's 50th birthday, December 27, 1997. The Wings won that night, 8–1 (a score that has familiar ties to Mickey and the Leafs that you will see in a moment). And we would return to Toronto that season on March 18, 1998, which is my birthday, and the Wings won that night 5–2. So the first two regular-season games we did together in Toronto were on our respective birthdays. Somehow the stars just aligned.

Mickey had gone through some tests the previous three years and found that he had celiac disease, an autoimmune disorder that primarily affects the small intestine and causes gastrointestinal problems.

Because of this condition, everything Mickey eats has to be gluten free. I wanted to do something special for old No. 20, now 50, and we searched out a bakery where we could get a gluten-free cake. We surprised him with it on air during our UPN–50 broadcast, and he blew out the candles, likely wishing for a Wings victory! Either that, or that he wouldn't get sick from the cake. The baker did a great job, but Mickey, still not sure he wouldn't become ill, abstained from tasting.

It was neat that we could celebrate at Maple Leaf Gardens, because the place meant a lot to the two of us. I worked my first NHL game there and Mickey called a lot of games from MLG for *Hockey Night in Canada*, and it's where he scored to become the first Red Wing to record a 50-goal season on March 27, 1973, in an 8–1 win over the Leafs. He scored that goal on Ron Low, who later became a Red Wing, and just happens to be a mirror image of Mickey himself. The resemblance is uncanny.

Dropping the Gloves

One fight we've never had is who calls the fights. When I first got here Mick said to me, "Do you like calling fights?"

And I said, like them? I've always called the start of them. It's just the way it's been. Mickey sort of gave me a look and said kind of sadly, "Oh, okay."

Right then, I knew to step aside when two players square off and drop the gloves and let Mickey go. Probably the most disappointing night for Mickey was the March 26, 1997, brawl with the Colorado Avalanche, when Detroit's Darren McCarty went after Claude Lemieux to avenge the vicious cheap shot Lemieux had given Kris Draper in the 1996 playoffs, and everyone on the ice dropped the mitts and went at it, including a sensational goalie fight between Detroit's Mike Vernon and Colorado's Patrick Roy.

Mickey saw every second of the action on the monitor in a studio but didn't get to say a word because he'd gone downstairs to do a between-periods interview. I was happy for him later on when the Wings and Avs brawled again and this time Chris Osgood was the one who went after Roy. Mick got to call that goalie fight. I knew he wanted it and knew just to back off and let him go at it. I managed to find a space when he took a breath so that I could fit in my five seconds' worth of commentary.

I don't condone the old donnybrook fighting, nor as you will see avenging a clean hit with fisticuffs, but I think it's a better outlet than somebody getting a stick in the face.

Take a Hit

While we're on the topic of fighting, here's another thought about today's game that really bothers me: why does every big hit, if clean, need a response with a fight?

I'd need a team full of gloves to count the number of times I've said that while calling games. The practice of having to answer for every hard, legal hit in today's game is ridiculous.

Certainly, there are times when a response is called for. In the first game of the 1969 Stanley Cup playoffs at Boston Garden, big, burly Toronto Maple Leafs defenseman Pat Quinn got his elbow up on Bruins star Bobby Orr. Orr was the key to their team, so that deserved a response from the Bruins.

The superstars of the NHL are a team's meal ticket, so they must be protected from cheap shots. It's why if you wronged Wayne Gretzky with the Edmonton Oilers in the 1980s, you answered to Dave Semenko. As former St. Louis Blues tough guy Kelly Chase once said, "If I cheap shotted Steve Yzerman in Detroit, I didn't have to wait to hear from [NHL disciplinarian] Colin Campbell to find out what the punishment was. The punishment was Bob Probert and Joe Kocur."

It was the same during the 2015–16 season when Evander Kane took a hack at Red Wings captain Henrik Zetterberg in the corner at the Joe, and Brendan Smith stepped in to protect Z. You don't want Zetterberg fighting Kane, and players need to know when they've been wronged and are in jeopardy that their teammates have their back. That's been part of hockey as long as there's been skates and pucks.

But today, when a player has his head down and gets caught by a clean hit, at least in a referee's opinion, the hitter still has to answer for what should be a beautiful part of the game and is well within the rules.

If there is no referee's arm in the air for a penalty on a hit, and a member of the opposing team challenges that player who delivered the hit to a fight, then the guy who started the fight should be ejected from the game, and his team should play shorthanded. The player who had to answer for a clean hit should get no penalty at all. He should be allowed a free fight.

If the league determines later that the official missed the call on the original hit, then the game misconduct for fighting can be rescinded, and perhaps then a suspension levied against the hitter. That's why we have supplemental discipline in the game, and that's why we have referees and hitting. Hits are allowed in the fastest game on earth. Let the refs determine if they are fair.

No Smoking

When we first started calling games together, Mickey was a big smoker, and he smoked Marlboro cigarettes. I was used to the Canadian cigarettes like du Maurier Special Milds, which weren't as strong. It was in November, my second month, and the darts during the play were getting to me. So I drummed up the courage and said to Mick, "Would you mind only smoking during the intermission and not during the period, because it's making me cough?" We were in that small booth at the Joe. I told him that I would leave during the intermission, and he could spark as many as he'd like.

He said, "Okay. That's fair." The next game, we went to a commercial break with two minutes to go until the intermission and Mickey lights up. I just gave him a look and said, "Really?"

He said, "Hey mister, you got 18 minutes. Don't push your luck."

That's how I came to know that if Mickey wants a little leeway, give it to him.

I'd often ask Mick when he was going to quit smoking, and he'd say, "Nobody likes a quitter." That was his favorite line. There were spurts when Mickey tried everything to stop. He tried going off cigarettes and having the odd cigar. One night he picked me up in his truck to go to the airport for a road trip. On our way there Mickey asked, "Do you want a cigar?" I said, "No, these cigars stink. What are you smoking?" He said, "I don't know. They're five-buck cigars." And I told him that a five-buck cigar should smell better than that. And he said, "No, no, no. Five bucks for the whole box." Okay, that explained it.

A little while after that he went on the patch for a time. One game he walked out of the booth during the intermission, left the press box, and went down the stairway. When he came back for the second period, I could smell the cigarette smoke. I asked him why he smelled like cigarettes. He said, "I just went out in the hall and had one." But you're on the patch? "Oh yeah. I forgot about that."

In 2002, he was diagnosed for the first time with cancer. So, the blessing in that scary situation was that it got him to quit smoking.

The doctors said his lung capacity was so good from his playing days that it actually helped him beat the cancer.

High Above the Ice

I have often said during the final season at the Joe, since I have often been asked, that it's that "smell" of the building that most comes to memory when I think of things I will miss from the old barn. I know what you're thinking. The smell? The urination left behind in stairwells, combined with spilled beers? (That, by the way, would be alcohol abuse.)

No. It's just a hockey rink smell. Not great. Not awful. Just a smell. And then there was the night there was a very distinct smell. And we noticed how distinct it had become during a third-period commercial break.

Our Fox Sports Detroit broadcast came out of that TV timeout with some of our players, pretaped, speaking about how they too, felt the smell in the building was something they would remember. Particularly Justin Abdelkader.

Our cozy broadcast spot at Joe Louis Arena for my first 20 seasons. The crowd is just a row beneath in section 208. (Courtesy of the *Detroit Free Press* / Julian H. Gonzalez)

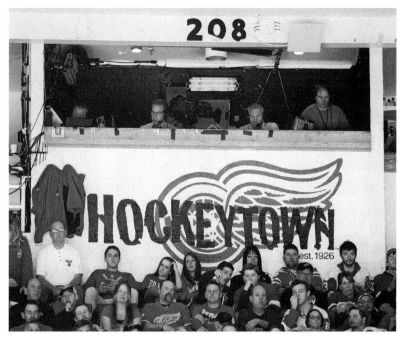

The view up to the booth. (Photo courtesy of Dave Reginek / Detroit Red Wings)

Playing off that, as only he could, Mickey said, "Oh, there's a smell all right. What's that Frank Sinatra song that goes [to the tune of 'Strangers in the Night'] 'doo-be, doo-be, do'?"

I held back my laughter, and noticed Number 25 of the Red Wings going back to retrieve the puck in his own zone. I immediately said, "As Mike Green goes back to get it, green, Mick, is prevalent in this building tonight." Yes that distinct smell was marijuana. (So I'm told.) My goal in moments like these is to see if I can get Mickey to lose it (and not on the refs). This time I did. His laughter is infectious, and as I looked over at him and our trusty booth sidekick Chuck Fair, I couldn't speak. For the next 20 seconds, as Mickey removed his headset, play continued. There was announcer silence.

Mickey finally regained his composure and emphatically stated, "Boy, am I ever going to miss this place!" Bingo, bongo, Mick.

Tire Fire

If I told you Mickey had a plow on his truck to not only remove his snow but also snow from his neighbor's driveways, would you be the least bit surprised? Of course not.

One afternoon, I'm on my way to the airport. The team is flying to Columbus for a game the next day. Mickey was planning to drive in the day of the game. I left myself some extra time that day. I don't know, maybe the gods told me to leave earlier, but it turned out to be a wise decision.

I hit one of those notorious potholes that are all over Michigan, this time on Southfield Road, and I really felt this one. But I knew I had a flight to catch, so I kept driving. The car was pulling a little bit but it was all right. Then the light came on in my car that the tire was underinflated. I kept going regardless. About two miles later, I'm on the Southfield Freeway, a mile shy of I–96. By now, it's really pulling. I thought, *this isn't good*, and then I feel that rumbling that is the sound of a tire going flat. I'm in the left lane and I pull over to the right-hand lane and get into that triangle of space that's on the highway by an on-ramp. I'm still halfway into the right lane of the highway, and as I'm slowing down I hear a bang and the tire just flies off. I put the flashers on, but I'm stuck. It's a rainy, slushy, crappy day, and I'm starting to panic. I see in my rear-view mirror all these cars coming up quickly, and I think if anyone's not paying attention, I'm dead because they're going to run into me.

I'm calling my car dealership to get them to send out a tow truck. I still needed to get to the airport ASAP. I called Mickey and told him I had a flat tire. All he says is, "Where are you?" I tell him the approximate location and then I hear, "I'm on the Lodge. I'll turn around. I'll come and get you."

There's still about 45 minutes until the plane leaves for Columbus. I'm sitting there waiting and a police car comes up behind me. Now I've got that safety net of a police vehicle with its lights on behind me, so I'm a little bit relieved at that point. He comes up to the car and he recognizes me. He says, "You going to the airport?" I said yeah and asked him how he knew to get there to help me in my emergency situation. "Somebody called 911 and said there was a tire on fire." I said, "You mean it was actually on fire?" "Yeah." You hear about a team blowing up and having a bad game and we may refer to it on the broadcast as a tire fire? Well, this was my tire fire.

Not long after that, Mickey shows up and the police officer obviously recognizes him. Mickey is ready to take me to the airport, but we can't leave because I need to be there with the vehicle when the tow truck shows up. Now we're wasting precious time, so I call Todd Beam, the Wings' director of public relations, and tell him that I'm going to get there and can he give me a few minutes? He said, "We'll do our best."

The tow truck shows up, and by now we've got about 20 minutes to spare. I said to the cop, "Can you give us an escort to the airport?" He said, "Normally I would do that for you guys, but I can't. It's such a lousy day on the roads today. There's just too many accidents out here." He said, "How long you got?" I looked at my watch and said, "15 minutes." "You'll never get there," and Mickey said, "Yes we will."

I got in Mickey's truck, and off we went. The plane left at 2:00 PM and we got there at 1:59. Announcers, we're always on time.

169

Sometimes to the last second but we're always on time (except for Ken Kal, but more on that later). So I got on the plane, and obviously, Jeff Blashill and Ken Holland knew what was up and asked me what happened. They were concerned, which was very nice. When you're not the main guy, when you're riding their coattails, you don't want to be slowing them down.

The next day, I'm having a coffee at the hotel and Red Wings defenseman Nik Kronwall comes along. He said, "Was that your car on Southfield?" I said yeah. "E [Wings defenseman Jonathan Ericsson] and I were driving, but we were in the left lane. We saw you and we said to each other that we thought it was Ken, but there was nowhere to pull over to help you." Just like many NHL games, trapped!

Chef Mickey

Due to his issues with celiac disease, it's hard for Mickey to travel. He has to bring his own food. Even in the booth at Joe Louis Arena, Mickey is sure to pull out a salad midgame brought from home. Chuck Fair, our amazing right-hand man in the JLA booth for 20 years, and I marvel at Mick's culinary skills. We joke that Mick is carrying a Coleman stove on the road. In his own room, he'd have a cook plate. Now the hotel kitchens try to help out, and they put a bigger fridge in his room to hold all of his food. In some cities, if we're going to be there for a few days, such as during a playoff series, he'll find a market in town and buy some food. Even on the plane they'll have salads for him that aren't contaminated.

Mickey has to be sure of everything he puts into his mouth. Items the rest of us take for granted—things like mouthwash, toothpaste, over-the-counter medicines—can cause serious problems to a person suffering with celiac.

I remember during the 2001 playoffs in Los Angeles, Mickey had been cooking in his hotel room. We were sitting out by the pool, and one of the service managers came down to find Mickey because the maids had freaked out. They were going to kick him out of his room because he was sauteing in there. They could smell the food. I never saw Mickey move faster in his life. Scotty Bowman was holding court before we were interrupted and in typical Bowman tone he asked a question that needed no answer, "He's really got a tough life, doesn't he?"

Whenever you get off an elevator in a hotel where the team is staying, you can always tell where Mickey's room is. Just follow the garlic. Or the smoke. One afternoon in Columbus, we were on the same floor in our respective rooms and I hear a smoke alarm going off. I open up my door and thought that it's got to be Mick. I head down the hall, letting the smell lead me, and I see Mickey with the door open on a chair with a towel, trying to wave away the smoke. And now, the maid has joined me in staring at this scenario. I'll never get that sight out of my head. He sees me standing there and he just starts to laugh. That's the chemistry we have on the air. We have more fun together, whether it's on the air or off the air. Mickey is just the most wonderfully unique human being I've met in my life.

Losing His Chiclets

Since Mickey began dealing with celiac, he doesn't make a lot of the road trips to call games, which has led to others filling the seat next to me in the booth. Of the nine analysts I've worked with in my 20 seasons of Red Wings hockey, only one dropped his teeth.

Mickey has broken a few. But Pat Verbeek's bridge fell out, right before we went on the air in Anaheim.

Our talented Fox Sports Detroit crew enjoying a day off in Whistler, B.C., snowmobiling. Director Brian Maas (he crashed), me, producer Mark Iacofano (he laughed...a lot), and Trevor Thompson (he stalled).

During his career, Pat was known as the "little ball of hate," a mean SOB to play against. But to work with, he was gem. A wonderful guy, and to this day I consider him to be a good friend.

Just as we were getting set to go on air at Anaheim's Honda Center in one of the NHL's smallest broadcast location, Pat turned to me and said, "Oh my God, my teeth just fell out!"

After our game producer Mark Iacofano stopped laughing, we had to decide what to do. Mark said, "First off we will pre-tape it (meaning record it early rather than go live) and I'll bring you guys on camera, and you introduce Pat. He'll nod, and then we can go voice-over the rest of the way." In TV terms, that meant we wouldn't be on-camera again. That worked for me. Pat actually did want to go live. I just thought he had better not. It would be a funny moment but a moment that could haunt him forever.

And Then Pat Said...

And then there was the night I noticed Brett Hull's white tape on his stick.

It was during the 2003–04 season that Brett Hull was in a lengthy goal slump during what would turn out to be the final season of his fabulous career, other than a brief five-game comeback he made with the Phoenix Coyotes in 2005–06. Brett hadn't scored a goal since December 10, 2003. It was now January 22, 2004, and Brett had gone goalless for 20 games. The Wings were playing in Los Angeles at the Staples Center.

Brett had tried everything to snap out of his slump, and in a moment that I still can't explain, I noticed that to start the second period Brett had white tape on the blade of his stick.

I felt at the time it was the first time (later to be confirmed) that Brett had ever used white tape on the blade of his stick rather than black tape.

And two shifts later, Brett scored on the power play, 3:47 into the second period to tie the game 2–2. The white tape proved to be the slump-buster.

I must say I was pretty proud that I noticed the switch, which led to a TV close-up of Brett sitting on the bench with the butt-end of his stick facing us.

Which in turn led to the following discussion.

Ken: "Pat, Brett may have switched to white tape on the blade, but as you can see he still has that Red Wings red tape on the end of the stick."

Pat: "That's not red tape Ken, that's pink."

Ken: "That's not pink. Come on. That's red—just like the Wings red."

Pat: "Ah, no it's not. Look. I've put enough tape on the end of my knob over the years, to know what pink is."

I've got nothing here. Silence. Crickets. All I can hear in my ear (headset) is the laughter of my producer, Mark Iacofano. Then Pat starts to laugh, and I start to laugh. We're hitting our mute buttons and there's dead air.

And at that point, I looked over to my right to Pat as the play continued on the ice beneath us, and Pat was the brightest shade of red—or was it pink—I had ever seen, thus proving my point!

Analyze This

As I noted, I've worked with plenty of analysts over the years, and there have been many since Mickey decided to cut back on travel due to his celiac disease. Just because a player had been in the NHL, however, doesn't mean he can talk about the game. It's not easy. As an analyst or play-by-play guy, a key when talking to players in preparation for the game is to immediately condense a story they are telling for a minute into a 20-second version to tell on the air.

Sometimes Mickey and I do go on a tangent. He could be referring to a funny story during the play. That drives some people crazy, I know! But it happens. You've got pictures in front of you. I don't think we get too carried away too often. Sometimes it's a 5–1 game, or the Red Wings are losing and there's nothing happening. You're trying to entertain the people. I don't think you have to stick to play-by-play every second of the game.

And sometimes, the play-by-play guy will say nothing for two full minutes. Yup. It happened. Mick and Larry, who was in his first year on the job, got to "flapping," and Mickey made the mistake of asking Larry, who was between the benches, a follow-up question to his first one as the power play began. By the time these two were done, so was the Wings' man advantage, just as the goalie held the puck. That's when they both ran out of things to say. I wasn't bailing them out at that point. Mickey looked at me and laughed knowing full well I would continue to be silent until play began again.

The good analyst will work at his craft. And right from the start Pat Verbeek worked at it. He would have been great at the job had he chosen to stay with it, and he asked the executive producer at the time for more games to get better but didn't get them. So he went to scout for the Red Wings and then moved on to join Steve Yzerman when Stevie took over as GM in Tampa Bay.

A recent analyst who has worked well for us on the broadcasts is former Wings goalie Chris Osgood. Ozzie has a great gift of gab (or as he calls it, "flapping") and he's not afraid to speak his mind.

What Red Wings Hockey Is All About

When I first arrived in Detroit I immediately realized what a closely knit Red Wing hockey community we had. The Wings, especially the crew at UPN-50 TV, would be deluged with requests for birthdays and on-air hellos, mostly for when we were on the road. Sometimes the game would get in the way of our greetings and salutations. Even Jean Martineau, the smart-aleck PR guy with the Avalanche, would say to us, "My first cousin's first cousin has a birthday next month. Can you get it in tonight?"

When we started getting razzed by the likes of him and a team from Colorado, it was time to pull in the reigns. And that we did. But we still leave room for birthdays within the Red Wings organization or for those who need a mention most. Sometimes it truly comes down to life and death. And here is where we can make a difference; that makes our job so worthwhile. This request was sent to our communications director, Courtney Welch, during late March of 2017.

Hi Courtney,

I'm sure you receive many requests for acknowledgments. I fully understand if there are any policies regulating on-air conversations not pertaining to the broadcast and/or their interests. However, I hope that exceptions can be made for a die-hard 90-year-old Red Wings fan who's living her very last days.

Mary Ann Petrie (Pee-tree) is my wife's grandmother. She is a HUGE Red Wings fan. She watches all the games and reads anything with "Red Wings" attached to it. She also genuinely loves Steve Yzerman...Seriously! She can discuss the Wings at a deep level—and not just about their record, but their system and individual players. It's amazing! Her family loves the game as she does. Her children, grandchildren, and great grandchildren played and/or coached at high levels, including college.

Unfortunately, she was diagnosed several years ago with lymphoma, causing her to develop a weakened heart. She fought hard for a few years. However, within the past month, she and her doctors decided to stop treatment, knowing full well these will be her final days. A few days ago we were informed that, according to hospice, Mary Ann's time will be any day. She is currently surrounded by her family in her condo in Westland, MI.

Undoubtedly, THEY WILL HAVE THE RED WINGS GAME ON TONIGHT! Although she's quiet and flies under the radar, I know she would LOVE to hear one of Mickey's "shout-outs." That would be a great send off for a great Red Wings fan!

Courtney, anything you can do would be appreciated. Sorry for the blabber, but I actually kept this as simple as possible.

Kindest Regards,

Eric Kuciban

I showed this to Mickey, and he immediately took control. We promoted the fact going to a break that we would be sending out a special hello when we returned to the game, so as to give the family a heads-up. With tears in his eyes, Mickey spoke about Mary Ann and thanked her for her tremendous support and sent our Red Wings love her way.

We received this response two days later from Eric.

Hi Courtney,

The acknowledgment from the broadcast was WAY MORE than we could have imagined. I was told Mary Ann tried to smile and speak; this is clearly a positive response from someone who could no longer communicate. Our family is so appreciative of that final joy she experienced.

As anticipated, it was her last game. Within 24 hours, Mary Ann passed away peacefully in her home. Mickey's words proved to be the sendoff she was looking for.

On behalf of the entire Petrie family, THANK YOU! Please send our gratitude to everyone involved.

Best Wishes, Eric Kuciban

To that, the game takes a backseat.

Appearing and Disappearing

The analyst starters manual should read: "How and why. Get in and get out. If they do those four things early on, they could be outstanding. You can decide who has grasped it." This is what makes Mickey so good. If a goal is scored, he's going to get three looks at the goal. Maybe a high wide, then maybe a game shot, and then an iso shot or a close-up. You've got to say the same thing three different ways in 15 to 20 seconds.

An analyst has to decipher how a play happened. Was it a bad change? Did a guy not pick up his man? Did he make a nice move off the boards and maybe his man didn't get inside position on him?

And the position to my right or left in the booth over my 28 years of play-by-play has been occupied by Bill Watters, Gord Stellick, Howard Berger, Bob McGill, Jim Peplinski, Brian Hayward, Dick Irvin, Greg Millen, Harry Neale, Ryan Walter, Cap Raeder, Tom Reid, John Garrett, Mickey Redmond, Mike Greenlay, Doug Brown, Shawn Burr, Pat Verbeek, Larry Murphy, Darren Pang, Pierre McGuire, Joe Micheletti, Andy Brickley, Daryl Reaugh, Manny Legace, John Keating (for the third period of a game when Mickey lost his voice, and the first thing John did was ask Mickey a question on the air), Craig Simpson, Bill Jaffe, Fred Pletsch, Trevor Thompson, Lyle Phair, Darren Eliot, and Chris Osgood. Ray Ferraro also joined us for a game at JLA when his son Landon made his NHL debut with the Red Wings.

That was very cool, since it came in the same building where Ray's career finished, with Landon in the seats watching his dad. To see the pride and fear in Ray's face as the game went on was something I will always cherish. Ray is one of the great guys of the game.

With Mickey Redmond in February 2016, prior to the Coors Field outdoor game. (Photo courtesy of Mark Iacofano)

People who sit at home and watch and think, "This guy's not a good analyst," well, they ought to give it a try. (Or play-by-play for that matter.) It takes work and it takes practice. You've got to be prepared and think quickly on your feet. It's apparently very easy from the couch.

Mickeyisms

The love the Red Wings faithful express for Mickey stems from his long-standing ties to the organization, his obvious passion for what he does, and perhaps most of all, for the unique way he has of expressing himself.

They've come to be known as Mickeyisms, and over two decades together, I think I've heard them all. But these are some of the best:

"Black puck, white net, red light, embarrassed goalie."

"They're giving the goaltender a sunburn on the back of his neck."

After a spectacular Sergei Fedorov goal: "Coast to coast, like buttered toast."

On Patrick Kane: "What a set of hands you'd like to have on your stick every day."

"[Jimmy] Howard said no like a sponge."

"Couldn't hit a bull on the butt end with a banjo."

On Pavel Datsyuk: "More moves than a monkey on a high wire and a toolbox most players would only dream about."

When a defenseman is badly beaten: "His jockstrap is hanging out there somewhere on Woodward Avenue."

"Bingo, bango, bongo."

When a player takes a dive: "And then down he goes like he's been shot with an elephant gun."

When a fight breaks out: "And all 19,000 fans are hating this, right?"

After a veteran makes a smart play: "He was born at night, but not last night."

When a player wades into a scrum late and scores: "Sometimes it's the last man to the dinner table who gets the biggest pork chop."

After Brendan Smith came off the bench and immediately scored a goal: "He came down from the popcorn stand to score that goal."

When Jordin Tootoo reacted angrily to a penalty call: "He's not saying Happy Thanksgiving, I can promise you that."

"He was shooting the puck so badly, if he was standing on the end of a pier he couldn't hit the water."

With my great friend and broadcast partner during a speaking engagement in January 2017. (Photo courtesy of Jim Jacek / "Photos to Go")

Describing Joe Kocur's punching power: "That jackhammer works on any kind of cement."

On Slava Kozlov: "The kid's got eyes in the back of his head, and he's a waterbug."

During playoff overtime: "This is no place for a nervous person."

Describing Igor Larionov's stickhandling skills: "Don't play the puck against this guy, boy, or you'll end up short of equipment."

On Anthony Mantha: "He's breathing different air than most people at 6–5."

"A hockey player without a stick is like a duck without wings."

"Statistics are for losers...unless you have good ones."

When the Red Wings are certain of victory: "You can head for the parking lot, folks. This one is over."

CHAPTER 6
SCOTTY BOWMAN, GENIUS?

*How often do you get to spend so much time
with maybe the smartest hockey person of them all?*

Lessons from a Legend

One of the best things about calling Red Wings games was the daily chance to interact with perhaps the greatest mind in hockey history, that of Scotty Bowman, Detroit's coach from 1993 to 2002.

I'd often join the coaching staff and Ken Holland to go watch other games on the road the night before ours. This was long before the NHL Center Ice package was available everywhere.

Scotty and I were at the ESPN Zone in Denver, in town to play the Colorado Avalanche, and we got a small booth where we could put on the Blues game, our next opponent, on a small screen right beside us. It was March Madness and there was basketball on every other set in the place.

The joint just goes wild and Scotty looks up at the basketball game on the big TVs, looks around at all the people going crazy, shakes his head and says, "For F-sake, it's 5–2. The score is 5–2!"

Seekers

One thing we always say about the Red Wings is that they travel well—there are always plenty of Red Wings fans in visiting arenas. And no matter what time our bus pulls up to the hotel—even at 2:00 AM—many would be outside waiting. But these wouldn't necessarily be Red Wings fans, these would be the seekers. The autograph seekers. This would always get Scotty pissed. "There they are. Look at them. They want you to sign. And it will be on eBay in 30 minutes." Scotty would then get off the bus, grumbling, while asking, "How much, how much?"

Late Arrival

My first season in the booth calling Red Wings games began without Scotty behind the bench. He was recuperating from off-season heart surgery as well as a knee replacement, and associate coaches Barry Smith and Dave Lewis guided the Wings to a 4–1 record working as co-interim head coaches.

When Scotty returned to work, there was no group hug, no sentimental speech. He wasn't about that kind of stuff. But the players knew the foundation was stable again.

"It's like adding another veteran superstar to your lineup," was how forward Doug Brown explained Bowman's return. "Someone who knows the league, who is going to keep finding new ways to win."

With Scotty Bowman in Washington in June 1998, after the Wings captured a second straight Stanley Cup. It was the first celebration for me. (Photo courtesy of the Detroit Red Wings)

Bowman, who was 65 at the time, wondered what all the fuss was about, indicating that he never had a doubt that he would return to work.

"What else would I do?" Bowman asked. "It would be a pretty long winter."

Detroit general manager Ken Holland remembered sharing his players' delight at the return of their world-class bench boss. "There was nobody like him in the league, with his presence behind the bench and attention to detail," Holland said.

The Greatest Motivation

Scotty coached a record nine Stanley Cup winners, but of all those wins, he's always counted Detroit's 1997–98 championship as the most memorable.

The Wings had lost All-Star defenseman Vladimir Konstantinov to a career-ending brain injury suffered just days after their 1996–97 Stanley Cup triumph.

"We never replaced him," Scotty Bowman said. "Having to play without him, that team dedicated that season to Vladimir Konstantinov and Sergei Mnatsakanov [the team masseur, who also suffered a debilitating brain injury in the same crash]. Arguably, I think Vladimir was ready to become the next Norris Trophy winner. We were all concerned about both of them and wondering how we were going to exist after losing him. They found a way, and I think the motivation of that team was so strong."

Pittsburgh Similarities

They persevered through a horrible tragedy, had a legendary coach at the helm, and overcame occasionally erratic goaltending. They were sparked by an offensive catalyst whose passion for the game was often questioned. And they repeated as Stanley Cup champions.

Prior to the 1997–98 Red Wings, the 1991–92 Pittsburgh Penguins were the last National Hockey League team to win back-to-back Stanley Cup titles.

"It had a similar tinge to it," Scotty Bowman admitted. He'd also coached the 1992 Penguins, coming into the position under difficult circumstances. In August 1991, Penguins coach Bob Johnson, who was preparing Team USA for the Canada Cup at the time, was diagnosed with cancer—an inoperable brain tumor.

"We didn't find out about Bob until just before training camp," Bowman recalled. "When we realized the severity of his illness, everyone was stunned.

"With our Red Wings team, we dealt with the situation [with Konstantinov and Mnatsakanov] all during the summer and the season. In Pittsburgh, Bob passed away in November and we lost him. With Vladi and Sergei, we're still able to see them, to talk to them. We saw improvement."

Pittsburgh struggled at times during the 1991–92 campaign and no one really expected the Penguins to repeat, especially when they fell behind 3–1 to Washington in the first round of the playoffs. Detroit also had its difficult periods in their '98 Cup season and trailed Phoenix in the opening round of the playoffs.

Both teams overcame a rash of injuries early in the postseason. Pittsburgh swept Chicago in the final. Detroit swept Washington in the Stanley Cup final.

Pittsburgh's offensive leader was Mario Lemieux, a Hart Trophy winner whose love and desire for the game was questioned by many. Detroit's offensive leader was Sergei Fedorov, a Hart Trophy winner whose love and desire for the game was questioned by many.

Also a question mark on both teams was goaltending. But just like Tom Barrasso in Pittsburgh, Detroit's Chris Osgood endured the criticism.

Captain Steve Yzerman was the conscience of the Red Wings, a quiet leader not unlike Pittsburgh's Ron Francis.

Pittsburgh center Bryan Trottier had plenty of success with the New York Islanders before moving to the Penguins.

Detroit's Igor Larionov had a great run of success with the Soviet National team before he came to the Red Wings.

Pittsburgh had Larry Murphy. Detroit had Larry Murphy.

"I think there were definitely similarities," Murphy said. "I think that both teams had something to rally around—persevering through tragedy."

He credited Bowman with being the guy who brought them over the hump on both occasions. "Scotty did a great job with that team," Murphy said. "From Day 1, he emphasized that this was Bob Johnson's team and that we should never forget what he had meant to our success."

"We pretty much stayed with the same systems Bob had used the year before," said Bowman, who had Barry Smith as an assistant coach with both teams. In each case, the team responded. "It's a situation where you realize that life must go on, but the memory of what happened doesn't ever go away."

A Steal at Number Five

And speaking of the Penguins, it was during the 1990 NHL Draft that the Pittsburgh Penguins took Jaromir Jagr with the fifth overall pick. Scotty Bowman could be heard leaving BC Place in Vancouver saying, "I can't believe we just got the best player in the draft at number five." It turns out Scotty was right again. Jagr has more than 1,900 career points—second all time. Only the great Wayne Gretzky is ahead of him with more. Jagr is the all-time NHL leader in game-winning goals, and only Chris Chelios at age 46 while with the Wings was older than Jagr when he scored a game winner. Chris scored his in February of the 2008 Cup year and broke his leg in the next game. Chris joked, "We had so many injuries to our D that month, our top four were all hurt, and according to [Wings coach Mike] Babcock, I was still our sixth best!"

Gordie Howe and Chelios are also the only players older than Jagr to have scored a goal in the NHL! The top four taken in the draft before Jaromir weren't bad either—Owen Nolan, Petr Nedved, Keith Primeau by Detroit, and Mike Ricci. Fourteen of the first 21 first-round picks in the 1990 Draft went on to careers of at least 500 games. But only one was still playing at the age of 45!

It's Not Over

The clock was counting down the final seconds of Game 4 of the 1998 Stanley Cup final and the Wings, up 4–1 in the

189

game on the Washington Capitals, were about to win their second straight Stanley Cup and first with me as their play-by-play voice.

On the bench, there was jubilation. The players had already dropped their sticks and tossed their gloves, ready to pour over the boards in celebration.

Scotty Bowman took his focus away from the ice for a second and noticed what was happening on the bench in front of him. "What's going on?" he asked. "What are you doing? The game's not over."

Forward Marty Lapointe later revealed that "we were just praying there wouldn't be a whistle. We knew that son of a gun would change lines, just so we'd all have to scramble and try to find our sticks and a pair of gloves to wear."

Numerology (Part 1)

When the Wings acquired Dmitri Mironov from Anaheim at the 1998 trade deadline, forward Tomas Holmstrom relinquished sweater No. 15 to the veteran defenseman, opting to don No. 96.

"Why did you pick 96?" Scotty Bowman asked Holmstrom, who answered, "Because that's the year I came here from Sweden."

"You should have taken 98," Bowman said, "because that's when you're going back."

Bowman claimed that Holmstrom chose his new digits for an entirely different reason.

"He thinks he's Bure," Bowman said, referring to then Vancouver sniper Pavel Bure, who wore No. 96 until switching to 10.

"I don't know what we're going to do," Bowman said. "Our No. 10 is up in the rafters" in honor of Alex Delvecchio.

After toying with his emotions, in the next breath, Bowman opted to praise Holmstrom.

"Here's a tip," Scotty said, pointing toward Holmstrom. "Take this guy in your playoff pool. He's going to be on the power play."

During his rookie NHL season in 1996–97, Holmstrom played one playoff game as Detroit won the Cup. In 1997–98, my first season, the Wings defended their title and Holmstrom finished tied for third in postseason scoring with 19 points. Scotty the pool shark.

Numerology (Part 2)

Scotty Bowman dreads the number 13. He won't even stay on the 14th floor of a hotel because he knows it's just the 13th floor under an assumed name. And he won't stay in any room number that adds up to 13, such as 904.

He cringed when forward Slava Kozlov joined the team opting to wear sweater No. 13.

"I have a lot of superstitions," Bowman said. "That's one of them. I don't know how it started, but I don't like that number."

Except, perhaps, when it was on Kozlov's back.

"It worked good for him," Scotty had to admit. And it worked even better for Pavel Datsyuk when he arrived in 2001.

Numerology (Part 3)

Why did Sergei Fedorov take No. 91? Because he came to play for Detroit in 1990. As he told me, it's not how you start but how you finish. And Sergei finished his rookie season in 1991 with

31 goals and 79 points in 77 games played. He finished his career not in Detroit, but as Scotty would tell you, Sergei was one of the greatest Red Wings of all time.

The Human Touch

As demanding as Scotty was on his players, he also had a compassionate side. He frequently visited defenseman Vladimir Konstantinov and team masseur Sergei Mnatsakanov, who suffered closed head injuries in a limousine crash a week after the 1997 Cup win.

The day after Detroit won that 1997 Cup, Scotty loaded Lord Stanley's mug into his car and drove it across the border to Windsor, Ontario, Canada, visiting with Jimmy Skinner. In 1954–55, Skinner had been the previous coach to lead the Wings to the Stanley Cup.

Scotty does a lot of nice things, he just doesn't make them public knowledge. He prefers to keep people guessing.

Be Like Mike

Scotty made a career of winning mind games with athletes, but he probably shouldn't have tried to go one-on-one with Michael Jordan. The retired Chicago Bulls superstar was a visitor to the Detroit dressing room after a game against Chicago. Jordan was there to chat with close friend Chris Chelios shortly after the 1999 deal that brought Chelios to the Wings.

Spotting Jordan, Bowman asked if he had shown Chelios his championship rings and got him ready to win a title with the Wings. Jordan told Bowman, that yes, he had shown Chelios his championship rings, but added that it was Bowman's job to get Chelios a championship.

Of a Different Mind

Scotty loved to play mind games with everyone—the players, the officials, the media—it didn't matter.

Our Red Bird plane was in for maintenance so we had to charter an aircraft, which meant players were in different seats. Video coach Joe Kocur had returned from the back of the plane and Bowman asked, "Where are the rookies sitting?"

Kocur said, "They're at the back."

And Scotty went, "What the hell are they doing at the back? Who's up front?"

"Yzerman and Shanny and Fedorov," Kocur answered.

Bowman said, "I don't give a crap where Fedorov is sitting. Where are Shanny and Lidstrom and Yzerman sitting?" Obviously, Scotty was unhappy with Fedorov for some reason at that juncture and that was his way of getting that message delivered.

"He had a mystique about him that all of the players in the league were aware of, whether they played for him or not," former Detroit defenseman Bob Rouse said of Bowman. "He liked to keep his players on edge.

"Everyone in our room felt Scotty's wrath. We all had our turns in his doghouse. How you reacted to that, how you responded to it, determined how much you would play."

We were into the second round of the 1999 Stanley Cup playoffs when Wendel Clark, who'd been acquired by the Wings about two months earlier at the NHL trade deadline, allowed that Scotty still hadn't said a word to him.

Most of of today's NHL coaches are hailed for their strong and open communication skills, but that wasn't Scotty's style. After Aaron Ward was traded to Carolina by Detroit, he said that Hurricanes coach Paul Maurice spoke more to him in their first meeting than Bowman and he spoke over the course of Aaron's eight years as a Red Wing. But Scotty also had a rule that after mid-March, while readying for a playoff run, stay off the radio. Aaron didn't abide by that. Loving a microphone as evidenced by his post-playing career, Aaron could occasionally be heard on an all-sports radio station on a game day. Scotty would catch that, or someone would tell him. He would turn on the radio and then turn off Aaron in more ways than one.

"Scotty was quietly calculating," Kocur remembered. "He'd always keep you thinking."

Bowman felt that keeping the players at arm's length also kept them guessing, kept them on their toes.

"I didn't just sit down, hold a guy's hand, and tell him, 'This is what we're going to do,'" Bowman said.

Love and Hate

Another NHL star who was taught the ways of the game the hard way by Bowman was Hall of Famer Dave Andreychuk. Andreychuk, who'd go on to score an NHL-record 274 power play goals, was Buffalo's first draft pick in 1982, when Scotty was coach and GM of the Sabres.

There was a time when the mere mention of Scotty's name made Andreychuk's blood boil. Today, it only warms his heart.

"I'd heard a lot of stories about Scotty Bowman," Andreychuk said. "They were all true."

Bowman was persona non grata in Andreychuk's world for quite some time.

"For the years from 18 to 21, he was probably the most hated person in our household," Andreychuk said.

Andreychuk had much to learn, whether he wanted to admit it or not. "I was young and immature," Andreychuk remembered. Eventually, logic replaced pride. Andreychuk came to realize Bowman wasn't playing games with him, the coach was seeking to teach him how the game should be played.

Andreychuk stopped sulking and started listening. He developed into a player.

"Scotty taught me how to play the game without the puck," Andreychuk said. "He showed me there was two ends to the rink, and both were equally important."

Discovering methods to keep the other guys from scoring enabled Andreychuk to stay in the game long enough to score more than 600 goals of his own. But that wasn't all Bowman instilled in him.

"Scotty was big on preparation," Andreychuk said. "His dedication and passion for the game was immense and he passed that kind of passion and dedication on to the players he coached. I played 23 years in this league, and he was a big reason why."

The Secret

Since he was the greatest coach in the game, every up and coming NHL coach viewed Scotty as the benchmark, the litmus test of your abilities as a bench boss.

"This is part of the dream, that when you get to the Stanley Cup final, the guy on the other bench would be Scotty Bowman,"

Paul Maurice explained when he guided the Carolina Hurricanes against Bowman and the Wings in the 2001–02 Stanley Cup final.

Looking for a word to describe what it was like to coach against Bowman, Maurice was left in a state of wonder.

"*Intimidating* is a good word, but it's not the right word," he said. "*Awe*, I think, is maybe the word. Statistically, the two of us, when you put the records and our games side by side, the difference would be very noticeable.

"There are very few times in sports that you can watch something unfold and say, 'We're never going to see that happen again.' I'd have to coach 50 years to match what Scotty has accomplished."

Bowman kept everyone on edge but especially the other coach. "There are two ways to play hockey," Stanley Cup–winning NHL coach Ken Hitchcock said. "An easy game and a very hard game. Scotty made his teams play the very hard game. To get a team to do that, you have to be determined. You have to be demanding. You have to be very combative and very stubborn. But when you make your team do that, you play winning hockey."

Proud Papa

We were in Carolina on a road trip and Red Wings equipment manager Paul Boyer got us tickets to see Billy Joel at the Hurricanes' home arena the night before the game. Scotty's son, Bobby, was on the trip with him, and Scotty said that his son loved Billy Joel. We agreed to take him to the concert.

"You'll look after him?" Scotty asked. Sure we will. The whole day, Scotty was like that doting father. He called me. "What time do you want Bobby?" he asked. "I'll bring him up to your room. What time are you coming back?"

In that moment, he wasn't the NHL's greatest coach, he was just a concerned parent. When we got back, Scotty was waiting up for us. But this time, he wasn't waiting to make sure his players all made it in before curfew. He was waiting in the lobby for his son to get home from a concert.

Marriage Counselor

Scotty would go for a walk late at night to see if any players were out. On a road trip in L.A., a bunch of us were out for drinks at a great local spot called Chez Jay in Santa Monica. I was in there with Ken Kal, our radio voice, and some of our P.R. staff and trainers.

We were talking at a table with a few women, when who walks in but Scotty.

There was nothing going on other than some friendly conversation. Scotty walks up to the table with his jaw pointed upwards and says, "Let me tell you right now," and he starts pointing at all of us. "He's married, he's married, he's single, he's divorced." Scotty went through everybody at the table and then turned around and walked out. Classic. I was the divorced one, by the way.

Grading Papers

Scotty could also lead you astray. We're on the plane, flying to a road game, and I was sitting up front with the coaches. Scotty's got the newspaper out, and all I heard was, "Are you kidding me? Are you kidding me? I want Ted Kulfan as my teacher. I want Ted Kulfan as my teacher," referring to the Wings beat writer for the *Detroit News*. When I asked why he would want that, he responded, "He gave Brendan Shanahan a B-plus." And he repeated, "He gave Brendan Shanahan a B-plus. F-me!"

He was reading Ted's midseason grades for Red Wings players. Shanny would have been in Bowman's bad books that week.

That Scotty, he'd read everything and critique it.

Who's the Boss?

Scott Oake from *Hockey Night in Canada* wanted to talk to Scotty for a piece on the state of the game. Scott calls me and says, "I've been trying to get through to John Hahn, who won't get me through to Scotty Bowman. I'm having trouble getting through your P.R. people to Bowman." I wrote down Scott's number and walked down to Bowman's office.

It's a game day, but it's four o'clock in the afternoon. I knock on the door and Scotty answers. I walk in and tell him Scott Oake wants to get a hold of him. "Yeah, yeah," he says. "What's he want?" Right away it's *Hockey Night in Canada* and that's big for Scotty. He's trying to get a hold of you through John Hahn. And Scotty says, "John Hahn? I didn't get the message." I tell Scotty that Scott wants to come down to Detroit to interview him for a piece on today's players and the state of the game prior to the Olympics. He says, "Okay, okay. What's his number?" Scotty picks up the phone and calls Scott Oake. "When are you coming down? Thursday. Yeah, that should be good. Okay. We'll see you then."

Now it's after the game that night. I go down to the room and Scotty's standing there with John Hahn. Right in front of John Hahn, Scotty says—because he knows that Scott Oake has been trying to get a hold of him through John Hahn—"Kenny, when is that Scott Oake coming? Is he coming Thursday? Is that what we decided? I'm meeting with him Thursday, right? Four o'clock Thursday." "I don't know Scotty, you were on the phone with him." "Yeah it's Thursday, four o'clock."

And then he goes off to another conversation. But he wanted to make sure that John Hahn knew. That was just Scotty's way of saying, "Don't block me."

The Plane Truth

On January 16, 2001, we had a rough night. We were scheduled to fly from San Jose to Vancouver on Redbird II, the team's private plane—Redbird I was retired in 1999. We were leaving San Jose for Vancouver, but we ended up in Sacramento, which was a lot better landing spot than where we could have come down on the ground if things had turned out worse.

We were in the air, about 45 minutes into the flight, and both of the engines on the DC–9 went quiet. We lost both engines. We hit some turbulence and you just sort of felt these vibrations and then you heard a bump, bump noise and then everything went quiet. Then the plane started to go down slowly, not at any fast rate of speed. I guess what they do in that situation is bring the plane lower to go into a controlled glide. Once the plane leveled out, you felt the vibrations again. By this time, between the bumping noises and the quiet, I knew this wasn't turbulence. Something was seriously wrong.

I do remember at the front of the plane there was Scotty yelling at assistant coach Barry Smith, "Barry, Barry. What's going on?" I could hear Scotty constantly yelling at Barry. Finally, Barry turned to Scotty and said, "What am I, the damned pilot? How the hell should I know what's going on?"

199

I was sitting with Mickey. It was quiet, and things seemed to be under control after the initial panic, but you are worried and you are thinking about your family. It does help to put things into perspective. I remember looking at Mickey, and I could see the worry in his eyes. Mickey isn't the most organized guy in the world. He looked at me and said, "I don't know what's going to happen, but I know Arlene's screwed."

"Why's that?" I asked him.

"Because I've got documents in more places. She's never going to know where to find them."

I was a little surprised that when the plane finally landed, there was no loud applause or any sort of elation among us. But I guarantee you everyone getting off that flight was a much whiter shade of pale than when they boarded the plane. And we couldn't help but notice as we deplaned that parked next to the airport shuttles waiting to transport us to the hotel were fire trucks and emergency crews.

The gallows humor didn't take long to emerge. The Wings didn't have a new deal signed with winger Marty Lapointe yet, and GM Kenny Holland walked up to me and said, "I think we should throw a contract under Marty's nose right now." Defenseman Larry Murphy walked by me, and as he's coming down the steps he said, "I'm getting off this plane, and then I think we should all sign it and put it on eBay."

We spent the night at the Hyatt Hotel in Sacramento and boarded another flight at 11:00 the next morning to go to Vancouver. We were able to borrow a charter that had taken the Pittsburgh Penguins to Phoenix and was waiting to fly them to their next game in Dallas.

I came down the elevator the next morning, and Barry Smith was waiting for the elevator to go back up to his room to get something. As he gets on and I get off, he said, "You better look out."

"What?" I said.

"Scotty's on the warpath."

"For what?"

"I don't know, something you said on the radio."

Starting in 1999 and covering a five-year span, I went on the radio with J.J. and Lynne on 94.7 FM in Detroit. Twice a week I would do Red Wings updates in the morning, and in the afternoon I would do a segment called "Electric Moments" with Ken Calvert as the station would play my goal calls of the week. It proved to generate a lot of publicity for the Red Wings.

I finally run into Scotty and he said, "You had to go on the radio. You had to go on the radio and say what happened." I told Scotty that I think everyone knows what happened. It was on the radio first thing in the morning according to my wife back in Detroit. I went on the radio at 4:30 AM our time. It was 7:30 in Detroit, my usual scheduled time slot. I wasn't going on there to break news. There were news crews on the runway when we got off the bus upon landing around 3:30 AM Detroit time. The story was out there. I didn't say anything wrong. I told people what happened and that everything was handled very well. It was calm.

I didn't say anything that wasn't out there. And Scotty said, "Who are you working for? Are you working for the Red Wings or are you working for the media? People heard back in Detroit, and they're not happy with you." I told Scotty that I was an employee of the Red Wings, but I do this on the radio every week. I didn't say anything I shouldn't have said.

Now I'm angry, and I told Scotty where he could go! Brent Gilchrist and Mathieu Dandenault were in shock and likely would have applauded if Scotty weren't still standing there. I didn't talk to Scotty for a long time. I avoided him. I thought he was unfairly rude to me. We were all having a rough day. But Scotty decided that day that I was the guy that he was going to pick on.

I remember we were in Boston maybe six weeks later and Scotty was standing by the elevator and it was our first direct eye contact in all that time. He looked right at me, and I went the other way. About five minutes later Mickey comes over to me and he says, "Bowman finally said it."

"What's that?"

"He said, 'Your broadcast partner is pissed at me. Hasn't talked to me in weeks.'"

Okay good. Scotty knows now. Over the next few days we started to say hello, and we've been wonderful ever since.

There's a funny conclusion to the plane incident. Later during the Arizona leg of the same road trip, the plane had been repaired and was ready to go. Ken Holland showed up at practice to tell the players. The guys balked at getting back on that plane when Holland told them it was again fit for air travel. They put a simple question to Holland—would he be willing to get back on that plane?

"No, I have to fly to California for our scouting meetings," Holland said, before adding, "You couldn't get me on that plane with a cattle prod." The entire team burst out laughing.

Wrong Turn

Scotty did so many things behind the bench, sometimes I think he just did it to screw with the other coach. Longtime NHL coach Ken Hitchcock used to say that he was exhausted after a game of trying to match wits with Scotty behind their respective benches. There's usually a method to the madness, but sometimes, there was no method to Scotty's madness. He'd just do it to see how the other guy would react. I think Mike Babcock does the same thing. So did Mike Keenan. All the great coaches probably do.

Scotty would change lines so much that half the players throughout the game would be asking, "Who's up?" Scotty would tell them who was up with a second left before the change was made. He'd then grab a guy's jersey and pull him back from going over the boards, say, "No, no, no," and change things up on the fly. There was always mass confusion on the bench, and the players just learned to live with it.

There was a game where the linesman didn't call an icing. Scotty was peeved about it. The linesman came over to the bench and Scotty said, "That should have been icing." The linesman said, "Steve Duchesne turned the wrong way." And Scotty said, "Turned the wrong way? I'm here to tell you he can only turn one way."

The players on the bench had their faces buried in their gloves, trying not to laugh. Scotty made them laugh lots on the bench, and many times it was unintentional.

One Man Short

There are games I miss due to a national network taking over. One such game was March 31, 2001, and the Wings had just lost in Philadelphia 1–0 mustering only two shots on goal in the third period. Bowman couldn't have been happy. Jenna Osgood, the wife of Wings goalie Chris Osgood, who played that Saturday afternoon, was expecting their first child. Jenna had paged Wings trainer John Wharton to let him know to tell Chris she was in labor. Bowman wanted to get out of Philadelphia quickly. Ken Kal and Paul Woods were doing their postgame show on the radio. Paul was done and headed to the bus, but Kal had to wrap and wasn't aware of the urgency. Mike Kuta, the P.R. guy, said, "Kal's not here," and Scotty said, "I don't care. We're leaving." And the bus left. Kal got there about 45 seconds after the bus was gone.

Kal went upstairs outside the arena to try and find a cab to get to the airport and maybe catch the plane before it left. He ran into Wings captain Steve Yzerman, who wasn't going back with the team. Steve's wife, Lisa, was there and they were flying back on his buddy's private jet. Steve said, "Why don't you come with us?" It was a huge break for Ken.

The kicker to the story was when I went into Kal's office back at the Joe the next afternoon prior to that night's game against Washington. Not aware of what went on, I asked Ken what time he got back from Philly, and Ken started cussing me out. I asked him what kind of response was that? He says, "Yeah, like you don't know." I knew nothing and asked him what he was talking about. "Scotty left me behind," he growled. Seriously, I had no idea. I was just trying to make casual conversation.

Ken told me the whole story and said, "Do you know how much that would have cost us by Scotty doing that? It would have cost me an extra night's hotel. It would have cost me a plane ticket to come home. It would have cost the team per diem. For 45 seconds, he couldn't wait."

I told Ken he was 100 percent right, and that he should go tell Scotty that. So after a little convincing—okay, maybe a lot—we walked down to the dressing room now three hours before game time, and out of the sauna walks Bowman with a towel around his waist and shaving cream still on his face. And to his credit, Ken stood up to Scotty and started in on him as the two walked into Bowman's office and closed the door. The F-bombs were launching. Stevie peeked around the corner and laughed. Out walked Dave Lewis from the video room, and as Kal appeared Dave said, "You're my hero!" Each man had his say. Pros that they are, they did the pregame radio coach's comment segment once Scotty got dressed after the undressing.

The happy news was that daughter Mackenzie Osgood, Chris and Jenna's first child, was born on April 1.

Blues Clues

When Scotty Bowman made his NHL coaching debut with the St. Louis Blues on November 22, 1967, Vince Lombardi was still coaching the Green Bay Packers, and Casey Stengel wasn't long removed from his tenure as baseball's sage manager.

Bowman lived by a simple philosophy—the comfort zone is not a place where anyone around him should reside.

This theory was easily maintained in St. Louis, when coaches had complete control. Once, Bowman came upon a group of Blues enjoying a night out. He didn't say a word, just sauntered over to the jukebox, made a selection, and left.

Fats Domino singing "I'm Going to Kansas City" soon filled the room. The Blues' minor league affiliate was located in Kansas City.

In the modern era of no-trade contracts, Bowman's options were limited, but he still found ways to keep people on their toes.

He'd often call players into his office, grilling them on the state of the NHL. Who won last night's games? What were the scores? Who had the goals? Believe you me, you had better know the answers. He was always thinking hockey, and he made sure they were, too.

Bowman felt he was gaining an edge by keeping them on edge. On road trips, Bowman would leave a stick with the hotel front desk at curfew time, asking the clerk to get players to sign it. It was his simple way of deciphering which players were coming in late.

"If anybody asked me for an autograph late at night, I always signed 'Darren McCarty,'" Brendan Shanahan laughed.

Bowman's ability to succeed through changing times was remarkable.

"The only thing that changes about Scotty is that he gets older," Jimmy Roberts, who played for Scotty in St. Louis and Montreal, once remarked.

As talented as any coach to pick up a whistle, Bowman is remembered as much for his success as for the complex personality that operates beneath his unique hockey mind.

Scotty lived for the attention to detail. The competition, the games. It was his time to flourish. He liked the pressure, and that's what made him such a good coach. He got better and better the further you got along in the grind toward the Stanley Cup final.

He knew more about the game, and he knew more about the players in this league, than anybody. Scotty never believed he'd figured it all out, that there weren't other avenues that could give him an edge.

He was never afraid to experiment or to try new innovations. He stayed on top of things, and that's why he was so successful.

Scotty was the first coach to lead three different teams—Montreal, Pittsburgh, and Detroit—to the Stanley Cup. He was the first NHL coach to win 1,000 games.

He was an old-school guy who adjusted to new-school personalities. Amazingly, Bowman had performed these alterations without weakening his ability to motivate players. His fire and determination to win have never waned.

Former Blues defenseman Bob Plager recalled a specific time when Bowman was unhappy with their collective effort and called a 9:00 AM practice.

"We had to drive all the way to the rink in rush-hour traffic," Plager said. "He skated us for a couple of hours and then told us not to leave the rink, there was a team meeting at 2:30. We waited around and waited around while Scotty was in his office. What we didn't know was that Scotty's office had a window that looked out on the freeway.

"He was watching the traffic, waiting for it to build up again, and then he came down and told us the meeting was cancelled, but we were to go straight home because he'd be calling us in half an hour and if we weren't there, we would be fined. We all raced home, and when Scotty called, he said 'What did you think of that traffic? How'd you like to battle that traffic twice a day, every day? Now do you realize how lucky you are?'

"He was tough all right, but then every June, you'd get a big check for the playoffs and you'd look at that check and think, *That Scotty, he's not such a bad guy after all.*"

There may not have been a love affair between Bowman and his players, but there was respect.

"His mind works like a computer," Shanahan said. "He'd articulate to us a team's tendencies, and sure enough, we'd go out on the ice and that team was doing it."

Bowman listed a simple formula as the key to his success. "I was blessed with three constants everywhere I've coached: great, supportive ownership; fantastic goalkeeping; and a structured defense," he said.

Of course, he forgot one other pertinent detail—a brilliant hockey mind to run the show.

The Shoes Fit

Longtime St. Louis GM Ron Caron once relayed a story about Bowman's first training camp as coach of the Montreal Canadiens in 1971.

"After practice, he told the players to put on their tracksuits and get ready to go for a run," said Caron, who was a member of the Montreal front-office staff. "A few of the veterans said they'd really like to run, but they didn't have any running shoes."

When the players arrived the next day, they found 30 dozen pairs of running shoes waiting to be tried on. "Find a pair that fits," was all Scotty said.

Burning Down the House

After a 5–1 win over the St. Louis Blues March 9, 1972, when Scotty was coaching the Montreal Canadiens, the players and staff were slumbering at the St. Louis Hilton Inn, when the shrill sounds of the fire alarm awoke them.

"I opened my door, which was a big mistake, because the flames were right out in the hallway," Scotty remembered.

Fire engulfing his room, Bowman sought refuge on his fourth-floor balcony. "I wasn't going to burn to death up there," Bowman said. "I was getting ready to jump. There was a pool, but it didn't have any water in it."

He wasn't panicking, simply dissecting the situation and weighing his options.

Scotty's lasting recollection of that St. Louis fire after the rescue squad saved his life was that defenseman Serge Savard suffered an 18-stitch cut while kicking out a window.

"We lost him for the playoffs because of that," Bowman said.

With Scotty, everything comes back to hockey. Always has. Always will.

Love at First Tie

In Scotty's world, even romance was measured at ice level. His love connection with his wife, Suella, was certified early in their relationship as Suella waited to pick up Scotty at the airport following a tie game on the road.

"She didn't know a lot about hockey, and she told me she wasn't sure if she was supposed to be happy or sad because we had tied," Bowman said, recalling that day.

"She decided she should be sad. Right then, I knew she was the one for me."

Russian Five

Bowman embraced the Russian philosophy earlier than most hockey people, and that was why he created the Russian Five unit of Sergei Fedorov, Igor Larionov, Slava Kozlov, Viacheslav Fetisov,

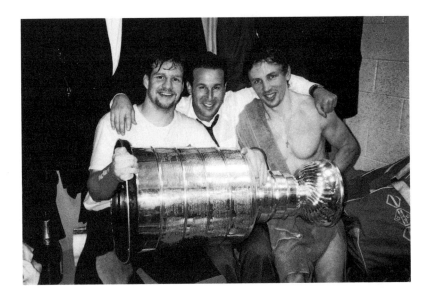

With Brent Gilchrist (left) and Igor Larionov celebrating the Stanley Cup win in Washington in June 1998. (Photo courtesy of the Detroit Red Wings)

and Vladimir Konstantinov to help the Wings win the 1996–97 Stanley Cup.

He thinks many Canadians still don't comprehend how much Russians are like them. "They love the game as much as we do, and they have 10 times the population of Canada, so it's only natural that they are going to produce great players," Bowman said.

A Career Coach

Scotty tried his hand at scouting and was a GM in Buffalo, but he never liked the fact that in those aspects of the game, your work never seemed to end. As a coach, he had his summers to himself and his family.

"I enjoyed the games more than anything," he explained. "How are you going to work your lines? How are you going to get the right guys on the ice at the right time?"

A lot of it was guesswork, obviously, but that's what he enjoyed the most, the feeling that he could do something to maybe get a player who was having a good night a little more work, do a little wrinkle. But he also was careful not to overcoach.

Rain Man

Scotty is always thinking. He'd often ask me as he saw me approach, "What do you think?"

I had no idea about what he was thinking I should be thinking about, but I also knew he only partly cared. It was only a test to see what was going on in the game. He knew the game and there was nothing I could tell him, but for him it was just for a pulse of what's happening around him. A crazy thing (among many) about Scotty was that someone would ask him a question, and if Scotty didn't want to answer that question, he'd turn it into something he wanted to talk about. In the end, you'd be impressed more often than not with what you just heard, even though it was never in your thought process to hear about it.

Scotty has had so many ideas about the game, but one he had years ago has not gained any traction, but I wish it would. It would be a line from the top of the face-off circles in each end. Not right across the ice, but just from the side boards extending about five feet from each side. That would be the indicator line for a linesman that the defenseman would have to reach to make a pass to a teammate across the center ice line. This would force the defenseman to carry the puck to the top of the circle to make a lengthy pass, rather than just wiring it from his own corner to the opposition blue line 125' away. It would create more of an opposition forecheck and perhaps more mistakes with a defenseman forced to carry the puck a bit and think about making an accurate pass. Without the center ice line now for the purpose of a two-line pass, the game has just become a long-pass, chip, and chase game. This wrinkle may help change that.

Scotty and Mike

Playing for Mike Keenan in high school and working with Scotty Bowman in Detroit for five seasons, I've been blessed to learn from two of the greatest and more unique minds to ever grace the game.

Just as Toe Blake mentored Scotty, Scotty mentored Mike.

"He's unto himself," Keenan said of Scotty. "The accomplishments that Scotty has achieved will never be matched."

Bowman certainly was Keenan's coaching guru. "Scotty Bowman gave me my first pro coaching job," Keenan recalled. When Bowman was coach-GM in Buffalo, he hired Keenan to coach the Sabres' Rochester farm club. "A lot of what I know...I've learned from Scotty."

Scotty recalled what stuck with him from his first dealings with Mike.

"He didn't like to lose, that was the biggest thing," Bowman remembered as the quality that stood out most in the young Keenan, a trait both men continue to share today.

In short, that is what Bowman was and is all about, what he thrived on. Winning. "I'm not a good loser," he frankly admitted. "I'm not a lot of fun to be around when I lose."

Their mutual respect for each other developed into a lasting friendship.

"I think he probably saw some of himself in me," Keenan recalled. "There were nightly phone calls, usually lasting at least an hour. He certainly gave me a lot of insight about coaching men and coaching pros."

There has always been a unique bond, both in the personal and esoteric sense, between Keenan and Bowman. Both men took the Peterborough Petes to the Memorial Cup before moving into the pro ranks. Keenan also shared with Bowman the habit of chewing ice, the same stoic pose behind the bench, and shockingly similar receding hairlines. Adding to these bizarre similarities, as I've pointed out before, Keenan hails from Bowmanville, Ontario.

Like Bowman, Keenan is known as much for what is often viewed as a dictatorial off-ice demeanor as he is for his success, and Scotty felt this portrayal of Mike was a misnomer. "I think it's been unfair," Bowman said of the criticism of Keenan. "I think a lot of it has been stretched out. A lot of it has been the figment of somebody's imagination. I think it has detracted from [Keenan's accomplishments]."

It was also Bowman who helped open the door for Keenan to his first NHL head coaching position with Philadelphia in 1984.

"[Flyers GM] Bobby Clarke phoned [about Keenan]," Bowman said. "I told him he couldn't find a better guy for his team."

Skating with Scotty

In 2002, I was privileged enough to strap on the blades and skate alongside Scotty on Ottawa's famed Rideau Canal for a special segment we filmed for Fox Sports.

Some of Scotty's revelations that day follow.

Skating Outdoors as a Kid

"All the time," Scotty said. "The biggest thing for me was the weekends. I was fortunate. I lived in Verdun, a Montreal suburb, and I could put my skates on at home, skate up the streets and through the back lanes and five minutes later I was at the park. We skated from eight in the morning until dark, and that was every Saturday and Sunday. I don't know what we did for lunch, but we sure were on the ice."

Coaching in Montreal

"When I first got there, I was returning to my hometown, and they were coming off a Stanley Cup win," he recalled. "At the beginning it felt like pressure. The fans were so committed to that team, and boy if you didn't have a good season and play-offs, you couldn't wait to get back to start the next season. In Montreal, you either won the Stanley Cup, or you had a tough summer. We had guys like Guy Lafleur, Steve Shutt, Larry Robinson, and Bob Gainey, who all came in at the same time. They just got hungrier and hungrier. The excellence of those players is what I remember most. They went into every game expecting to win."

Best Goal Scorer He Ever Saw

"It's tough to compare eras," Scotty admitted. "Growing up in Montreal, I saw Rocket Richard and Boom-Boom Geoffrion. Bobby Hull in the late '50s and up to the time of the WHA was a tremendous goal scorer. He had the shot. In later years it was Lafleur and Mike Bossy. Bossy's record is phenomenal, and then obviously Wayne Gretzky. He did it better than everybody, and he did it over a longer time."

Best Defenseman He Ever Saw

"I grew up watching the Canadiens in the 1950s, and there was not a defenseman in the league that was even close to Doug Harvey," Scotty said. "He was the leader of those Canadiens teams that won five straight Cups. He played for us in St. Louis in 1967–68 and 1968–69, and he was 44 and was phenomenal. Bobby Orr, for his 10 years, when people talk about great players, you put him right at the very top."

Toughest Player He Ever Saw

On this topic, Scotty sought a caveat. "How do you define tough?" he asked me. "I think toughness is playing with pain. Steve Yzerman and Chris Chelios were two guys who could play through incredible pain. In terms of plain toughness, John Ferguson was pretty tough to beat. He came up at a time when the Canadiens were getting pushed around, and he turned them into Stanley Cup champions."

Best Player He Ever Coached

Not surprisingly, having coached as long as he did, Scotty couldn't narrow it down to one player. "In St. Louis we had Glenn Hall," Scotty noted. "What a goaltender, probably in the top three of all time. In Montreal Lafleur was the player of the 1970s. Mario Lemieux for what he did with that Pittsburgh team, and he didn't have as much support as guys with other teams, you had to admire him. In the '91 and '92 playoffs, you saw how he just lifted the whole team. We won 11 straight games in the '92 playoffs, and Mario was the reason, really."

Dangerous Practice

There was an off day during the first round of the 2002 play-offs when it was an optional skate, and we didn't think Bowman was around. Not that we thought he'd care, but you always liked to clear things through Scotty before you did them, just to be safe.

Anyway, Ken Kal and I went out on the ice. There were a bunch of kids out there as well, so it wasn't just us. We saw Bowman come out to the bench. Kal and I were on the far side of the ice and the two of us took off to the near corner, so Scotty maybe wouldn't look down to his left and see us. We were sort of hiding, because with Scotty, you never knew. Anything you did could just set him off.

Scotty left, and we skated down toward the bench. Assistant coach Barry Smith said, "You better get off the ice. Scotty's not in a good mood. I'll cover for you." We took off down the hallway, and Barry went into the dressing room to make sure Scotty wasn't coming out. Kal and I went down into the room because we had our stuff in the Red Wings dressing room. We went to another room and took our skates off and came back and got the rest of our stuff later when Scotty wasn't there. You had to hide from Scotty at times. You had to pick your spots.

Make Them Laugh

The Wings were slated to play Colorado in Game 7 of the 2002 Western Conference final. The winner would be in the Stanley Cup final, and let's face it, these were the two best teams in the NHL, so the winner would be lifting Lord Stanley's Cup in a couple of weeks.

Bowman knew exactly how to get his team ready.

"He told us stories about his seventh-game experiences," Wings defenseman Steve Duchesne said. "Some of them were pretty funny. It was lighthearted. By game time, nobody was tense. Everybody was relaxed and ready to go."

Just ask the Avalanche how ready the Wings were. Detroit won that Game 7–0.

It was just before that deciding game that Scotty recited a story about an unheralded player he had coached in junior who scored a big winning goal for his team, and then added, "He had great hands. Just like you Drapes!" The room lost it, because the last thing Kris Draper was known for was his finishing touch around the net. Then the Wings went out and won it. Handily.

"Some nights there was a little more tension than others, and that night I could tell, I could feel the tension," Scotty explained. "It was Toe Blake who mentioned to me that in crunch time if you could ever crack something that might make them laugh, you've got it made. If your team can laugh in a situation like that, they're probably going to have a good night."

Scotty and Toe

It didn't matter to Scotty after he won his ninth Stanley Cup as a coach with the Wings in 2001–02 that he had surpassed Toe Blake to become the NHL coach with the most Cup wins. What mattered to him was fondly reflecting back on all he'd learned from Blake, who'd been his coaching mentor in Montreal.

"He was my idol," Scotty said. "I think he was far and away the best coach that's ever coached in the league."

Their offices were down the hall from each other in the Montreal Forum, when Blake was coaching the Montreal Canadiens and Scotty was coaching the Montreal Jr. Canadiens. "The Canadiens would practice in the morning, around 10:00,"

Bowman remembered. "He would leave after that—he had another business he ran—but he'd come back in the afternoon. We practiced after school and sometimes, he'd watch us work out. Afterward, we'd talk about things in the game."

Blake, who died in 1995, won eight Stanley Cups as coach of the Canadiens. After an All-Star career as a left-winger for the Canadiens, skating alongside Maurice (Rocket) Richard and Elmer Lach on Montreal's famed Punch Line, Blake took over as coach of the Canadiens in 1955.

A year later, the organization hired Bowman, who was just 23 at the time, to work with their junior club in Ottawa.

"The first five years [Blake] was in Montreal, the Canadiens won the Stanley Cup every year," Bowman said. "Chicago put together a big, tough, dirty team, and they were able to win a Cup in 1961 and beat Montreal in the semifinals by just beating up on them physically. Montreal lost in the semifinals for four straight years, and they were pretty tough years. People were saying that Blake had lost it, that he didn't have the touch anymore. What had happened was that Montreal had developed too many of the same type of skill player, and the team had gotten too small.

"Sam Pollock took over as GM in 1964, and they knew the team had to get tougher. They brought in people like John Ferguson, Ted Harris, and Terry Harper, and Blake won three more Cups in the next four years. The hockey world had written him off, but he had reinvented his team."

Both men had their playing careers halted by serious injury. Blake broke an ankle in a 1948 game against the New York Rangers. Bowman suffered a fractured skull when hit by the stick of defenseman Jean-Guy Talbot while playing for the junior Habs.

In a town where the French-language press was always ready to sacrifice an English-speaking player, Blake was never concerned about the origins of his players. "I didn't care what language they spoke, as long as they backchecked," he once said.

Bowman credited Blake for many of the on-ice devices he employed.

"Toe Blake was a great innovator," Scotty said. "He doesn't get the credit for that, but he was the first coach to match lines and the first coach to put his best defensemen against the other team's top line. A lot of the stats that the league hands out today—plus-minus, power plays, penalty killing—they didn't have them back in those days. He kept them himself. In his office, he had charts covering every game, every goal—who was on the ice, how it was scored."

In 1968, Bowman—a rookie coach in the league—guided the St. Louis Blues to the Cup final, where they met Blake's Montreal Canadiens. It would be Blake's last Cup.

"We knew before the series that he was going to retire," Bowman recalled of going head-to-head for the Stanley Cup against his mentor, a series that Montreal won in the minimum four games. "Being eliminated was tough, and being swept was even more difficult to take. But over the years, knowing that it was his last one, it's softened the memory a little bit."

When the end came for Bowman, he showed he'd absorbed another lesson from his teacher.

When it comes time to go, go out on top.

Farewell Skate

Scotty isn't the sentimental sort, at least not outwardly. Scotty knew since February of that year that he planned to retire from coaching following the 2001–02 season, but he didn't tell anyone until the Wings were on the ice celebrating their Stanley Cup win over the Carolina Hurricanes.

I went down on the ice. I didn't call the games because by that stage of the playoffs the networks had taken over, so I was in the seats for the Cup win. Scotty had gone in the Red Wings dressing room, and in a first for him he put on his skates so that he could carry the Cup, wearing that camel brown sweater vest he rarely took off due to his superstitious nature. When he returned to the JLA ice I watched him hug Sergei Fedorov. I saw Sergei's reaction, and I believe Sergei may have been the first player he told. I happened to catch Scotty talking to Sergei and I saw Sergei sort of taken aback. In the moment, I thought nothing of it. And then about five minutes later Barry Smith came up to me and said, "Bowman's done." Done what? "He's finished. He's retiring."

That's when I went up to Scotty and asked him if he was really finished. And we hugged one another and he said, "It's just the right time to go. I'm done." I was very happy for him. I don't think he wanted to take away from the celebration at that moment, but in the emotion of it all he just started to tell people.

CHAPTER 7
THE GREATEST TEAM
EVER ASSEMBLED?

*I looked around and it was as
if I were at the NHL All-Star Game.*

Hardware and Tear

A dressing room for the aged and ages.

The two Norris Trophy winners—Nicklas Lidstrom and Chris Chelios—sat side-by-side along the back wall. The three Hart Trophy winners—Dominik Hasek, Brett Hull, and Sergei Fedorov—were interspersed throughout the room. Steve Yzerman, the Conn Smythe Trophy winner, suited up next to Luc Robitaille, one of the club's three 500-goal scorers.

I looked around, and it was as if I was at the NHL All-Star Game. And the best part was they didn't play like they were at the All-Star Game. There was a special feeling in the room. I knew that Robitaille and Hull would balance the attack and that Hasek would give the Wings a chance to win every game.

Since the Wings won consecutive Stanley Cups in 1997 and '98, the team had suffered three disappointing playoff campaigns. By the time the postseason would roll around that spring, both forward Igor Larionov and defenseman Chelios would be past 40, so the Wings seemed to realize that the time to win was of the essence.

Realizing its window of championship opportunity was closing rapidly, Wings management went out in the summer of 2001 and acquired two right-wingers with 60-plus goal seasons on their resumes—Robitaille and Hull—along with Hasek, the world's best goalie, and defenseman Fredrik Olausson, who formed a solid top pairing with Lidstrom.

The additions were part of a summer spending spree in which GM Ken Holland acknowledged that there's no time like the present. Or, in the case of this team, there's little future past the present.

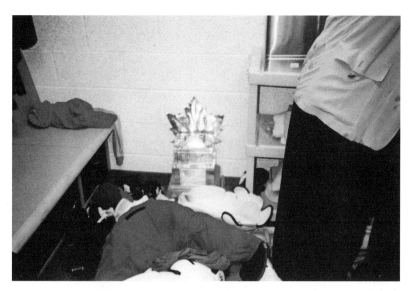

Washington, 1998: Conn Smythe needs a place to sit. The trophy is waiting among the sweaty equipment worn by Steve Yzerman to return to his stall.

Hull was 37, Hasek 36, and Robitaille and Olausson were each 35. Captain Yzerman was 36 and two years away from completing his personal goal of 20 NHL seasons. Defenseman Uwe Krupp, returning after missing two full seasons with a back injury, was also 36, as was defenseman Steve Duchesne. In total, 14 Red Wings that season were 30 or older.

They might not be over the hill yet, but they sure didn't require binoculars to see the crest of that hill. Bifocals, maybe. But not binoculars.

That team realized that their future was now, and what a bright one it was.

Detroit's 2001–02 lineup included 33 Stanley Cup rings. Three players—Krupp, Hull, and right-winger Darren McCarty—had counted Cup-winning tallies. Five players—Fedorov, Yzerman,

Robitaille, Hull, and left-winger Brendan Shanahan—had posted 50-goal seasons.

Yzerman joined Hull and Robitaille with 60-goal campaigns, while Hull had also ascended to the 70- and 80-goal plateaus.

That season, Robitaille joined Yzerman and Hull in the NHL's exclusive 600-goal club. The Wings would be the first team to suit up three 600-goal scorers. Bowman even experimented with them as a line at times, the most productive trio since the Three Tenors.

The veteran leadership in the room ensured that the final objective was never forgotten.

"Our whole goal was to win 16 games in the playoffs," said Hull, part of this group that could have assembled a hardware section to rival Home Depot.

Besides Hasek's six Vezina Trophies, Hasek, Fedorov, and Hull all owned Hart Trophies. Lidstrom and Chelios had Norris Trophies. Robitaille captured the Calder Trophy, Hull had a Lady Byng Trophy to his credit, Yzerman had won the Conn Smythe Trophy, and Fedorov and Yzerman both had Selke Trophies. Bowman had won two Jack Adams Awards, and Fedorov, Yzerman, Hull, and Hasek all had captured the Pearson (now the Ted Lindsay) Award.

There were World Championship, World Cup, Canada Cup, and Olympic Gold medal winners littered among the Detroit players. Eleven of them had skated in the NHL All-Star Game, and they'd earned two-dozen NHL First All-Star Team selections.

"I figured Detroit would be a top team when I signed," said Olausson, who was the first of the four newcomers to ink a deal. "As the summer went on and they added the other guys, I just kind

My first season in Detroit, and I'm drinking out of the Stanley Cup! (Photo courtesy of the Detroit Red Wings)

of said, 'Wow.' We've got a lot of world-class players here. We've got quite a few to choose from."

Normally, mixing this many egos into such a confined space as an NHL dressing room might be a recipe for disaster, but it was never a problem in Detroit, where Bowman was a master at ensuring everyone remained on the same page.

"People make too much out of chemistry," Yzerman suggested. "You can hate a guy, but as long as he comes to the rink and does his job every day, that's all that matters."

Everyone in that room knew that they'd have to sacrifice personal goals in favor of the team objective, and for all their star power, each was fine with that recipe.

The Wings also scoffed at detractors who suggested that they were buying a championship.

"We didn't care," Hull said. "How can you hold it against a team for trying to be better? I guarantee you the other players in the league wished their GM had done it."

Besides, it wasn't true. The nucleus of that team—Fedorov, Yzerman, Lidstrom—were all Detroit draft picks. All Holland did was go out and fill in the holes with the blessing and the bank account of team owner Mike Ilitch.

And what an array of glory they assembled. Entering the 2001–02 season, here's how it all added up for the Red Wings:

Stanley Cups (33)—Scotty Bowman (9); Mathieu Dandenault (2); Kris Draper (2); Fedorov (2); Tomas Holmstrom (2); Larionov (2); Lidstrom (2); Kirk Maltby (2); McCarty (2); Brendan Shanahan (2); Yzerman (2); Chelios, Brent Gilchrist, Hull, Krupp.

Olympic gold medals (3)—Larionov (2), Hasek.

Canada Cups (3)—Bowman, Larionov, Yzerman.

World Cups (2)—Chelios, Hull.

Hart Trophies (4)—Hasek (2), Fedorov, Hull.

Vezina Trophies (6)—Hasek (6).

Norris Trophies (4)—Chelios (3), Lidstrom.

Lady Byng Trophies (1)—Hull.

Conn Smythe Trophies (1)—Yzerman.

The Dominator

That sensational 2001–02 season all started in the first week of July. I was out golfing, and my wife called me and said that Kenny Holland's secretary had called looking for me. I was with a buddy at the time, and if Kenny wanted to talk to me, I didn't need my friend hearing our conversation because I didn't know what it was about.

When I got home I called Kenny and asked him what was up. "What if I told you we could get Dominik Hasek?" he said.

I think I remember saying that I'd think he was the king if he could get Dominik Hasek.

"We'll, you can crown me," Holland said. "I think we can get him. What do you think we'd have to give up?"

I said, "Fedorov?"

"Hell no, not Fedorov. [Slava] Kozlov. Kozzy and a pick."

I said to him that I guessed he was doing the deal.

"Yes we are." That's how I found out we'd got Dominik Hasek.

The Wings played the St. Louis Blues in the second round of the 2002 Stanley Cup playoffs, and that was a scary moment because it could have easily been Dom who was guarding the Blues' net in that series.

With the Dominator during our 2002 postgame Stanley Cup celebration. (Photo courtesy of the Detroit Red Wings / Dave Reginek)

If St. Louis GM Larry Pleau were more open to conversation, Hasek likely would have been more open to the idea of making St. Louis his new home. It was his first choice.

Hasek saw Al MacInnis and Chris Pronger on the Blues defense and he saw nirvana. What right-thinking goaltender wouldn't want to perform behind two Norris Trophy winners in the prime of their careers?

Pleau learned the ways of the game from then New Jersey Devils GM Lou Lamoriello, who believes that there is only one thing you should tell anyone about your team, and that would be nothing.

Faced with the chance to add a guy who almost never lets in goals, Pleau refused to let his guard down. He didn't inform Hasek that St. Louis was on the brink of acquiring center Doug Weight from Edmonton, which was basically a done deal at the point when the two discussed the possibility of Hasek becoming a Blue.

Hasek then met with Holland, who opened up the books on every intricate detail of the Wings' plans to get back to the top of Lord Stanley's mountain. Very soon thereafter, a deal was bartered between the Wings and Buffalo.

If Pleau hadn't opted to play mum, then Hasek might have decided he enjoyed the Blues' tune.

Losing an Ace

A season that began with so much excitement and hope quickly turned somber while the team was in training camp in Traverse City.

There were so many compelling reasons to be excited about the opening of training camp. The arrival of goalie Dominik

Hasek and wingers Brett Hull and Luc Robitaille ignited a buzz.

So much to talk about, made so meaningless by the Tuesday, September 11, 2001, terrorist actions in New York and Washington, D.C., when airplanes were crashed into the World Trade Center towers and the Pentagon.

It was Brendan Shanahan who broke the news to me. I had no cell reception that morning driving to Traverse City and little in terms of radio reception so I was listening to CDs in my car between 6:30 and 10:00 AM. As I walked into the hotel lobby, Brendan was the first person I saw watching TV along with a full throng. To which I asked, "What's going on?"

As we watched the news reports and began to understand the scope of the carnage, the prevailing wisdom among all who gathered for camp—players, coaches, media—was simple and straightforward.

"What are we doing here?" was the most commonly asked question by everyone. "It seemed so insignificant," was how Detroit forward Kirk Maltby remembered it. "We're playing a child's game which seemed so unimportant in comparison to the tragedy and suffering people were enduring in other places."

Athletes lead fairly sheltered existences. Reality seldom enters their realm. Mortgages, car payments, credit-card bills, these are of no concern. But it was clear at that moment in history from talking to players, from looking into their eyes, at their devastated expressions, that the pictures we'd all been viewing on television had also impacted them.

Just like you and me, they were stunned, they were scared, and most of all, uncertain about what the future held for the world. "I can't remember a time in my life when it was so hard to shut the TV off," Maltby recalled. "The whole team was affected by this awful thing."

It was crushing emotionally.

A couple of dozen Wings donated blood during camp. You just felt so helpless, you wanted to do something to try to find a better way.

These tragic occurrences were so unbelievable, they couldn't possibly be true.

That was what we felt until we all had a face to link to the tragedy, a man we all knew, a member of the close-knit hockey community. Garnet (Ace) Bailey loved life—a life that was snuffed out by heartless terrorists, as he was among those killed on the aircrafts. Ace was director of pro scouting for the Los Angeles Kings, a former NHLer, and ex-Red Wing. Ace was a very close friend of my broadcast partner Mickey Redmond and former housemate of Mick's during his two years in Detroit.

Suddenly, it was too real to stomach. Ace was a character, someone who always left them laughing. And Ace was well known to many of the Wings. Luc Robitaille and Steve Duchesne shared stories of time they spent with Bailey in Los Angeles.

"He was always laughing," Robitaille related. "Ace was the kind of guy who came into the room and right away, had everybody smiling."

The nature of their profession, the movement between teams, the travel between cities, makes any sort of air disaster register just a little more in the case of an athlete. "Whenever a plane crashes, I think about how much time I spend on planes," Detroit GM Ken Holland commented. "I like flying, but I like flying best when we touch down."

Holland got to know Bailey well during his own scouting days. "He was a popular guy," Holland said. "You always knew when Ace was in the room. He had a real presence and a great sense of humor."

Bailey was best remembered from his days as a gritty winger with the Bruins, winning two Stanley Cups with them.

Except this day. It was difficult for those who knew him to think about Bailey and not wonder about the terror he and the other passengers endured. "It was just so devastating," Robitaille said.

Robitaille's wife, Stacia, was scheduled on September 11 to take a Detroit-to-Los Angeles flight. "Those flights which were hijacked were going to Los Angeles," Robitaille recalled. "That really shook us up."

The Wings pondered whether to open training camp as scheduled. "In the end, we decided to go about and do what we do," Holland said. "I don't know what the right answer was.

"No one knew the right answer. All we knew was there was no explanation, no rationalization available for such violence against innocent people."

No Goal

America's foremost proponent of the First Amendment, Brett Hull, had nothing to say.

Dominik Hasek, hockey's most renowned rubber rejector, admitted there was something he'd allow to be put behind him.

The topic was Hull's controversial Stanley Cup–winning goal for the Dallas Stars against Hasek's Buffalo Sabres in the 1999 final, a moment etched in hockey infamy. When Hull tallied in overtime for a 2–1 victory, his skate was clearly in the crease. NHL officials ruled he'd followed the puck into the crease and counted it. The entire rule was ludicrous from the beginning.

Two years later, the central figures in the controversy now found their focus centered on a common goal—to win the Stanley Cup for the Red Wings.

Their coming together provided a compelling plot but a short story as far as the principals were concerned.

"I think we'll just leave that one alone," Hull said.

Scrunching his face in the international symbol for "Here we go again," Hasek also wanted no part in any reminiscing.

"No, we never talked about it, and I never asked him to talk about it," Hasek said at the time. "I won't talk about it because I don't see any reason. We are teammates and whatever happened two years ago, it doesn't matter. I always look ahead."

In a dressing room filled with an eclectic collection of superstars and super egos, Hull and Hasek stood out—for what they'd shared, for what they'd accomplished, and because of who they were. Simply the best in the NHL at what they do.

Employing a style that was part butterfly, part Baryshnikov, and part Gumby, Hasek won six Vezina Trophies and back-to-back Hart Trophies as NHL MVP. "He was second to none in the game as far as goalies are concerned," Hull said. "But I liked to think I could score on anyone."

In Hull, Hasek saw the NHL's most dangerous sniper, whose 86 goals in 1990–91 remain an NHL record for right-wingers.

"He had everything you need to score the goals—he could shoot hard and accurate and he didn't need any time," Hasek said.

Hull also shot from the lip with frequency, saying what he thought, but no such malady afflicted him during that 2001–02 season.

"There's people that will be on the bench in situations where they're used to being out there," Hull said. "For the good of the whole, you have to realize that next time, you'll be out there."

Hull's eccentricities stemmed from his work ethic. Hasek's work ethic allowed him to stand out in the crowd. Even in practice, he strived to be unbeatable.

"Hockey is supposed to be fun," Hasek explained. "For me, fun was stopping all the shots."

Starbucks...Four Bucks...Five Bucks

I'm a big Starbucks fan. I've owned their stock for many years, so keep it going. I thought for a while there I was addicted to Starbucks until the lockout year came and I wasn't being paid, so I stopped going. I found without a latte a day—and I counted up the days—I saved about $1,700 that year by not going to Starbucks.

It's an old Jerry Seinfeld joke. "My friend goes to Starbucks, but he calls it four bucks because whatever you order is probably about four bucks." I used to call it four bucks all the time, and Dom would laugh. He was also a fan of the Starbucks ritual. On the road before we boarded the bus, there'd usually be one nearby because there's a Starbucks every 20 feet, right?

Dom and I would often be in there, and whomever was in line first would buy for both. I always felt Dom should pay, because he was making significantly more than I was, but anyway, we would do that. One day I'm on the bus and we're in Arizona and Dom boards and says, "No more four bucks. Now five bucks," as he holds up the cup looking at me. We both had to laugh.

A Different Kind of Cup

Coffee is often a starting point for a lot of the players and broadcasters on the road. Trevor Thompson and I had made a Starbucks stop in New York City a season ago. As we were walking down 6th Avenue a guy walks past and says, "Hey Ken!" Trevor and I were both astonished and Trevor says, "How the heck would he know who you are?" And I thought maybe he has the NHL package and is a hockey fan. But a few blocks later as I turned my Starbucks cup in my hand, I got my explanation. There it was. Written in bold letters: Ken. Wise guy. The only Cup a name should be written on is Stanley!

Start the Bus

How valuable did the Wings view Hasek to their cause? We're on the bus in Vancouver, waiting to leave GM Place after morning skate and Scotty said, "Let's go. What are we waiting for?" John Hahn, the team's P.R. director at the time, said, "Some of the players aren't here yet."

Scotty tells Hahn to go in and check and see who's missing. John goes back in, and only one guy comes out and it's Hasek. Bowman turns to me and says, "Good thing I had him go look. Good thing we waited."

If it was any other player, Scotty wouldn't have cared. But he took full credit for the situation.

The Wings knew that they weren't going anywhere without Dom.

Olympic Glory

Before they'd chase a silver mug together, they briefly separated in pursuit of gold. Ten Red Wings played at the 2002 Winter Olympic Games in Salt Lake City. That led to some entertaining banter inside the Red Wings dressing room as the Games approached.

"Almost every day, we'd talk about the Olympics," Hasek remembered. "There were lots of jokes."

Often, the butt of these jokes was Hasek, the man who'd had the last laugh four years earlier in Nagano, Japan, backstopping the Czech Republic to a stunning Olympic gold.

Facing pranksters like Canada's Shanahan and Hull of the United States, Hasek deflected their verbal barbs as deftly as he blocked pucks in Nagano. Then he'd go on the offensive, happily chiding Canadian teammates Shanahan and Yzerman, reminding them about the immense expectations placed upon their shoulders by a hockey-mad nation. "Canada almost has to win," Hasek would say with a cackle.

As things would turn out, four Red Wings ended up in the gold-medal game, as Shanahan and Yzerman and the Canadians beat the United States of Hull and Chris Chelios 5–2. Sergei Fedorov, Pavel Datsyuk, and Igor Larionov won bronze medals with the Russian team.

Hasek and Swedes Nicklas Lidstrom, Fredrik Olausson, and Tomas Holmstrom all came home empty-handed, as did another Swede who'd soon become well known in Hockeytown, a kid by the name of Henrik Zetterberg, who was the only non-NHLer to make the Swedish team.

Yzerman estimated that the sensation of being part of Canada's first Olympic hockey golden moment in 50 years will never fade. The gold medal, coupled with the Stanley Cup they'd win in June, at the time allowed Yzerman and Shanahan to join Ken Morrow (USA, New York Islanders, 1980) as the only players to win an Olympic gold medal and a Stanley Cup in the same season.

The moment he cherished the most? The 5–2 victory over the U.S. in the gold-medal match. A close second? The dressing-room atmosphere following the game.

"Access is pretty restrictive at the Olympics," Yzerman recalled. "After the game, we just sat in the room for about two hours—players, coaches, and trainers—talking about what we'd just accomplished.

"It was something I'll never forget." And something that was over in the blink of an eye. Six games in 10 days. Pick up your medal, then go home.

The NHL quickly resumed its schedule, and teammates once again became bitter rivals. Such are the strange bedfellows created by this midseason marriage of NHL players and the Olympic movement.

"In the room afterwards, we jokingly suggested a truce for the rest of the regular season," Yzerman said of his Canadian teammates. "We won't hit each other until the playoffs."

As close as the Canadians grew, trade secrets on NHL teammates skating for other nations weren't available at any price. "We asked [New York Rangers players Theoren] Fleury and [Eric]

Lindros where to go on [Rangers teammate and U.S. goalie Mike] Richter, but they wouldn't say," Yzerman said.

"Guys were asking me about Dom before we played the Czechs, and I just said, 'I don't know.' But if we'd gone to a shootout, I would have opened up the book on him."

He closed the book with a golden moment, one that Yzerman still slotted fourth in his memory bank behind his three Stanley Cups.

"We've only thought about the Olympics for the last 8–10 years," he said. "We've thought about winning the Cup since we were three."

That might explain the quiet, reflective nature of the Canadians after capturing gold, quite unlike the on-ice pandemonium that unfolds during the Stanley Cup presentation.

"The Stanley Cup is such a journey," Yzerman said. "You've got the regular season, then four rounds of playoffs.

"Once you win it, the emotion of the accomplishment just explodes from within you. The Olympics are a different situation. When you win, there's no parade. You go home and go back to work."

Goat

That 2001–02 Red Wings team was billed as the greatest hockey team ever assembled, and they certainly did everything in their power to live up to that billing. Bursting from the gate, the Wings won eight of their first nine games. They had more overtime wins in the month of October than they had total losses.

The Wings were 22–3–1–1 over the first two months of the season, and at that point, every other team in the league knew that they were playing for second place. There was a 9–1–2 12-game stretch in January, and then the Wings won 10 of 11 games in another streak that began in February and extended into March. They were home and cooled out so quickly as Bowman was able to rest many of his stars down the stretch, while other teams battled for their playoff lives. And back then, the league didn't like the Wings resting stars for a competitive balance with others trying to make the playoffs.

Everyone contributed. Backup goaltender Manny Legace posted a 19-game unbeaten streak. And there was this dazzling rookie forward named Pavel Datsyuk, who could make the puck dance on the end of his stick. I just knew that he was headed for greatness. Datsyuk played on a line with Hull and Boyd Devereaux that Hull dubbed "two kids and an old goat."

Milestone achievements were happening everywhere you looked. Hull became the highest scoring active player in the NHL, and Robitaille passed Brett's dad, Bobby Hull, to become the highest scoring left-winger of all time. Yzerman became the ninth player in NHL history to accumulate 1,000 career assists.

As the playoffs got underway, the magical moments just kept happening. Hasek set a club record with six postseason shutouts. Hull scored his 100th career playoff goal in the Stanley Cup final against the Carolina Hurricanes. Chelios won his second Cup, to go with the one he'd captured with the Montreal Canadiens in 1985–86, and the 16-year gap between titles at the time was also a record. When Detroit lifted the Cup, Bowman surpassed his mentor, Toe Blake, by winning his ninth Stanley Cup as a coach.

We Won't Lose

As great as that season was, as with any championship run, and Michigan roads, there were potholes that had to be navigated and overcome along the path to glory. The playoffs certainly didn't get underway as the blueprint for success would have been laid out.

The Vancouver Canucks were the first-round opponent for the Wings, and they wasted little time displaying that they weren't going to be easy pickings. In fact, they scared the living daylights out of the Red Wings faithful.

The eighth-seeded Canucks came into Joe Louis Arena and won Game 1 by a 4–3 verdict on an overtime goal by Henrik Sedin. Then in Game 2, Todd Bertuzzi had a goal and an assist and the Canucks were easy 5–2 victors.

We were down 0–2 heading to Vancouver and things were looking bleak. We boarded the plane, and Scotty Bowman was already seated before me. I got on Redbird, and then Steve Yzerman walked on right after me. Stevie turned to Scotty and to Ken Holland, who was right across from him, and said, "We're not losing this series." I could hear the determination in his voice. That made me feel a whole lot better going back to my seat.

We landed in Vancouver and took the bus to the hotel. A few cars must have been at the airport and they followed us back from there to the hotel. They had Canucks flags waving out the windows and they were yelling, "Go Canucks go. Red Wings suck."

Everyone on the bus took all of this in, and I could tell that the players were pissed off. Looking out the window, it was just two or three cars filled with a bunch of kids in their late teens or early twenties. I thought right at the time that this was a good thing. Those foolish kids thought they were taunting the guys, but if anything, it just revved up the team.

The Turning Point

Game 3 of the Wings-Canucks series was tied 1–1 in the final minute of the second period when Nick Lidstrom gathered the puck in the Detroit zone. I can still hear my call of that next moment in my head because as much as any play that spring, it certified the Wings as a championship team.

"Lidstrom carries to center...long shot...scores! From center ice! That's just the break the Red Wings needed." Mickey Redmond would just say, "Oh my," but really, what else could you say to analyze that goal?

Vancouver goalie Dan Cloutier had been sensational up until that point, but that terrible goal just seemed to break his back and break the hearts of the Canucks. Brendan Shanahan made it 3–1 in the third period, and then Hasek stopped Bertuzzi on a penalty shot.

Yzerman scored the winner in Game 4, a 4–2 Wings victory, and it was back to Detroit tied 2–2. Hasek turned in a 25-save shutout in Game 5 at the Joe and the Wings made four first-period goals stand up for a 4–0 victory. Hull scored a hat trick in a 6–4 victory in Game 6, and the first hurdle was cleared.

Stevie Y had vowed that the Wings would not lose, and they backed up their captain's confidence with an impressive showing on the ice.

I Got It...No You Don't

St. Louis was ousted quickly in five games, and it was on to the showdown all hockey fans awaited, the Wings versus the Colorado Avalanche in the Western Conference final. For all intents and purposes, this was the Stanley Cup final, because no team in the East would be able to overcome either of these powerhouse squads.

It was as tight as you would have expected. Each team won once in the other's rink through the first four games, two of those tilts being decided in overtime. Game 5 was at the Joe and went to overtime tied 1–1. But when Colorado's Peter Forsberg scored 6:24 into the extra session, the Avs returned home with a chance to eliminate the Wings.

Once again, Detroit's mettle would be tested, but it was a case of mental fatigue...or was it overt bravado...from the Wings' long-time Colorado nemesis that would turn the tide.

The game was scoreless in the last minute of the first period when Avs goalie Patrick Roy made a glove save on Yzerman. Ever the showboat, Roy held his trapper skyward to remind Yzerman of the robbery he'd just committed, but on the way up, Roy dropped his bounty. The puck fell out of his glove to the ice, and Brendan Shanahan slammed it into the net for what would prove to be the winner in Detroit's 2–0 victory.

Sevens Are Wild

It was Game 7 between the Avalanche and Red Wings at Joe Louis Arena...or was it seventh heaven? Wings fans would go with the latter.

When it was done, the Wings had rolled the Avs in Game 7 by a 7–0 count. You imagine and you pray for something like that, but realistically, you don't ever think that it's going to happen—the reality would prove so accommodating to the dream sequence.

Detroit's Larionov, at 41 the oldest player on the ice, was winning draws before Colorado's Riku Hahl was born. Larionov cleanly won the puck from Hahl at the dot, and Tomas Holmstrom deflected a Steve Duchesne slapper through Roy just 1:57 into the game. It was 4–0 by the 12:51 mark of the opening frame. Detroit got three goals from its fourth line of Larionov, Holmstrom, and Robitaille.

The Avs were done, and so was the debate over which of these clubs was the NHL's best. The Wings took the league's second-best squad, the defending Stanley Cup champions, and turned them into something resembling the pre–Hanson Brothers Charlestown Chiefs.

Roy, so often the cause of sleepless nights and frustration in the lives of Red Wings fans, was simply finished—pulled after Fredrik Olausson's second-period goal increased the Wings' advantage to 6–0, en route to a 7–0 rout and a ticket to the Stanley Cup final.

Roy didn't even follow the goaltender's handbook and wait until replacement David Aebischer arrived at his goal crease. Roy nearly reached the bench before Aebischer was ready.

It was the fastest a Colorado player had moved all night and, for the first time ever, made Roy a wanted man in Motown.

"We want Roy," the Joe Louis Arena crowd chanted as the game continued.

Sometimes, being wanted isn't all it's cracked up to be.

It looked hauntingly similar to that December 1995 night when Detroit blew nine goals past Roy. Leaving the ice, Roy told Habs president Ron Corey he was done in Montreal.

"I remember thinking the next day, *They're going to trade him. This could be bad for us,*" Bowman recalled. "And it's been bad for five years, until we got a hold of Dom."

With Detroit's season on the line, without another loss to give, Hasek didn't surrender a single goal in the last two games of the Colorado series.

At that point, I knew that the Stanley Cup was coming back to Hockeytown. Sure, the team still had to deal with the Carolina Hurricanes in the Cup final, but when you'd knocked out the Mike Tyson of Stanley Cup netminders, dealing with Andrew Golota was going to be a picnic.

Hurricane Warning

Stanley Cup series can be funny animals. On paper, you look at the 2002 Cup final and the Wings dispatched Carolina in five games. Easy, right?

No, sir. The Hurricanes gave the Wings everything they could handle, even winning Game 1 at the Joe with a 3–2 verdict on a Ron Francis goal less than a minute into OT.

The Wings were 3–1 winners in Game 2 thanks to Grind Liners Kirk Maltby and Kris Draper, who each came through with a goal, but it was another OT battle in Game 3 that proved to be the defining moment of the series.

When you're a local TV broadcaster, you don't get to call the final three rounds of the Stanley Cup playoffs. That's just a fact of life. The networks take over, and you are left on the sidelines to watch and sweat it out like the fans do watching at home.

Game 3 of the 2002 final led to plenty of squirming for a lot of people. Tied 2–2 after regulation thanks to Hull's goal with 1:14 left in the third period, the teams battled through two scoreless OT sessions. Finally, at 14:47 of the third period, Larionov cut across the front of the Carolina net and lifted a backhander over Hurricanes goalie Arturs Irbe to end what was the third-longest game in Stanley Cup history.

From that point, Hasek took over. He allowed just one goal over the final two games, posting a 3–0 shutout win in Game 4. Hull got the winner in Game 4, and then Shanahan scored twice in a 3–1 win in Game 5, including the Cup winner.

Looking back over all the machinations of that masterful 2001–02 season, I was reminded of that famous line uttered by John (Hannibal) Smith, George Peppard's character on the *A-Team*—"I love it when a plan comes together."

The plan had come together. Stanley was coming back to Hockeytown.

Like Fine Wine

As Larionov aged, he upped the octane level, but it would be difficult to argue that he wasn't as energy efficient as he used to be.

The Wings center once allowed that the secret to eternal youth was two glasses of red wine every day. "Since I turned 40, I've increased it to 2 1/2 glasses a day," he confessed during the 2002 playoff run.

Two and a half glasses a day. But never on a game day. The formula never changed.

Neither did Larionov's plans following what he described as "the biggest goal of my career"—that overtime winner in Game 3 of the Stanley Cup final at the Raleigh Sports and Entertainment Centre.

The most fervent Manchester United supporter ever to sit in the Red Wings dressing room, Larionov's late-night performance didn't alter his early morning plans the next day to watch World Cup soccer in his hotel room.

He was glued to the set about five hours after netting his game-winner to watch his homeland of Russia drop a 1–0 decision to Japan. Soccer was his version of must-see TV.

Larionov insisted he'd never sit and watch a hockey game on television, and the way this Stanley Cup was being played out, who could blame him?

With their frustrating, smothering style, the Hurricanes were embedded in their system and managed to even dull the excitement of triple overtime, normally an edge-of-your-seat experience.

It was a system Larionov warmed to about as affectionately as he cuddled up to the coaching philosophies of Viktor Tikhonov when he was playing behind the Iron Curtain in the former Soviet Union.

Larionov spoke out as fervently against the neutral-zone trap as he did against the Soviet sports system, calling it "destroy hockey." He viewed that 2002 Stanley Cup final as being a duel of good versus evil and felt it was imperative for the future of hockey that Detroit's style of puck possession and emphasis on skill over interference emerge triumphant.

In sports, mimicry is the sincerest form of flattery, and teams that win set parameters for the rest to follow. But more than systems, what swung that set in Detroit's favor was depth, the same element that proved to be Colorado's undoing in the conference final.

The Wings didn't flag mentally like Toronto and Montreal ultimately did while battling through Carolina's frustrating roadblocks earlier in the playoffs. Detroit kept battling and found a way.

Captain Courageous

Nick Lidstrom was deservedly awarded the Conn Smythe Trophy as the MVP of the 2002 Stanley Cup playoffs, but if there was an award for the most courageous performance of the postseason, Wings captain Steve Yzerman would have proven a runaway winner.

What Yzerman was able to achieve during that spring's playoff run was nothing short of remarkable and will live on in my mind as one of the bravest performances an athlete has ever turned in during a championship season.

Stevie shared his ordeal in vivid detail—every grimace, every anguished stride was captured by the lens.

On the ice, the Captain wasn't anywhere near the All-Star player he'd been during a Hall of Fame career. His value during the Stanley Cup final against Carolina existed as a faceoff man and penalty killer. He contributed one goal during his last 13 playoff games.

Off the ice, he was never better.

As far as I'm concerned, Yzerman was best leader I've ever seen. Yzerman wasn't a gung-ho guy. When he did speak, the message was clear.

Moments after Detroit took a 3–1 lead in the Cup final set, Yzerman stepped up to his impromptu podium in the Wings' dressing room. He realized there were two off days before Game 5 in Detroit and that the city would be bubbling with enthusiasm over the impending Cup verdict. He knew this was a dangerous equation.

His advice to his teammates? Don't talk to anyone. Don't answer the phone. Ignore the doorbell. Keep the focus on winning Game 5.

He had that team ready for the next game the instant they won Game 4. He was in complete control the entire playoffs. It was a magnificent performance.

It was all the more amazing considering what Yzerman endured daily to keep himself in the game. His right knee, surgically repaired earlier in the season, was reinjured during the Olympics, but Yzerman kept playing, determined to gain gold for Canada.

Mission accomplished, he returned to Detroit and received the bad news—his knee was an absolute mess. He rested it the remainder of the regular season, playing just once in preparation for the playoff run.

Everyone—Yzerman included—was uncertain as to whether he'd be able to survive the grind.

Acknowledging the pain, but refusing to be overwhelmed by it, Yzerman persevered. He never missed a shift, let alone a game, leading the Wings by example as well as in playoff scoring with 23 points. He was a true leader for the team to follow. He showed a tremendous commitment in the playoffs, playing through injury, through pain.

"All I did was play the games," Yzerman recalled, downplaying his accomplishment. "At the time, I didn't realize it, but it was the beginning of the end for me.

"I played on a line with [Brendan] Shanahan and [Sergei] Fedorov. We played the trap, so I would glide around and force the play one way or another, and then they would do most of the work."

During the Cup celebration, Yzerman brought his children to ice level to live it with him, and held hands with his oldest daughter, Isabella, as they came out together to accept the Stanley Cup from NHL commissioner Gary Bettman.

He called it the most enjoyable year he'd had in hockey as he reveled in the celebration of Detroit's third championship in six years.

He shared his pain and he shared his jubilation in a performance that no one will ever forget.

That 2002 Stanley Cup Was Ahhhhhh Lock...Literally

From that first September day in 1997 when I began with the Wings, I've been spoiled. Sure it took months to see Sergei Fedorov play, since he was idled by a contract dispute that ended when the Ilitches matched Carolina's colossal offer. But the sheer skill and determination of this team that would eventually defend their Stanley Cup hold was a pleasure to take in on a nightly basis.

As broadcasters, we have nothing to do with the team's wins or losses. As I've mentioned elsewhere in these pages, nothing we say can influence the outcome of a game. I honestly thought the term "jinx" ended in third grade. But I guess not. At any rate, what we do have a part in, after the team on the ice prevails, is that we get to party! Not only do I own three Stanley Cup rings, of which I had no part but enjoyment, but I have also been granted days with the Cup. Teams are not obliged to give their broadcasters a day with the Cup, but the Wings do. We are usually the last to get time with it, after it has traveled with the players and staff throughout the summer and all over the globe.

But that worked out well for me in both 2002 and 2008, since I was able to surprise both Jamie and Arlyn with the Cup at their respective schools. In October of 2002, both of my kid's schools were holding a "Red Wings Day," which I had organized ahead of time with the respective school principals. Even the teachers didn't know until the Cup arrived. Everyone had their picture taken with it. Sharing that Cup and seeing all those smiling faces allowed me to feel like a winner.

At my daughter, Arlyn's, Doherty Elementary school in West Bloomfield, the arrival of the Cup went much more smoothly than its departure. As we were preparing to take the Cup to some of my friend's homes, the Cup keeper (that guy who wears the white gloves), Mike Bolt, realized that the Cup and his keys were both inside his rented SUV and the doors were locked.

Good thing it wasn't recess. Those kids would have had an entirely new spelling bee game. We called the local police department, and as dispatch put out the call that the "Stanley Cup was locked in a vehicle we needed access to," the patrol cars began rolling in. They were both serving and self-serving. Cup photos aplenty. That was the least we could do.

My 2008 backyard party at my Farmington Hills home paled by comparison, but was a whole lot of fun.

Hall of Fame Confirmation

Scotty Bowman was already enshrined when the Wings won the 2001–02 Stanley Cup, but before long, he'd have plenty of company in the Hockey Hall of Fame from among the roster of that Cup-winning club.

"At the time, you don't really think about it," Robitaille said. "But looking back, I think that was a dressing room with 10 or 11 potential Hall of Famers in it."

Igor Larionov was the first team member inducted when his name was called in 2008. An entire forward line of left-winger Robitaille, right-winger Brett Hull, and center Steve Yzerman followed in 2009.

Hull joined his father, Bobby, in the Hall, the only father-son combination in league history to each score more than 600 goals and register over 1,000 points.

Robitaille finished his career as the NHL's all-time scoring leader among left-wingers, but it's his first season in Detroit he remembers most fondly.

"I was a free agent [in 2001] and my wife [Stacia] asked me, 'Which team do you think has the best chance of winning the Cup?'" Robitaille recalled. "I said, 'Detroit,' so she said, 'Why don't we start with them?'"

"My agent called, and was I ever excited when I found out they were interested."

The 2001–02 Wings are just the third Cup winner to have at least three of its members occupy the same Hall of Fame class, joining the 1943–44 Montreal Canadiens (Toe Blake, Elmer Lach, Butch Bouchard, Kenny Reardon in 1966) and the 1925–26 Montreal Maroons (Punch Broadbent, Nels Stewart, Reg Noble in 1962).

With great hockey minds, Red Wings Executive VP/GM Ken Holland and Scotty Bowman, on December 31, 2009, at Wrigley Field in Chicago. The Red Wings won the game 6–4.

Defenseman Chris Chelios and left-winger Brendan Shanahan were inducted in 2013 and goalie Dominik Hasek in 2014. Defenseman Nicklas Lidstrom and center Sergei Fedorov, who joined the Wings via the 1989 NHL entry draft, joined the Hall together via the class of 2015.

You know there's a place reserved in the Hall for Pavel Datsyuk when his time on the ice in Russia is up, which will make Robitaille prophetic. That will put 10 players in, and Bowman makes it 11. Mike Ilitch is already there, along with Jimmy Devellano.

So what's the final verdict? Were the 2001–02 Red Wings hockey's greatest team?

I'll defer to someone whose opinion I respect immensely to answer that question.

Yzerman, ever the voice of reason, won't put his squad above all others.

"I think of those Edmonton Oilers teams in the 1980s, who could put a power play out of six of the best players in the world," Yzerman said. "And I think those Montreal teams in the 1970s and the Islanders teams that won four Cups in a row in the 1980s with the same group of players. They were better.

"We had a great team, but a lot of our players were at different stages of their careers."

Yzerman, as usual, registers a valid point.

But what a great team to call and recall fondly.

Editor's note: Following more than 3.6 million votes cast over a six week period from April 13 to May 25, 2017, the National Hockey League announced in June that the 1984–85 Edmonton Oilers have been selected by fans as the Greatest NHL Team of All Time.

CHAPTER 8

THREE CUP RINGS
IN TWO DECADES
OF BEING SPOILED

The wonderful Wings I've had the pleasure to know and call

He's Great

I first met Brett Hull while I was working in Toronto with the Maple Leafs and Brett was with St. Louis. There may be no "I's" in team, but there are two in *invoice*, and I was asked by my good friend and Toronto agent Rich Caplan if I would be the voice-over guy for a Kellogg's commercial featuring Brett Hull. I wasn't the voice of Tony the Tiger saying, "They're Great," but I did the rest. St. Louis was in town, so I went down for the morning skate and introduced myself to Brett, telling him something corny as in how we were both flakey, if you know what I mean? I asked if he would sign the script, but he thought I said "stick," so I ran with it.

"Yeah, a stick would be great," I told him. He said, "Come down after the game, and I'll autograph a stick for you."

Brett did, and I still have it. I already had one of his dad Bobby's signed, game-used sticks from the '60s. So I then called Bobby's brother Dennis, who was the first Hull to play for the Wings when he joined Detroit in 1977–78. I knew Dennis from many of his hilarious speaking engagements, and I asked Dennis if he had any game-used sticks at home that I could get him to sign to complete my Hull hat-trick collection. He said, "Your collection?" in that gravelly witty voice of his.

I explained that I had one from his nephew Brett and one from his brother Bobby, to which Dennis said, "Then what the hell do you want mine for?" That was Dennis' sense of humor.

I met Dennis out by St. Catharines to pick up the stick that he signed for me. It's now part of my Hull family set.

Brett came to Detroit in 2001 and played a key role in the Wings' Stanley Cup win that spring, but the 2003–04 season was not a good year for Brett. He's an avid golfer, and he was definitely putting on 18 that season in terms of his hockey career.

After the Wings were eliminated by Calgary in the second round of the 2004 playoffs, as Brett got on the bus, I shook his hand and told him what a pleasure it was over the years, both getting to spend time with him as well as the treat of getting to watch him play, just in case I didn't get to see him again. And he said, "Don't worry. You won't."

He was right. Brett was done with the Wings. As a postscript Brett didn't sign that commercial script I asked him to sign because he never heard me say it, until his jersey retirement night in St. Louis in December 2006.

The Greatest High Five

It was an honor to be asked by Nicklas Lidstrom to host his retirement night in 2013 when his No. 5 jersey took its rightful place among the best. I made a joke that night that Nick had a choice of two hosts, either Tomas Holmstrom or me, but seeing as he wanted everything to be understood, he made the right choice. Fellow Swede Holmstrom was Nick's best friend, but the players used to jokingly refer to his fractured English as Swenglish.

I will never forget the night Nick walked onto Redbird after a game and stopped at my seat and said, "How many goals in my career do you think Holmer (Tomas Holmstrom) has cost me?"

Tomas was one of the best in NHL history at pestering goaltenders, but he would have a tendency to literally step over the line. Tomas was often called for goaltender interference for being in the crease. I thought maybe 15 goals, but Nick insisted, "I told

Holmer on the way out here, it had to be over 20." Nick may have been right, but Holmer's ability to screen goalies maybe got him another 60.

When Nick's jersey banner went up, I remarked to the sold-out crowd, "The greatest high five in Detroit sports history." Which it was in more ways than one. With all the winning the Wings did while Nick was here, there was a lot of high fiving going on in the city.

The afterparty, seeing Nick so loose and in a completely different light than we were used to seeing him, it was a heck of a lot of fun. Nick was a generational player, a seven-time Norris Trophy winner, and the best defenseman I'd seen since my boyhood idol Bobby Orr.

With Nick Lidstrom in Washington following the 1998 Stanley Cup win. Nice way to begin a career with the Red Wings. Nick wouldn't win his first of seven Norris Trophies until three years later. (Photo courtesy of the Detroit Red Wings)

Near-Death Experience

The last thought that would cross my mind when I get to the booth to call a game is that I might have to talk about an unfolding tragedy, but that's what happened at the Joe the night of November 21, 2005, when Detroit defenseman Jiri Fischer went into cardiac arrest and collapsed on the Wings' bench during a game against the Nashville Predators.

As it happened, I remember saying, "Uh, oh, something's going on over at the Red Wings bench." The game is going on, and you could see the frantic movement taking place in the entrance to the hallway next to the bench, the walkway leading to the Detroit dressing room.

I was thinking at the time, because from my vantage point the view was somewhat blocked, I didn't know whether a fan had fallen over the railing and gone down or if someone had collapsed in the hallway. Jiri was down by the bench door, but I couldn't see him, I could just see everybody scurrying about.

At the time we were so careful. I think my network training kicked in to just be very aware of how it's being interpreted. That was really my first thought. We are on live television, I have to be careful here for everyone's sake. No guessing. From where our camera angle was, through our producers, maybe within two minutes we knew who it was. I could see the No. 2 on the sweater. We were pretty sure it was Jiri Fischer. But until I got the go-ahead, we let the pictures tell the story.

The first rule of broadcasting is don't speculate. Don't blurt out something that you're going to regret later. Go with the facts.

really nobody needs to see. I think we handled it very well, very professionally, but it's a moment you can't prepare for and let's face it, you're not prepared for.

The sadness that emerged was that even though Jiri recovered and still works with the Wings organization, he could never play again. The good thing that came from it was it led to the installation of defibrillators in hockey rinks. That started a big awareness of defibrillators, and we need more of them.

Unearthing a Rare Gem

The tale of the arrival of Pavel Datsyuk in Detroit is a spectacular combination of intrigue and subterfuge.

Detroit scout Hakan Andersson was getting on a flight in Russia to go to the outskirts of the country to watch Pavel play. He was going to scout him for a second time, and there was a bird dog from the Calgary Flames getting on the plane at the same time. Hakan was a little concerned, because he was certain that no one else had seen Pavel.

Turns out there was bad weather and the plane never did take off. He was actually thankful because the other scout never got to see Pavel, so he was still there for the Wings to steal in round six of the entry draft.

The Datsyukian Deke

Danny Gallivan, the great voice of mostly Montreal Canadiens' games on *Hockey Night in Canada*, had coined many phrases during his 32 years and more than 1,900 games called. From "scintillating" to "larcenous," or "caught up in the paraphernalia his 32 years and more than 1,900 games called. From "scintillating" to "larcenous," or "caught up in the paraphernalia [equipment]" or "cannonading drives," describing the velocity of a shot, Danny could always find unique ways to express himself. The former high school teacher from Nova Scotia once got a letter from a viewer saying there was no such term as "cannonading." Danny wrote back, "There is now."

Danny would call a spin move a "spinorama," an entry that is now included in the Canadian Oxford Dictionary. That term began as Danny was in Los Angeles on a game day, where he noticed that there were many signs of "Bowl-a-rama" or "rama" this or that. So with Danny's dandy use of alliteration (see what I just did there?), his thoughts turned to future Hall of Fame defenseman Serge Savard of the Canadiens and his penchant for spinning away from a checker. With that, he came up with the "Savardian spinorama."

I will often mention Danny's name when using one of his terms within a game, and Mickey loves to play off that because he loved Danny, who was calling the games when Mickey won his two Cups with Montreal, two of the 16 Stanley Cups Danny called while with the Canadiens.

So with that in mind, an Urban Dictionary online site chose to acknowledge "The Datsyukian Deke" origins.

> Pavel Datsyuk is a Russian-born NHL hockey player for the Detroit Red Wings. Wearing Number 13, as a centerman, Datsyuk has played in three Stanley Cup championship series, winning two Stanley Cups to date (2002 and 2008).
>
> He is known for his excellent skating, lightning quick hands, and ability to steal pucks with ease. His moves

were described as "Datsyukian" by Red Wings television announcer Ken Daniels. "Datsyukian" has become
a term to describe any unbelievable dekes or moves during a hockey game by Datsyuk or any other player.

I tried asking Siri on my iPhone the question "What is a
Datsyukian deke?" It was a phrase I coined for Pavel's penchant of
"undressing" opponents, but Siri couldn't quite grasp the language
adjustment on that question.

However, if you were to ask Siri, "Who is the Magic Man?"
(a phrase coined by Mickey Redmond), she will reply "Pavel
Datsyuk," with information and a picture.

And here's a story about Siri you may not know. The woman
behind the voice is the former wife of ex-NHLer Curt Bennett, a
forward with the Atlanta Flames during the 1970s. If you believe the
voice is somewhat condescending, that might explain the "former"
part.

Pavel could dazzle one-on-one like no player I had ever seen.
Mario Lemieux was also magnificent in that way. Pavel Bure and
Rick Middleton and Wayne Gretzky and Bobby Orr were great,
as well. But Pavel was jaw-dropping.

Pavel came on the scene in 2001. In his rookie year, he was
on a line for part of that Cup season with Brett Hull and Boyd
Devereaux. Brett coined the line "Two kids and an old goat," with
Brett being the latter. Brett, when things weren't going well, or the
pass wasn't right where he'd wanted it, certainly wasn't shy about
letting his linemates know. Pavel part of the time would claim
ignorance and the language barrier. We all believed that Pavel

grasped the English language at a much quicker rate than he ever let on. He was smart, even as a rookie.

I tried not to overuse the Datsyukian deke phrase. You could have probably used it two or three times a game with that guy, but I tried not to use it more than once every eight or nine games. I didn't want to overplay it.

A few years after I started doing it, I asked Pavel if he knew the phrase I used when he made a nice move. He said, "Datsyukian Deke. I love that." It was nice to hear that. And Pavel heard what was being said about him even in his rookie season. I got on the bus one night after a game where I had lovingly described Pav's skating style as being sort of like an orangutan, the way his arms would swing out to the side and a little bowlegged. Igor Larionov, who sat with Pavel right behind me on the bus, tapped me on the shoulder and said, "Pavel doesn't like the reference to a monkey." I reminded Igor it wasn't a monkey it was an orangutan. Igor said, "Pavel is serious." Okay, then. He wasn't monkeying around.

Pavel Does the Gordie

Pavel Datsyuk and Anaheim's Corey Perry have had their issues. Perry was wearing a mic one game and was caught on sound after tangling with one of the Wings saying, "Tell Pavel he's next."

The night Pavel got into the fight with Perry, he had a Gordie Howe hat trick—a goal, an assist, and a fight in the same game. The Red Wings got Pavel a framed picture, with his fight in the middle and the game sheet showing the Gordie Howe hat trick— and Gordie signed it for him.

A month or so later he came out of the dressing room with a large wrapped package. I asked him what it was, and he unwrapped it. Pavel said, "So proud. Best picture I own." He said, "This goes right up in the foyer of my house." Just to see how his eyes lit up, I knew it was a special moment for him. He'd got a Gordie Howe hat trick and had been in a fight with Corey Perry and he did okay. He held his own. He loved that photo.

Beast Mode

When you put together a short list of the greatest people I've known in the game, Brad McCrimmon is right at the very top. What a great guy, and such a funny dude. Brad was always so upbeat and positive, and he could spin a yarn better than anyone.

Everyone called him Beast, not Brad. He came to the Wings late in his career as a defenseman and later as an assistant coach under Mike Babcock. Brad was as far from a beast as anyone you'd ever meet—although I'm sure the forwards who had to try and get past him on the ice would disagree. Beast was the nickname Brad picked up when he was playing in Philadelphia because evidently he bore a striking resemblance to a Sesame Street muppet known as the Beast.

Brad was always smiling and carried himself with an every-man effervescence that never suggested he'd ever been an NHL star. Beast wouldn't even wear his 1988–89 Calgary Flames Stanley Cup ring. He didn't like to wear jewelry. Instead, he had it put on a chain so his wife, Maureen, could wear it as a necklace.

He was always looking at things the positive way, trying to encourage players when things weren't going well.

Brad wanted to be a head coach. He wanted to see what it would be like, and he wound up being a head coach with Lokomotiv Yaroslavl in Russia's Kontinental Hockey League.

On September 7, 2011, the Lokomotiv team boarded a flight headed to their first game of the season, but the plane barely got off the ground and crashed, killing everyone associated with the team.

McCrimmon died along with former Wings defenseman Ruslan Salei and goalie Stefan Liv, a onetime Red Wings prospect from Sweden who was close with many of Detroit's Swedish players.

Back in 1991, then-Detroit GM Bryan Murray acquired former NHL All-Star McCrimmon from the Flames, deploying his veteran presence as a soothing partnership for a rookie learning the ways of the NHL by the name of Nicklas Lidstrom.

"He was more of a stay-at-home defenseman, and that gave me a chance to be part of the offense," Lidstrom recalled. "He was my partner for every game my first year.

"He was that steady defenseman who stayed home all the time. He would protect me in situations when things got heated."

Off the ice, the two lived in the same area, so they carpooled to games. Their wives also bonded into a friendship.

"He helped me out a lot my first year in the league," Lidstrom said.

That was Beast. He was there to help everyone, and he never expected anything in return.

The day that his plane went down I was at the broadcast meetings in New York, and we were waiting for NHL commissioner

Gary Bettman to come in and talk to us. It was about 9:15 in the morning, and our phones started going off. You could hear a pin drop in that room. That was a very sad day for all of us.

People may not know this about me, but I guess I can have a foul mouth and swear with the best of them. I've never come close to swearing on the air and never would, but it's common around my friends and because I've been around the hockey world—they all do—and Beast was probably the best of the bunch. He could fly the F-bombs better than everybody. He could tell a story better than anybody. And we'd be brought to tears with laughter. Beast brought us to tears the day he left us. And when Joe Louis Arena bid farewell to hockey on April 9, 2017, Brad's wife Maureen brought us to tears that night too. She brought Brad's ashes with her to the Joe. Brad wanted to say goodbye too. As did Dani Probert, Bob's widow. A sprinkle of Bob's ashes were placed in the penalty box. Bob was "home" again.

Slow Ride to the Hall of Fame

One thing former Wings defenseman Larry Murphy never feared was having the wheels come off his game.

"That's impossible," said the slow-footed defenseman for the Wings, who estimated the only folks who might identify with his foot speed were "senior citizens."

Underestimated and undervalued during his career, Murphy was living proof that to the steady goes the race. During his time in Detroit, the solid, reliable rearguard surpassed Tim Horton, setting the record for the most games played by a defenseman in NHL history.

Being able to last a lot longer than a number of other players, Murph took a lot of pride in that accomplishment. His lack of speed made Murphy an easy target for fans. They'd mock him in Toronto and Washington, two of his previous NHL stops. But those inside the game pointed out how Murphy's sharp hockey mind made him a valuable part of four Stanley Cup championships squads—two with Pittsburgh in 1990–91 and 1991–92 and two with the Wings in 1996–97 and 1997–98.

Jaromir Jagr called Murphy the smartest player he'd ever seen. Detroit coach Scotty Bowman used Murphy and partner Nicklas Lidstrom, another thinking man's defenseman, to put the Philadelphia Flyers' Legion of Doom unit of Eric Lindros, John LeClair, and Mikael Renberg out of commission during the 1997 Cup final.

"We looked at the pairings, looked at what [Murphy] could and couldn't do, and thought we had an advantage," LeClair said. "But it turned out very bad for us."

The strategy, clearly a victory of brains over brawn, led to a Detroit sweep. "Murphy and Lidstrom made a joke out of that forward line," remembered Hall of Fame defenseman Denis Potvin. "They were three steps ahead of them, four games in a row."

The end result turned LeClair into a Murphy believer. "He was incredibly smart and very gifted with the puck," LeClair said. "That made it extremely hard to play against him."

Lidstrom, a perennial Norris Trophy contender and one of the game's most solid blueliners, marveled at Murphy's consistency. "His game was so steady," Lidstrom said. "He was so smart with the puck. He seldom made mistakes, and his positioning was perfect."

It wasn't always so smooth. Murphy was such a poor skater as a youngster, he was the last player picked in the draft for his house league in the Toronto suburb of Scarborough, Ontario. His coach wouldn't let him skate out past his own blue line because Murphy wouldn't be able to get back to his defense position if the puck was turned over.

By the time he was a midget, Murphy was helping the Don Mills Flyers to the Canadian title and a trip to Russia. Two years later, he was part of a Peterborough Petes team that won the Memorial Cup.

As a rookie with Los Angeles, Murphy set NHL rookie records with 60 assists and 76 points. "He reinvented excellence," suggested Bill Clement, who played in the NHL against Murphy. "He was the perfect example that you don't have to follow a prototype to be successful, but it took him years to get everybody else to believe it."

His self-effacing attitude helped Murphy laugh off his critics, but don't be mistaken—this guy who played with the Jack Dempsey style haircut was always a battler.

"We can't all skate like Howie Morenz," said Hall of Fame defenseman Harry Howell, who like Murphy and Horton, played over 1,400 NHL games. "Some of us had to find other methods to be successful. And Larry Murphy is a perfect example of someone who found those methods."

The Hockey Hall of Fame agreed with that assessment, inducting Murphy in 2004.

Murphy Made It Happen

Wayne Gretzky's fondest memory of Larry Murphy played out on an international stage.

Most hockey fans remember the pass Gretzky fed to Mario Lemieux for the winning goal against the Soviet Union in the final game of the 1987 Canada Cup. Few recall that it was Murphy who helped create the sequence that led to the goal by jumping up to join Lemieux and Gretzky on the rush.

"He made the whole play happen because he went to the net," Gretzky said of Murphy. "That created an opening. I faked the pass to him, and then I passed it to Mario."

Murphy admits he sometimes wonders how his fate would have changed if Gretzky had dished the rubber to him.

"I could have been a national hero," Murphy said with a smile. "Instead, I was the greatest decoy in hockey history."

Papa Bear and the Professor

That first season I did play-by-play for Wings games in 1997–98, I had a chance to call the names of two of the greatest ever to play the game in Igor Larionov and Slava Fetisov, known simply as The Professor and Papa Bear in the Detroit dressing room.

They were not only hockey superstars, they were two of the bravest people I've ever met, and that bravery had nothing at all to do with their exploits on the ice.

After helping their country to Olympic gold at Calgary in 1988, Fetisov and Larionov demanded changes and sought the opportunity to move from behind the communist Iron Curtain and pursue a career in the NHL. They were threatened with imprisonment for speaking out. Their families were shunned. Friends stopped coming by. When the doorbell did ring, Fetisov feared that it would be KGB agents coming to take him away.

Privileges were taken away. The advantages offered to elite athletes were no longer afforded those who spoke out against the system.

"We were no longer allowed to go abroad for almost a year," Fetisov said. "It was a critical moment in our lives. We were going up against a very scary monster."

Other than his family, and Fetisov's longtime friend and teammate Larionov, Russian chess master Garry Kasparov was the only voice to join their battle.

Fetisov would tear up at this thought. "They are my closest friends," he said. "They supported me all the way."

The Fetisov and Larionov–led campaign against the Soviet sports system in 1988 eventually led to Russian players being freed to play in the NHL. To them it was about standing up for what they believed in, literally putting their lives on the line.

"We had enough bravery to go against the Soviet system," Fetisov said. "Believe me, there were some pretty scary moments for all of us."

Larionov attacked national team coach Viktor Tikhonov and the Soviet communist sports system in editorials and magazine articles.

"They could have done anything they wanted to us, especially since we were in the army," said Fetisov, who admitted images of Siberia crossed their minds. "The army could send us anywhere, anytime."

Papa Bear and The Professor continued to fight and slayed the mighty Russian bear. "When they gave me a passport, and I got on that jumbo jet for the trip to North America for the first time in my life, I felt I had some freedom," Fetisov said.

More than the Stanley Cups, the Olympic and world titles, and numerous individual achievements, this moment provided Fetisov with the greatest joy.

"This is my biggest accomplishment," Fetisov said, while understanding that it couldn't possibly register with the same resonance with me.

"You have had your freedom your whole life. I waited 31 years for freedom."

Dallas Wanted Stanley

It all began for Dallas Drake in Detroit. He was a sixth round draft pick of Detroit in 1989, the greatest draft year for the Wings in their history. (That year, besides Dallas, the Wings selected Mike Sillinger, Bob Boughner, Nicklas Lidstrom, Sergei Fedorov, and Vladimir Konstantinov.) The hard-hitting forward broke into the NHL with the Wings in 1992, but he was traded away long before the team encountered Stanley Cup glory.

When Drake came back to the Wings as a free agent in 2007, it was with one objective in mind—to get his name inscribed on Lord Stanley's mug.

For Drake, as much as it broke his heart, each spring the Stanley Cup celebration was always must-see TV. He wouldn't miss it for the world.

"I'd always try to find a way to watch the Stanley Cup and see who'd hoist the Cup," Drake said.

On a warm spring night in Pittsburgh in 2008, he had the best seat in the house: front-row center, as Wings captain Nicklas Lidstrom accepted the Cup from National Hockey League commissioner Gary Bettman.

Much to Drake's surprise, Lidstrom skated toward him. "The guys kept pushing me out there, so away I went," Drake said. "My legs were real shaky, and I was just doing my best to hold it over my head.

"What an honor."

What a night. What a story.

Ask any NHL champion and each will tell you the Cup is like their children. Every one is special and none are more spectacular than the others. That's why for the guys who are experiencing this for the first time, the veterans will go out of their way to make it memorable.

In his 16th NHL season, Drake came back to Detroit and ascended the mountaintop. "It was a relief for me," Drake said. "I can't put into words how it felt."

As time wound down on the clinching game, on the bench, Drake remembered how his heart was beating and time seemed to stand still. "The clock wasn't moving," Drake said. "I was staring at my skates, hoping the clock might move faster, but it wouldn't."

Drake skated through 1,009 NHL regular-season games and 90 playoff contests before getting the first chance to get his hands on the Cup.

Mission accomplished, Drake hung up his skates that summer, retiring a champion.

Cheli's Calling Card

Be mean to outsiders. Be nice to insiders. And cheat whenever possible.

Biologist Lyall Watson's rules for genetic survival could also be interpreted as the laws of hockey according to Chris Chelios.

Beloved by teammates, reviled by opponents, but respected by all, Wings defenseman Chelios made it his mission to antagonize anyone not wearing the same uniform as him.

And since Mike Keenan didn't wear a uniform, he was fair game. While the mere mention of Mike even to this day launches

Brett Hull into a rant, Chris sees things differently, even if he and Mike didn't always see eye to eye.

Chelios was a warrior. He played every shift as if it were his last. He was a Hall of Famer and probably the most legendary American-born player in NHL history. His first defense partner in Montreal was Larry Robinson. After being traded to Chicago for Denis Savard, Cheli made the mistake of smiling at Larry during the pregame warmup. That didn't sit well with Mike, who then benched Chris for most of the game. The next day, leaving practice early, Chris went in and destroyed Keenan's office. And just to be sure Mike knew who did it, Chris left a calling card. He stuck that black Sher-Wood into a ceiling tile.

He developed this intense, combative approach to hockey while watching a childhood hero perform in Chicago—only this American idol didn't wear skates.

"The Chicago Bears had a linebacker by the name of Dick Butkus," Chelios said. "He was the toughest, meanest, nastiest competitor I've ever seen. Every kid on the South Side of Chicago wanted to be like Dick Butkus.

"I try to play hockey the way Dick Butkus played football."

Only the foolish would suggest he didn't.

Home Cooking

During the 2011–12 season, the Wings set an NHL record, winning 23 consecutive home games.

It was an incredible run, as the Wings obliterated the previous mark of 20 straight home wins shared by the 1929–30 Boston Bruins and 1975–76 Philadelphia Flyers.

They didn't lose a home game in December (5–0) or January (5–0). Nothing was able to slow the Wings. Through Thanksgiving, Christmas, New Year's, and Valentine's Day, they maintained a winning roll. They didn't miss a beat when No. 1 goalie Jimmy Howard went down with a broken right index finger, turning to journeyman third-stringer Joey MacDonald, who won six straight home starts after his recall from Detroit's American Hockey League farm club in Grand Rapids.

"Two weeks ago when I was watching on TV, they had 17 straight wins, and I was amazed," MacDonald recalled after he posted the record-tying 20th win. "Two weeks later, I'm right in the mix of things."

The numbers spoke for themselves. Detroit scored 93 goals during the streak, an average of 4.04 per game.

They posted four shutout wins and allowed just 34 goals during the stretch, a sparkling goals-against average of 1.47. Only twice during the 21 games did Detroit permit more than two goals. A dozen times, the Wings netted at least four goals.

The streak started November 5, 2011, with Howard's 5–0 whitewash of the Anaheim Ducks, and then they edged Philadelphia 4–3 on February 12, 2012, for their record-tying 20th win.

The St. Louis Blues were victimized three times during the 23-game stretch. The Anaheim Ducks, Dallas Stars, Phoenix Coyotes, and Edmonton Oilers double-dipped in defeat.

"I think that was one of the most consistent teams I've ever coached as far as bringing an effort each and every day," Coach Mike Babcock remembered.

Avery's Atomic Energy

Wings captain Steve Yzerman was moving hurriedly through the Olympic Village early in the 2002 Winter Games when his cellphone rang. Only a few hours earlier, Canada was shattered 5–2 by Sweden. The last thing Yzerman sought was conversation, yet he grudgingly answered the call.

"You guys really have to play your socks off," a voice screamed passionately into Yzerman's ear.

It was the voice of Sean Avery. That would be Red Wings rookie center Sean Avery, calling his captain, doing what everyone in Canada wanted to do after that game, calling out one of the Canadian players and giving him a piece of their mind.

Thinking about that episode can lead you down one of two paths regarding Avery. Either this guy has a death wish, or a lot of guts. Yzerman chose the latter side of the debate. He admired Avery's courage, respected his bravado. They kept talking that night and before and after every game during the Olympiad.

To get Avery's critique of Canada's performance?

"No," Yzerman said. "To calm him down."

You see, Avery is an excitable fellow, a combination of speed, annoyance, and work ethic during his NHL career.

"A very edgy guy," was how teammate Sergei Fedorov described Avery.

On the ice, he was a going concern. An agitator, an antagonist, what hockey people like to call a shift disturber. I must say one of the best lines I've ever heard from a hockey player, relayed to me from the ice, was when Avery turned to 6'6" Chris Pronger and asked him, "Hey Chris, what are you flossing with now, 120s?"

273

This was in reference to the thickness of skate laces that would fit in the front gap of Chris' upper teeth.

You never had to ask if he was in the lineup. Avery always ensured that he would be noticed.

There was no doubt Avery skated within the gray area of the rules. He took dives to draw penalties. He definitely liked to get into the middle of things.

Ultimately, though, Detroit's brass decided Avery's extra-curricular activities made him too dangerous as a long-term investment, and they traded him to Los Angeles in 2003.

It was a wise decision. Over the next few years, Avery committed racial slurs and made lewd comments about women, embarrassing himself and the league and earning fines and suspensions for his offensive comments.

On a personal note, I was going out after a game at the Joe with a woman I'd been seeing in 2003, and a friend of hers, whom I had not yet met, joined her at the game. Sean caught us on our way out of the Joe and asked if he could tag along. I will summarize the date by saying, I heard the lewd comments firsthand.

The odd thing about Avery is he'd be the first to admit that often when he opened his mouth, all that came out was stupidity. He wondered aloud whether he should seek some sort of counselling.

"There's going to be times when I do cross the line," Avery said during his time with the Kings. "I think everyone knows that. I think I've tamed it a lot more now, but there's still going to be times when everyone goes, 'What the heck did he just do or say?'" I lived that part!

The same trait that got him to the NHL is what gets him into trouble. Avery learned to live with that, but the rest of the NHL couldn't.

One league executive, after the Wings traded Avery, suggested that he'd play 10 years in the NHL for 10 different teams. He made it to 10 years but only four teams, playing for Dallas and the New York Rangers after the Wings and Kings.

Dom's Debut

Long before the Wings got Dominik Hasek in that 2001 trade with Buffalo, prior to his six Vezina Trophies and two Hart Trophies with the Buffalo Sabres, Hasek broke into the NHL as a backup to Ed Belfour with the Chicago Blackhawks, and former Wings coach Scotty Bowman remembered it well.

Bowman was coaching the Pittsburgh Penguins and they had the 1992 Stanley Cup final well in hand, holding a 3–0 series lead and a healthy advantage over the Blackhawks in Game 4 when Blackhawks coach Mike Keenan inexplicably pulled Vezina Trophy–winning goalie Belfour from the net in favor of an unknown rookie.

The shock waves reverberated through the Pittsburgh bench.

"We were all looking at each other wondering, *Who is this guy?*" Bowman recalled.

A moment later, Pittsburgh right-winger Jaromir Jagr skated to the bench, his complexion pale as a sheet. "We have to win this game," a shaken Jagr said, pleading with his teammates, a look of terror encompassing his face.

Being a fellow Czech, Jagr not only knew who this new goalie was, he knew the incredible feats he was capable of performing.

He knew this was Hasek and that the Penguins were in trouble.

Pittsburgh hung on to win—barely, by a 6–5 count—and Bowman still shudders at the thought of what might have been.

"He was just like he was in his prime," Bowman said of Hasek. "We couldn't get the puck past him. I'm just glad they didn't decide to put him in for Game 1."

A Threepeat

Hasek twice left the Wings only to return to their net, and when he came out of retirement to join Detroit for a third go-round in 2006, Bowman was someone who thought it was a brilliant idea.

The man who coached Hasek when the Wings won the Stanley Cup in 2001–02 was also the man who in 1968 coaxed another legendary goalie back into the game when he convinced Jacques Plante to join the St. Louis Blues.

"I knew he could still play," Bowman said of Plante, knowledge he'd gained from firsthand experience. Shortly after Plante hung up his skates with the New York Rangers following the 1964–65 season, Bowman, coaching the Montreal Jr. Canadiens, convinced Plante to make a one-game comeback with his club for an exhibition match against the Olympic champs from the Soviet Union. Plante performed sensationally and the Jr. Habs stole a 2–1 decision.

Two years later, Bowman was hired by the expansion Blues, who reached the Cup final their first season of play behind the Conn Smythe performance of veteran goalie Glenn Hall.

Buoyed by the success of one old-time goalie, Bowman figured a 1–2 punch might take the Blues even further and contacted Plante to feel out his interest toward getting back to the NHL.

"He was 39, but he got knee surgery done after he retired and was feeling good physically," Bowman recalled. "He was a really good athlete, and he was definitely ready to return."

Bowman planned to quietly select Plante's rights from the Rangers in the June 12, 1968, NHL intra-league draft, but Plante, like Hasek ever the showman, had other ideas.

"He came to the NHL meetings and called a press conference to announce his intention to return," Bowman said. "We decided we'd better take him in the first round, before anybody else took him. It was lucky for us, too, because Minnesota was going to take him with the pick right after us."

Anticipating some rink rust on his new netminder, Bowman initially decided to handle Plante's comeback delicately.

"At first, we mostly played him against the other West Division clubs," Bowman said. "But it didn't take long to figure out he was going to be fine."

The Hall-Plante tandem worked better than Bowman figured it would. The second-year Blues won the Vezina Trophy, allowing an NHL-low 157 goals against in 76 games, finishing 39 goals better than the Rangers, their nearest rival.

Bowman felt that Hasek, 38 at the time of his latest comeback, would provide equal solidity to the Detroit net in tandem with Chris Osgood, another veteran Stanley Cup winner.

"They were different styles of goalies, but very similar in that they were both perfectionists, dedicated to fitness, and determined to always find ways to improve," Bowman said, comparing Hasek and Plante. "They're definitely unique individuals, but both men played the game with a lot of confidence."

Bowman proved to be right, yet again. The Hasek-Osgood duo took the Wings to the conference final stage in 2006–07 and all the way to a Stanley Cup title in 2007–08.

Interestingly, Hasek (2001–02, 2003–04, 2006–08) was the third Red Wing to serve three separate stints with the team, and all three were goalies.

Terry Sawchuk (1950–55, 1956–64, 1968–69) and Jim Rutherford (1970–71, 1973–81, 1982–83) were the others.

My Favorite Calls

If truth be told I have three favorite calls, but those were telephone calls made to me. One by Brian Williams when I was 17 inviting me to watch him do the dinnertime sports at CBC. Another came from the Oshawa radio station offering me my first job in the business. And a humbling call came from the Red Wings wanting me to be their play-by-play voice on television in 1997. Three memorable calls made to me.

Here are some of the more memorable calls I made from the booth.

Buzzer Beater

Talk about cutting it close, I still recall the goal Henrik Zetterberg scored to beat Vancouver 4–3 in overtime during the 2009–10 season.

There were .03 seconds left on the clock when it went in. As Zetterberg cut to the net from the boards, I was aware that time was of the essence and I said "better hurry" on the call. Who knows? Maybe he heard me.

Shoot the Puck

The Wings weren't scoring on the power play very often during the 2016–17 season and it was because they weren't shooting enough.

I'm calling the game and Mike Green got the puck in the high slot and I could see Thomas Vanek tapping his stick on one side and Gus Nyquist tapping his stick on the other side, both wanting a pass. I was so frustrated with the power play I said, "In front to Green. Shoot the puck! Scores."

I was thinking in my head, *Don't pass*. Stop the passing. It was one of those calls where you kind of anticipate the moment.

Round and Round He Goals

Probably the goal I called that I hear about the most is that incredible overtime tally by Gus Nyquist against the Ottawa Senators on December 27, 2014.

It was still four-on-four overtime then and Gus was just holding the puck and holding the puck. It wound up being 28 seconds of game time. It was all one sequence. I remember saying at the time, you could get dizzy watching this. It was probably the longest goal call I ever did.

Here's exactly how I described this remarkable goal:

"Nyquist forced on his backhand the whole way by MacArthur. And now back again. He's going to get dizzy. Now he'll go on his forehand. Now to the backhand again for Gus Nyquist. Trying to get away from Cowen. It's all Nyquist on this shift. He keeps on going. Nyquist has it. Nyquist shooting…scores! Game winner, what a shift! Gus Nyquist! 3–2 Detroit! They win it in Ottawa."

I was surprised he wasn't exhausted and that he was still able to shoot the puck.

Milestone Men

To call any milestone goal is so cool. You wait for it. You hope you get a good call. I think maybe on Brett Hull's 700th goal I got a little too high on it. You want it to be clean. You talk to them after they've seen it and you hope they come up to you and say, "Good call."

Steve Yzerman's 600th against Edmonton on Tommy Salo was a flukey goal from the side of the net. I wasn't even sure it went in. It was like Patrick Kane's Cup winner for Chicago in overtime in the 2010 final that nobody saw go in. That's probably my worst nightmare, as a play-by-play guy, not to see the puck in the net.

When it's a network game and we're not calling it, and somebody on the Wings is about to net a milestone goal, I'm thinking don't score today because I want to be part of it. Unless of course the team needs it for a win!

CHAPTER 9
COAST TO COAST

End-to-end rushes from my time with the Wings

This Is SportsCentre

My beautiful wife Rebecca had never been to the Hockey Hall of Fame. So in the summer of 2015, while visiting my family in Toronto, we made our way down to Yonge and Front Street. Years ago, when I was with CBC Television, director of corporate and media Kelly Masse and company were nice enough to let me into what they call the dungeon, where they store all of the artifacts not currently on display because only so much can go into the Hall of Fame at any one time.

There I saw Terry Sawchuk's 100th shutout stick on the floor with a bunch of other wood collectibles. I peeked into the drawers of old jerseys. I tried on Phil Esposito's old sweater from the wool days, and it was tight on me. I'm thinking, "Did these things shrink?" Esposito only wore the old shoulder caps, but even then, how did this thing fit him?

In the Hall, TSN had a makeshift studio where you could read off a teleprompter, and pretend you were hosting SportsCentre. (re for Canada, eh). They handed me a script outline for footage of Alec Martinez's 2014 Stanley Cup Game 5 overtime winning goal for Los Angeles against the New York Rangers. I'd call the highlights as if I were doing SportsCentre. I'd say something like, "Welcome to SportsCentre. I'm Ken Daniels and the Los Angeles Kings are reveling in their Stanley Cup victory...yada, yada, yada."

Now, I had done highlights for TV since 1985 at CBC, so I wasn't breaking new ground here. After I'm done and leaving their little studio set, the guy says to me, "You know, I've been here for a year and a half doing this, and you're the best one I've seen."

He had no clue who I was. But I took the compliment, and said thanks, knowing I still had it.

Split Jury

I've lived in Detroit since 1997. It was February 2016 the first time I was called for jury duty at Oakland County Courthouse. Now that I consider lucky.

It was a Monday afternoon in the middle of February, and the Wings had a game in Pittsburgh two nights later. We would be flying out Tuesday afternoon. Sometimes when you go to jury duty the cases start right away. I'm doing my civic duty, and people who'd been involved in this beforehand advised me to let the judge know that I've got a unique job where there's no one to replace me.

There's about 30 people waiting to be selected for jury duty, and I'm now in the box with 12 other people and the lawyers are determining which of us to keep and which of us to excuse. They are asking all of us questions to determine prejudice. Now the other side of celebrity comes into play because I didn't want to look like a jackass. I've got to say I was impressed with both the prosecutor and the defense attorney. They both knew the names of all the jurors in the box and I don't know how they memorized them all so quickly. And remember, I'm a guy who knows a thing or two about memorizing names.

The judge finally says, "Is there anything else that you prospective jurors have to say?" I put my hand up and I explained my situation without mentioning my exact job, but she basically told me that she didn't care. She told me it was my civic duty to serve and I should be honored that I'm here. This is what we all do regardless of our occupation. I was just going by what two other people in the legal industry had told me to do, but it didn't carry any weight with her.

I could see the prosecutor looking at me. I'm sitting there for another 10 minutes, watching as two other jurors are recused. I thought, *well, this isn't good.* I am so getting on this jury. I'm going to miss the game. One more juror was recused and then after that, the prosecutor stood up and said, "We'd like to recuse juror number three," which was me. I grabbed my stuff and as I was walking out, I looked at him and I said thanks, and he mouths, "You're welcome." So I believe he knew what I did for a living.

Here's the kicker—I had to go back to the jury room in case there's another jury I could be called for, but the room was empty. I figured everyone was at lunch. I walked up to the front desk and inquired and was told I could leave seeing there were no more cases for the day. I was good for another three years.

As I'm sprinting out of there, two of the guys who were recused before me were still waiting outside. One of them said, "You got out. We were worried about you, because we know you've got a game in Pittsburgh." I guess being known sometimes can help.

Datsyuk and 15%

I've changed seats a few times over the years on the team plane. When I first came to the Wings, Sergei Fedorov was seated across from me drinking his Vernors. Then I was in the broadcasters' section. Then I moved back to sit with Bill Roose, who was the team's website writer, and Dan Mannes, the team videographer. We had lots of laughs staying occupied.

Pavel Datsyuk's group sat in a foursome across from us with Justin Abdelkader and team masseur Sergei Tchekmarev, "Chica," as the players call him, and Alexey Marchenko. They would play dominoes from wheels up to wheels down. Pavel didn't feel like playing one night after a game and because Bill wasn't there, Pavel came and sat in the empty seat next to me.

I was watching video prepping for a Michigan–Michigan State hockey game at the Joe in 24 hours, and every once in awhile, Pavel would interrupt me and say, "Rewind. Let me see," and he'd make some jokes in his unique sense of humor about me doing too much work. Pavel wouldn't stop, and he was just driving me crazy. No one thought for sure in December 2015 that this would be Pavel's last season, but I had heard rumblings about it and was pretty certain it would be.

I made a joke about him not going to college and having to earn money the hard way, and he said, "I am earning a living the hard way. All that escrow. Way too much escrow—15 percent, 18 percent. Escrow is ridiculous." The players are required to pay a percentage of their salaries into an escrow account to guard against league revenue drops as of the 2013 CBA. I asked Pav, "Had enough?" And he said, "Oh I have had enough. No more escrow." And that's when I got the feeling that maybe Pavel was done, although ultimately I don't think it was escrow, I think it was predominately family.

I still think that what Pavel did, knowing his heart was back there in Russia, he should have signed one-year deals instead of the three-year pact he signed in 2014. Leaving a year before his contract was finished left the Red Wings in a huge bind, as per CBA rules when players don't honor contracts signed after age 35.

Wanting to go home, I get all that. I understand. But he probably wanted to go home before he signed the deal. As wonderful as it was to watch his incredible time with the Wings, that was a "Datsyukian deke" I didn't appreciate.

Coffee Filled to the Rimer

I start drinking coffee in the morning, and on game nights I don't stop until about midway through the third period. No wonder after a game I don't fall asleep until around 2:30 in the morning. As prep for a game, I'll watch video the night before if the other team had played within a couple of days. On game day, I work for about five hours on any one particular game doing notes. I arrive in the booth a couple of hours before the game to look over things that my producer needs me to see, and I will leave my notes out in front of me on the console. I've already got the cup of coffee next to me. Over the years it's become custom that the broadcast crews get together and shoot the breeze about their respective team they call, knowing what we should or shouldn't reveal. We are still more apt to get an honest assessment that way on players than we would from the opposing head coach. Jeff Rimer, the Columbus Blue Jackets play-by-play guy, comes into the booth at Nationwide Arena in Columbus to visit and Jeff's left hand knocked my coffee all over my notes. I was not happy. He apologized, but I never let him forget it. It has become a running joke between us now.

Burke's Bluster

Brian Burke was still the GM in Anaheim, but the rumors were swirling that he was about to leave. The Ducks were running into a lot of cap issues and weren't doing well. While calling the game in Anaheim, I said Brian Burke would be leaving the Ducks at an opportune time. Based on the way the team was structured with their cap issues, he would be getting out while the going was good.

Not really a big deal, I thought. The rumor was out there that he was going to Toronto. The next day we're in Nashville, continuing on our road trip, and Ken Holland calls me in my hotel room and says, "You'll never guess who just emailed me?" I said, "Who's that?" "Brian Burke. He's pissed." I said, "At what?" He laughs. "Whatever you said on the air." And what did I say? "Well, according to Burkie, he said, 'Tell that genius play-by-play guy of yours that it has nothing to do with getting out while the going is good. I have no intention of going anywhere.'" I laughed more than Kenny and I said, "We'll see." Months later, Burke was gone to Toronto. But his intentions of staying were good.

That's Burkie. He's a good hockey man, with a huge heart but likes to be a bully at times.

Brian also yelled at me years earlier when I was on the FAN Radio in Toronto. Brian was working for the NHL then in charge of player discipline, and he was on the air with us. There was a Leafs–Red Wings game and Sergei Fedorov's stick came up, hit the crossbar, and caught Toronto's Tie Domi in the face, and there was no call, no suspension. I asked him why there was no suspension and Burke said, "Because his stick hit the crossbar first and then came up and hit Domi." But I asked, "Doesn't a player still have to be responsible for his own stick?"

When I got off the air, having posed a question to Brian that he didn't like, I got back into my office and the intercom is on and our producer says, "Oh is Burke pissed."

When I asked why, the producer told me, "He said, 'Who the bleep asked that bleeping question of me about the stick going off the crossbar?'"

I said, "Did you tell him?"

He said, "No, I just told him it was the sports guy, and he hung up." Thankfully, Burkie wouldn't have known that he was mad at me. Until now.

Take the Long Way Home

Mike Babcock doesn't hang around any longer than need be at morning skates on the road on the day of a game. Like clockwork, he's off the ice within 20 minutes of getting on it at 11:30. He's quick primarily because he returns to the rink within three hours of leaving it. So instead of waiting for the players to change and taking the team bus at 12:30, Mike does his media briefing and hops in a cab and is gone by 12:10.

On this day, we were playing the Devils at the Prudential Center in Newark. I didn't feel like hanging around either, so Mike said come back with me. We hailed a taxi and I told the driver we were going to our hotel in Short Hills, New Jersey. This was late November of 2014. Mike was in the last year of his contract with the Red Wings and there was much debate about whether he would stay. I asked him that question, and he said he'd love to. He sounded sincere, and said he needed a six-year deal. He wanted to raise the bar for the coaching fraternity. No one could blame him for wanting that. He had earned that right, becoming a "free agent," just like the players. I said to him rather emphatically that he was going to Toronto. He said, "Not a chance." (Okay, Lloyd Christmas.)

Now, as time passed on our drive, Mike got on his cell with his wife, Maureen, and I realized this drive looked completely different. Wrong direction. The driver didn't have a clue where the hotel was. As I leaned forward to ask, Mike heard me, and in the midst of ignoring his wife, blurted out, "Where the hell are we going? Driver, I'm not a patient man."

I told the driver, "I can vouch for that!"

I then heard Mike telling his wife, with a slight grin on his face, that "Daniels got us lost," which wasn't true at all. A ride that should have taken 20 minutes took us 45. When we finally got to our hotel, all Mike said to me was, "You're damn lucky we beat the bus back here!" He paid. I got lucky twice.

It must have been the eight-year deal that made Toronto palatable.

Top Cat Toby

We lost a great guy when Toby Cunningham died early in 2017. I loved working with Toby. He was the man who did it all for our Red Wings UPN–50 broadcasts. We called him Top Cat. He produced, he directed.

But the one thing about Toby, he was always a company guy first.

The Red Wings had come back from an 0–2 series deficit in the first round of the 2002 playoffs to beat Vancouver in six games out in British Columbia. That was the game that Steve Yzerman broke Gordie Howe's all-time Red Wings playoff scoring record. It's 1:30 in the morning Detroit time when Toby and I are about to have a disagreement, the only blowup we ever had.

We still have a pretty big audience back in Detroit because the Red Wings are moving on, and four straight wins had people taking notice.

Veteran legendary broadcaster Ray Lane was on the ice with one interview live, when Toby said, "Okay, we're going off the air." I hit my talk back button, which takes me off the air and directly to Toby in the truck, and I said, "What do you mean we're going off the air?" Toby responded, "We're going off the air. The game's over. It's 1:30 in the morning." So what if it's 1:30 in the morning? Steve Yzerman just broke Gordie Howe's playoff record.

I just saw Ray on the ice interviewing Steve for playback, but I thought that would be in moments. Not 21 hours later. Toby told me, "We're holding the interview for news tomorrow [now tonight]."

UPN–50 only had 10 o'clock news, so I asked Toby, "You're going to hold this for 21 hours when we've got exclusive rights?"

He said, "Well, there aren't that many people up. Our viewership isn't going to be that great right now."

I said, "I'm not so sure. It was 1:30 in the morning, but people hanging in with us now would be more than will be watching the 10 o'clock news anyway. I think we owe it to the fans."

"No, we're going off the air" Toby insisted.

I asked, "To what? *Moesha?*" That was one of UPN's shows back then. Sure enough, we said goodnight. I did more than a Dave Hodge pencil flip. When I saw Ray after the game downstairs he was in a good mood until I told him his Yzerman interview that he thought aired, did not. Ray made a beeline into the truck to find Toby.

Toby was a fantastic guy, but as we say in the play-by-play vernacular I bet he'd like to have that one back.

Emmy Worthy

On December 12, 2006, I did play-by-play from where I was told it had never been done before—between the benches. I was squeezed in between the Red Wings and Ottawa Senators benches. Mickey Redmond remained upstairs. I would also be holding a camera they would cut to while I was calling the game. They called it the "Kenny Cam," and it gave a different view.

That's the game I remember Nicklas Lidstrom, who could thread a needle in the dark, passing from the far corner, through several pairs of skates, up the right wing perfectly onto Jason Williams' stick 90 feet away. Incredible.

You do lose perspective from between the benches. Looking to my right or the left, from the far goal post to the corner, it's a tough vantage point to see that area. You've got to go without notes, because there just isn't a place to put them.

I remember the next day, I was driving to the airport. Art Regner was on the radio and made mention about enjoying the broadcast but having one bone to pick. I wondered what bone could he have to pick? His complaint was that there was maybe a minute or so to go in the game and with the Red Wings trailing, Mike Babcock pulled his goalie and used his timeout to diagram where he wanted the players to be for a center ice faceoff. Pretty basic stuff.

As I'm saying what Mike's illustrating, the guys are coming out of the scrum and getting ready for the faceoff. Sure enough, they have a guy lined up wide left.

291

Between the benches in December 2006, doing play-by-play and operating the Kenny Cam, as Detroit played Ottawa. (Photo courtesy of the Detroit Red Wings / Dave Reginek)

And not only was I the play-by-play guy and camera operator, I also did interviews (here with Henrik Zetterberg) on the ice during the Red Wings–Senators game. Let's see Pierre McGuire do all that! (Photo courtesy of the Detroit Red Wings / Dave Reginek)

Art thought I was giving away game secrets. My point was how the heck was I giving away secrets? Did Art really think the video guy from the Ottawa Senators dressing room is running out to the bench as I'm saying that, yelling, "Hey coach, they're going to line up with someone wide left!" As if they can't see it and haven't prepared for all this? Visiting teams listen to their own play-by-play guys on video. Not the opposing team's feed.

I called the radio station to get on the air with Art to lay out my argument, thinking he was off base. As I get on the plane, Mike Babcock had obviously been listening on the way out and says, "Seriously? That's where he went with it?" And I said, "Thank you very much." Even Babs knew it was a ridiculous argument, and of anyone, he'd be the one with the most reason to be upset. People must have liked the innovation, though. On June 16, 2007, at the 29th annual Michigan EMMY Awards, I won my first local EMMY. I did not thank Art.

Five Minute Major for Charging

More often than not on road trips years ago I would find additional charges on my bill at checkout time. Obviously, I knew someone was using my name, but I had to find out who was doing it.

As I was meeting a friend for dinner in Washington I went through the lobby bar, and I saw a group of Red Wings staff—goalie coach Jim Bedard, assistant coaches Barry Smith and Joe Kocur, and some others. The next day checking out, I had a $70 bar bill. I asked them what time the charges were made. They asked me, "Can you sign your name?" so I did. They actually took my signature to compare with the one that was on the bill—and no other hotel had ever done that—and had one of their people come down to verify different handwriting. We are in Washington after all. "It's clearly not his," the verifier says. I said, "No it's not."

Later on that season, we're in Arizona, staying at the Wigwam Resort. I was working out in the fitness area and there were tennis courts not far off. I saw Joey and Barry come out after having played tennis. I figured this is going to be on my bill. Sure enough, as I checked out, there's 50 bucks for tennis court fees. Again I said that it wasn't me but told them who it was. I don't know if it wound up on their bill or not.

Our radio voice, Ken Kal, had charges on his bill, too—many times. I wonder who was doing that? At one hotel Kal had a fitness charge and he walked up to the front desk and said, "Seriously, look at me. Do you think I was in the fitness room?" They immediately took off the charges.

After Barry left us to go to Chicago, I said, by the way, thanks for putting all those charges over all those years on my hotel bill. And Barry threw Joey right under the bus. "It wasn't just me," he said. "It was Joey, too."

Ever since Barry and Joe left, Kal and I have never had any extra charges on our bills.

A Different Call

Getting a night off from a Red Wings game due to an NBC broadcast actually proved to be a lot of fun. The Wings were playing Pittsburgh at the Joe. Red Wings legendary public address announcer Budd Lynch couldn't do the P.A. that night so they asked me to fill in. I'd done P.A. early in my career before I got into play-by-play. I was working for Mike Keenan when he was coaching at the University of Toronto, doing P.A. for the Toronto Varsity Blues at Varsity Arena when they won the Canadian university national championship.

I was used to calling goals, but at the Joe you've got a lot of scripts to read and a little microphone feedback. It just means you have to speak more slowly with a pause. Erich Freiny, who does the P.A. now, does a lot of stuff during the games you wouldn't think about until you are actually doing it. People who were in the crowd later told me that they thought they recognized my voice, but they weren't sure it was me. Practicing with Paul Morris back in the '80s at Maple Leaf Gardens came in handy.

Father's Day

It was Hockey Day in Canada in 2008 and the Wings were playing in Toronto. My dad, Marvin, was 93 at the time. He was 45 years old when I was born. That seems young today, but back in 1959 it wasn't the norm to have a newborn at his age. My mom had four miscarriages between my brother Gary and me. Gary is seven years older, and my brother John is 11 years older than I am. There's 13 years between me and my sister Linda. When I was 10, my dad was 55, so I didn't spend a lot of time with him in those years. As I got older we got closer.

In my youth, my dad did a lot of golfing. His game was consistent. He was on a golfing weekend with friends at the Cutten Fields course near Guelph, Ontario, but found his diamond wedding ring was hurting his finger. So he put it in his pocket but lost it when he pulled out his handkerchief. The next day, he felt miserable about losing that ring but hit his tee shot 200 yards and a little too far right. When he went

With my wonderful father, Marvin, then age 93, at the Air Canada Centre in February of 2008. He loved it. I loved it more.

to inspect the ball to see if it was his, there was his ring 6″ from where the ball landed. Now that is finding a diamond in the rough!

My dad was always very proud of what I did. My brother brought him down to the Air Canada Centre for that game in 2008 because my dad had never seen me work live, he had only seen me on TV. We were standing in the Red Wings bench watching warm-up, and my father was fascinated by the speed and the size of the players. We put him on our pregame show, and I did a two-minute interview with him from the bench. You can YouTube it if you wish. He talked about the old days and how they used to use horse droppings for pucks. He said, "I don't know if I can say that on TV." Well, I told him, you just did. He was talking about

297

Busher Jackson and Charlie Conacher, his favorite Toronto Maple Leafs growing up. It was actually pretty enlightening talking to him about how the game used to be.

During the game he sat right between Mick and me, and in the second intermission he was my guest interview. As we came on camera I introduced him and asked him a question. There was this pause that seemed like an eternity, and I wasn't sure if he was going to speak. In reality it was maybe a two-second delay, and he looked up and started talking and it went well. As soon as the interview ended he said, "I'm so sorry about that."

"About what?"

"I paused. I didn't know what to say."

"How come?"

"Because I looked at the monitor, and I saw how old I looked."

I said, "Well you're 93 years old. What did you expect?"

Not being as close to my dad until I was maybe 15 or 16, to be able to do this with him and have him be there with me, gave me chills. To know that it meant as much to him as it meant to me at that point was wonderful.

He actually emailed me a note about the experience the next day.

Dear Ken,

Thank you for introducing me to the Air Canada Arena. I thoroughly enjoyed everything. The interview at ice level. I was thrilled to sit between you and Mickey while you were broadcasting. I want you to know that I am very proud of you, Kenny. I could feel the love and respect you showed towards me while introducing me to your friends. I love you. I was like a kid off the farm in the big city. Maybe I might make it again down the road when you broadcast from Toronto. It could happen. Mickey is a wonderful person. I really enjoyed his friendly company. I hope the interview with me went well.

Love,

Dad

I found out about the Detroit job while I was in Buffalo doing the 1997 Stanley Cup playoffs for *Hockey Night in Canada,* and in December 2011, in the same building, I'm sitting watching the morning skate with Ken Holland and my sister Linda calls me to tell me my dad had passed. I did the game in Buffalo that night—it was too late not to do it—but I did it with a heavy heart. It was a rough night. Ken Holland made the call back to the Red Wings and arranged a hotel and a flight for me so that I could go to Toronto.

Three weeks before, my dad, who was 96 now, was in fine health, and Kenny Holland was driving into Toronto a few days before our game there to scout a junior game. He said, "Why don't you drive in with me, and you can visit your dad. I'll drop you off." My dad was still living on his own and had a girlfriend named Mildred who was 91. (My mom had passed five years before.)

After Kenny took me to my dad's place my dad and I went for dinner (he drove), and then we went grocery shopping for him. We're in the supermarket and my dad holds up a bunch of bananas and says, "No one my age should be buying green bananas, should they?" We both laughed at that notion. A week later, my dad had a stroke. Had Kenny not suggested I drive in with him I wouldn't have had that time. Hockey gods. My dad was in the hospital and couldn't speak anymore. We weren't even sure if he was aware of what was going on around him.

In part, I owe the Detroit job to my father. He had been an American citizen born in Toledo, Ohio, where he lived until he was eight years old. My dad worked hard in the '90s to regain his U.S. citizenship, which he had lost, just in case I ever needed a green card to work in the United States.

Citizen Ken

The green card I had, in part thanks to my father, lasted until I decided to become a U.S. citizen in 2007. It was a nice ceremony in downtown Detroit, and believe me, my name was the easiest to pronounce among the hundreds there that day.

There was a fair bit of studying involved to make sure I passed that test. I was never a history major, unless it involved Gordie Howe and Johnny Bower. But it got me to thinking of the major differences between Canadians and Americans.

Sure the "out and about" sounds stand out, and the apology of "sorry" has a distinct Bobby "Orr" about it.

And as much as I am a U.S. citizen now, I will never forget Kraft Dinner as a main nutrient source. I know that Thrills gum tasted like soap, but I still chewed it for at least a few minutes. I know that Toronto is not a province. I know what a toque is. I still get excited when American television mentions Canada. Loonies and Toonies though, are much too heavy to lug around (they are the Canadian one and two dollar coins). I have adapted and dropped the "u" from color, labor, and honor.

But I have not adapted to calling it a "candy bar" rather than a "chocolate bar." We really need to make Coffee Crisp a must-get in the United States. And while we're at it, can we include Harvey's hamburgers? I do miss being able to get my milk in bags, and not just jugs and cartons. I finally spent all of my Canadian Tire money. And I got to start drinking legally as a teenager. Some things never change, eh?

My Cup Call. Almost...

I will never forget the phone call while sitting in my home office on the morning of the Stanley Cup final Game 6 of 2008. The program director on the Red Wings flagship radio station calls and says Ken Kal has lost his voice and would I do the game? Sure. Twist my arm. Really hard! Because we had finished our local Wings coverage and the network had taken over, I had been working with Dan Miller for Fox 2 doing live pregame and postgame shows.

I affectionately call Ken Kal "Schleprock" from the Flintstones cartoon. Schleprock is the guy who is followed around by a black cloud. Anything bad that can happen usually happens.

Ken had even gone to church that morning in Pittsburgh to try and will his voice back. The Red Wings were up in the series three games to two and could win the Cup that night, so they had hired a charter to bring the families down to Pittsburgh for the game. I got on that flight, but it wasn't leaving until 4:30. We'd get to the rink by 6:00 at the latest with the game at 7:00, so I was cutting it tight.

As soon as I got to the Igloo, I ran into NHL vice president Colin Campbell, who had played defense for the Penguins. I had no idea where I was going, so Colin led me up to the press box. He joked, "I used to be scratched all the time. I can get you up there!" He took me through the back way and through all the concession stands. I got up there before game time with enough time to prepare.

Working local TV, I never get to call games in a Stanley Cup final. They are always on the networks, so to call a Stanley Cup final was not in the cards for me. Until tonight. I thought on the way down that it wasn't really my domain. If the Red Wings won the Cup that night, it was not my place to call "that moment." I did have it in the back of my head that Ken Kal should bring the game to its conclusion. At that point, though, I didn't know how bad his voice was.

I'm doing the game with Paul Woods and Ken Kal is there, handing me all the cards because there's so many sponsor reads on radio. The Red Wings are up by one late in the game. There's maybe two minutes left, and Ken is 10 feet away from me, watching with a spare headset on so he could listen to us call the game. A timeout was called in the final minute of the game, and while Paul Woods was talking, I took my headset off and I motioned to Kal.

He took his headset off and I told him, "You're calling the final 15 seconds of the game."

He said, "No I'm not."

"Yes you are."

"No I'm not."

"Yes you are. Suck it up, put your headset on, and you're going to call the final 15 seconds of the game." He finally said, "Okay." He really didn't want to do it. He wasn't sure how his voice would hold up, but I had talked to him throughout the night and his voice wasn't great but it was okay.

We put our headsets back on and I said, "For the final moments to bring home the Stanley Cup, here's Ken Kal."

I wished I had given it to him about five seconds earlier, because it felt a little rushed. And then Marian Hossa for Pittsburgh sent the puck just wide of Detroit goalie Chris Osgood's net on the lip of the crease just as time was expiring.

As the puck is slithering wide, I'm thinking to myself as he's calling it, *Oh my God, if they score, Schleprock is going down as the biggest jinx in Red Wings history.* It was just right for Ken to call it, and he did just fine. As I listen back and hear that call, it still feels right. Too bad he lost his voice, but I was glad I got to be where I was and he got to call the final moment. That's the only way it should have played out. It brought me my third Red Wings Stanley Cup ring courtesy of the Ilitch family. As always, among the diamonds was my name on one side of it. And this time on the interior of the ring the inscription read "FAMILY." That always meant so much to Mr. I.

Babs

Mike Babcock, who coached the Wings from 2005 to 2015, comes across as a stern taskmaster. He has a tough, rough exterior, but he does so much behind the scenes for cancer causes and mental health such as "Bell Let's Talk" program in Canada, that you don't hear about. If you really get to know him away from the scenes, he's a different guy—still intense but different.

When my father passed, I was driving in for the Toronto funeral and Babs called me. When my son died, he did the same thing. And he led off his Toronto media session the next morning talking about Jamie. He said if I needed someone to talk to, I was to pick up the phone and give him a call. That's the side that you don't see.

White House visit with President Bush on October 14, 2008. An amazing thrill to be there personally for the first time. (Photo courtesy of the Detroit Red Wings)

One thing about Mike, he's honest. He'll always tell you the truth. Mike always says, "People need to know where they stand." Can he find a better way of saying it at times, even to me? Sure. Early on in his tenure in Detroit I was in the coaching office. My laptop needed charging, so I was borrowing Brad McCrimmon's charger. Babs wasn't in there—it was an off day—and I was sitting talking to assistant coaches Beast (Brad McCrimmon) and Paul MacLean.

Mike walked in and said, "Meeting in five minutes. How long are you going to be?" I told him I could leave. Mike said, "Okay." And he left. I'm still talking to McCrimmon, and Mike walked back into the room five minutes later, sees me still sitting there, and launched into a rant. "Did you think I was kidding?" he asked.

"Get the hell out of the room." I was pissed the way he handled it. Would I have done it differently? I like to think I would. But that's Mike. He lets people know where they stand, just like he let me know where I shouldn't sit.

I know he's changed a little bit since then. He' tell you that. He's going to turn that Toronto team into a Stanley Cup winner before his eight-year deal runs out there. He doesn't have the same veteran group he had in Detroit, so he can mold the kids before they grow tired of the same voice. Mike knew it was time to move on from Detroit. His personality is as big as Toronto. Just what the Leafs needed.

You Look Just Like...

I'm at a Steely Dan concert in 2010 with my good friend David Kamen and this guy walks up to me and says verbatim, "Did anyone ever tell you that you look just like Ken Daniels?"

For my birthday on March 18, 2017, the Wings decided to honor me by reminding me how much I looked like Ron Burgandy in 1990 while with the CBC.

And I said, "No, they haven't." Failing to comprehend that, he tries again. "Really, because it's amazing how much you look like Ken Daniels." And I repeated that nobody had ever said that to me before. Which they hadn't. No one had ever said to me, did I think I looked like Ken Daniels?

I paused, not sure whether to put him out of his perplexed state, when the comedic timing of a script you couldn't write actually happened.

An acquaintance of mine from a distance sees me and yells, "Hey Ken." And the other guy turns to his wife and says, "See honey. That guy thinks he looks like Ken Daniels, too." And he walks away. I so hope he's reading this book.

Mickey (with help from our excellent producer Tom McNeeley), presented me with two cupcakes on the air for birthday No. 58. Neither were gluten free.

Carrie'd Away

My friends and I have always enjoyed using the phrase, "outkicked your coverage." For us, it refers to either a male or female who found a partner who is either way better looking than they are or far beyond their realm financially.

As beautiful and sweet and talented as Carrie Underwood is, it's hard to say Mike Fisher of the Nashville Predators outkicked his coverage. He's a great looking guy, talented, genuine, personable, and more than financially secure in his own right.

Therefore, Carrie Underwood and Mike Fisher are a perfect couple—Hollywood, yet down-home Nashville.

I first met Mike while he was playing for Ottawa, and then more often with the Predators while the Wings were in the NHL's Western Conference.

In December 2013, Mike and I were talking at a morning game-day skate with the Wings at Bridgestone Arena. I asked him if Carrie was coming to the game that night, and if she were, would she mind signing a CD for my daughter, Arlyn, a huge fan.

Mike said that she would gladly sign and to come see him after the game.

Mike was working out postgame and wasn't ready to leave to meet Carrie in the wives' room. But Barry Trotz, the Predators' great head coach, was standing nearby, and said, "Come on, I'll take you down there."

So, nervously I made my way to meet Mrs. Fisher (street cred Mike), and as Barry and I approached, the wise guy head coach blurts out, "Ken, I know you don't know who this is, but this is Carrie Underwood." Just hilarious, Barry.

Meeting the superbly talented Carrie Underwood following a Red Wings game in Nashville. She signed a CD for my daughter, Arlyn (who I think loves her husband, Predator's captain Mike Fisher, more than her).

Carrie, ever gracious and noting that I obviously knew who she was, extended her arms for a hug, and said, "I have something here for your daughter Arlyn." Carrie had already signed a *Blown Away* CD.

We talked for a few minutes about Arlyn, as Carrie asked questions to make conversation, and then I had to bolt for our team bus, but not before I got a picture with her.

A little more than three years later, February 4, 2017, we were in Nashville again, and Mike was kind enough to do a video message for my daughter who is studying abroad in New Zealand with the Michigan State Conservation Medicine program.

He mentioned Carrie had just toured there, but it was a country he had never been to but was looking forward to visiting, and wished her success.

Following the game, and a Petr Mrazek 42-save 1–0 shutout of Nashville, we were waiting in the garage on the team bus, when all the guys who were getting on after me were saying,

Taking my daughter to work: Arlyn has seen many games by my side from our perch at Joe Louis Arena.

"There's Carrie Underwood," as the cell phones came out for pictures from a distance. No matter what one does for a living, greatness can always be acknowledged. Mike had now shown up to join Carrie, and had it not been for just a few guys left to get on the bus, I was ready to step off to go say hello. But it was too late at that point. I think our players would have given me the business for that, but maybe a few would have been "Blown Away."

He Slammed the Door Shut

Coaches always talk about a goalie standing on his head, bricking up the net, or shutting the door of his net to the opposition. Following a game at the Joe during the 2016–17 season, Boston

Bruins goalie Tuukka Rask accomplished the latter. He literally slammed the door shut. On himself.

It was January 18, 2017, and the Bruins had blown 3–0 and 4–1 leads and lost 6–5 to the Red Wings in a shootout. Tuukka is famous for his emotional outbursts when he's frustrated—just check him out on YouTube and you'll see what I mean—but this time, only a select few were privy to Rask's latest meltdown.

Normally, the dressing room door is open to reporters postgame to allow them to gather quotes for their stories, but on this night, all of the player interviews were done in the hallway outside the visitor's dressing room. A few feet away Tuukka was in trouble.

As Tuukka left the ice following the Bruins' heart-wrenching loss, he was so angry he roared into the dressing room, walked into an interior room, and slammed the door shut behind him. He closed the door with such ferocity, it broke the lock.

Here was Rask, all alone in a small change room in full equipment. The Bruins players in the main dressing room were getting changed unaware that Tuukka was locked in. The goalie didn't know himself—that is, until they needed to get on the bus but were now waiting for their goalie.

Red Wings assistant equipment manager Brady Munger was summoned. Brady got his tools, grabbed a ladder, climbed up to the ceiling, and lifted out one of the ceiling tiles. He climbed through the opening across to another ceiling tile inside the other room, removed it, and dropped down to find Rask seated now smiling sheepishly and only his upper gear off.

Brady used a hammer to knock the hinges out of the door and removed it, but it took some time and an additional hammer.

Reporters noting the unhinged door sought to get to the bottom of the story, but none of them could lock it down that what actually happened was that Tuukka, and then the door, became unhinged.

Coach Speak

Hockey fans will often ask if there is a difference for me doing play-by-play for a local Wings broadcast as opposed to calling two other teams for *HNIC* or NBC.

Well, obviously, a part of me roots for the Wings to win because the environment is better for everyone, including me, when they do.

There is a different level of excitement, though, if a Red Wing player scores. But a goal is a goal. The game is what matters. Barely acknowledging an opposition goal is a disservice to this great game.

On a national level, I am paid by the game, and it makes no difference to me who wins. No network broadcaster in any sport roots against any team. Announcers just want a great, exciting game to be able to call.

But we all choose our words a little more carefully when broadcasting our own team's game. We are employed by the team. Anyone who thinks otherwise and isn't self-employed should go to work and critique their bosses publicly and harshly and see how long they stay employed. We do have a tendency to give our players and management the benefit of the doubt. Heck, even coaches of a team try to protect their own players publicly.

If coaches were always truthful, here is what would be interpreted.

When a coach says, "He's great in the room," *what he really means is:*

"We should leave him in the room, because he's no good on the ice."

When a coach says a player is a "grinder," *what he really means is:*

"It's 50-50 he'll miss an empty net from three feet."

When a coach says a player is a "power-play specialist," *what he really means is:*

"We like to have an extra man out there to cover up for his screw-ups."

When a coach says, "He's a role player," *what he really means is:*

"We think he can play a role, we just haven't figured out what that role is."

When a coach says, "He's a stay-at-home defenseman," *what he really means is:*

"He can't skate and carry the puck at the same time."

When a coach says, "Our team has good chemistry," *what he really means is:*

"We may be lousy but we all get along."

When a coach speaks of a healthy scratch and says, "We're letting him see the game from the press box so he can learn," *what he really means is:*

"He pissed me off so much last game, I want him as far away from me as possible."

So Long, Joe

The 2016–17 season was my 20th season with the Red Wings, and it was also the team's farewell campaign at Joe Louis Arena.

Moving to Little Caesars Arena, the new facility will be a state-of-the-art palace with every bell and whistle imaginable and wonderful sightlines from the broadcast location. But will it have the character of the Joe?

That remains to be seen.

There was just something about the Joe. It smelled like hockey. And the people. Oh, the people. There were really some one-of-a-kind folks who worked there.

From the guys in the parking lot when you pulled in to get your day underway, there was a nonstop parade of pleasantries extended my way as I worked my way through the bowels of the stadium up to the broadcast spot on press row. It's not the games that make a place memorable as much as it is the people you meet, and the people I met at the Joe were second to none.

That's why it will always hold a special place in my heart. That, and because it was where I got my start as the Red Wings play-by-play voice. And you never forget the first time.

We of course made room for Nick Lidstrom in our little booth during his retirement night. (Photo courtesy of Dan Mannes / Detroit Red Wings)

A wonderful farewell to Joe Louis Arena. I had the honor of hosting the event on April 9, 2017, following a 4–1 win over New Jersey in the building's final game, ending a 38-year run. (Photo courtesy of the Detroit Red Wings)

From this shot, this booth looks much bigger than it really was. And we were 105 feet from the ice. We will be 65 feet from the ice at Little Caesars Arena. (Photo courtesy of Dan Mannes / Detroit Red Wings)

Mr. I

The saddest moment of the 2016–17 season wasn't when the Red Wings' 25-season run of playoff appearances came to an end. It was the day that Red Wings owner Mike Ilitch died.

I was fortunate to meet Mr. Ilitch a half dozen times over the course of my tenure with the team, and his touch with the Red Wings was always evident.

He never left any stone unturned in his bid to make the Red Wings the best in the NHL. When it was time to step up, Mike Ilitch stepped up as well as any owner has in professional sports.

But it was more than winning with him. He cared about Detroit. He cared about what his fans thought and what they wanted. The members of the team, everyone from the superstars to the fourth-line players, were embraced like family.

He watched cities like Baltimore and Atlanta be revitalized and was always certain the same could happen in Detroit. It's why he put his world headquarters in the heart of downtown in the Fox Theater and why the new District Detroit, which houses Little Caesars Arena, the new home for the Wings starting in 2017–18, was also created right there.

Actually, the father of seven always admitted it was not him, but his family, who encouraged him to get involved with downtown Detroit. Cement footings had already been laid for a new Little Caesars corporate headquarters in Farmington Hills, Michigan, when the Fox opportunity presented itself.

"My kids were the ones who wanted to come to Detroit," he explained. "They were raised affluent, born in the suburbs, but they wanted to come back to Detroit and be part of it."

It wasn't the first time Mr. I had consulted with his family, and it certainly wasn't the last.

"They've been my incentive since I started," he said. "They've always been my inspiration."

Mr. Ilitch sent his youngsters into the real world with just one piece of advice—"Be humble." Family came first with Mr. I, and he felt the same way about his business.

"You target your marketing toward the family, and your first priority is the youngsters," he'd say. "You can't tell me the kids don't decide where the parents go to eat."

Mr. Ilitch won the Lester Patrick Award for service to hockey in the United States in 1991. Mr. I was compared with Patrick, patriarch of hockey's royal family. There are those in Detroit who were quite willing to ordain Mr. Ilitch as patriarch of Detroit's first family, but he was always reluctant to wear the crown.

"You talk about pressure, that's pressure," he'd say. "I'm no savior."

A lot of people in the city of Detroit would beg to differ.

Thank you Mr. I for this great opportunity. I was lucky to know you.